C000261954

LIVERPOOL FC
THE OFFICIAL GUIDE
2010

Sport Media
A Trinity Mirror Business

HONOURS

LEAGUE CHAMPIONSHIP (18)
1900/01, 1905/06, 1921/22, 1922/23, 1946/47, 1963/64, 1965/66, 1972/73, 1975/76,
1976/77, 1978/79, 1979/80, 1981/82, 1982/83, 1983/84, 1985/86, 1987/88, 1989/90

DIVISION TWO WINNERS (4)
1893/94, 1895/96, 1904/05, 1961/62

FA CUP WINNERS (7)
1964/65, 1973/74, 1985/86, 1988/89, 1991/92, 2000/01, 2005/06

LEAGUE CUP WINNERS (7)
1980/81, 1981/82, 1982/83, 1983/84, 1994/95, 2000/01, 2002/03

EUROPEAN CUP/UEFA CHAMPIONS LEAGUE WINNERS (5)
1976/77, 1977/78, 1980/81, 1983/84, 2004/05

UEFA CUP WINNERS (3)
1972/73, 1975/76, 2000/01

EUROPEAN SUPER CUP WINNERS (3)
1977/78, 2001/02, 2005/06

FA CHARITY SHIELD WINNERS/FA COMMUNITY SHIELD WINNERS (10)
1966, 1974, 1976, 1979, 1980, 1982, 1988, 1989, 2001, 2006

FA CHARITY SHIELD WINNERS/FA COMMUNITY SHIELD SHARED (5)
1964, 1965, 1977, 1986, 1990

SCREEN SPORT SUPER CUP WINNERS (1)
1986/87

LANCASHIRE LEAGUE WINNERS (1)
1892/93

INTRODUCTION

Welcome to the fifth edition of Liverpool FC : The Official Guide, the essential club publication for 2010. We continue to provide you, the fans, with the very best there is to celebrate about the Reds, both on and off the pitch, and this year's offering is no exception. We have again utilised the statistical expertise of Ged Rea and Dave Ball, who have offered some fascinating statistical notes, gleaned from another impressive year by Rafael Benitez's side. We have also retained much of the exisiting format, with notes on the current playing squad, last season's performances, club records, European matches, opponents for 2009/10 and much more.

You'll notice a slight restructuring of content this time, with the plan being to further emphasise records created, existing club records and the focus on individual players. 'The Boss' section has been removed, with Rafael Benitez's impressive statistics now noted in the 'Club Records', while 'Top 10 Moments' has been changed to 'Six of the Best', now included in 'The 2008/09 Season'. Sami Hyypia's departure from Anfield after a decade's sterling service also merits reference, as do the continued high standards set by Football Writers' Player of the Year, Steven Gerrard.

Fresh content includes more in-depth explanation of statistics, a look back at the club's first European Cup triumph, 'Rafael Benitez's 250', 'Long-serving Reds', '50-Up' and for the first time, the club's complete record in all competitions.

We hope you continue to find this publication of interest and a major reference point, balancing as it does the best of Liverpool FC in the past, present and future, whilst also utilising some of the best pictures available celebrating the club's rich pedigree at home and abroad.

WRITERS

Ged Rea and Dave Ball are Liverpool FC's official statisticians. Ged's Liverpool FC records are the most accurate available, while Dave is a key researcher for long-running BBC TV show *A Question of Sport*. James Cleary has also played a major role in writing and researching key information.

Executive Editor: KEN ROGERS Editor: STEVE HANRAHAN
Production Editor: PAUL DOVE Art Editor: RICK COOKE
Sub Editors: JAMES CLEARY, ROY GILFOYLE, MICHAEL HAYDOCK, ADAM OLDFIELD
Design Team: BARRY PARKER, COLIN SUMPTER, GLEN HIND, LEE ASHUN, ALISON GILLILAND,
JAMIE DUNMORE, JAMES KENYON, LISA CRITCHLEY
Liverpool FC Writers: CHRIS McLOUGHLIN, DAVID RANDLES, GAVIN KIRK, JOHN HYNES, SIMON HUGHES

All Rights Reserved. No part of this publication may be reproduced, stored in a retrieval system, or transmitted in any form, or by any means, electronic, mechanical, photocopying, recording or otherwise without the prior permission in writing of the copyright holders, nor be otherwise circulated in any form of binding or cover other than in which it is published and without a similar condition being imposed on the subsequent publisher. Liverpool FC logo and name are registered trademarks of The Liverpool Football Club and Athletics Grounds Ltd and are reproduced under license.

ISBN 978 1 9068 02226
Photographs: PA Photos, Trinity Mirror, John Cocks, John Powell
Printed and finished by Korotan

CLUB TELEPHONE NUMBERS

Main Switchboard	0151 263 2361
Customer Services	0844 844 2005
International callers	0044 870 220 2345
Ticket Office	0844 844 0844
International Ticket Office	+ 44 870 2202151
Mail Order Hotline (UK)	0844 800 4239
International Mail Order Hotline	+ 44 1386 848247
Club Store (Anfield)	0151 263 1760
Club Store (Williamson Square - City Centre)	0151 330 3077
Club Store (Liverpool One - City Centre)	0151 709 4345
Club Store (Chester)	01244 344608
Conference and Banqueting (for your events at Anfield)	0151 263 7744
Corporate Sales	0151 263 9199
Development Association	0151 263 6391
Community Department	0151 264 2316
Museum & Tour Centre	0151 260 6677
Membership Department	0844 499 3000
Public Relations (including all charity requests)	0151 260 1433
Digital Media (online, TV and mobile)	0151 293 8720

BECOME A MEMBER OF **ALL RED**, the new LFC Official Membership Scheme.
To join, visit **www.liverpoolfc.tv/ALLRED** or call 0844 499 3000.

SUBSCRIBE TO THE OFFICIAL **LFC PROGRAMME AND WEEKLY MAGAZINE**
To take out a subscription please call: 0845 1430001

LIVE AND BREATHE LFC 24/7
Official Club Media

Online – visit the official club website at **www.liverpoolfc.tv** for breaking news,
views, match reports, interviews, statistics, history and more.

Watch goals, highlights, interviews, press conferences, reserve matches, classic matches and
listen to commentary of every game with an e-Season Ticket – visit **www.liverpoolfc.tv/eseason**

TV – the official TV channel (LFC TV) is broadcast every day from the heart of your club. Available by
satellite, cable and online – visit **www.liverpoolfc.tv/tv**

Mobile – take LFC wherever you go. Download player animations, videos, games and our new
iPhone app or get the news as it happens with SMS alerts – visit **www.liverpoolfc.tv/mobile**

CONTENTS

Pages

Liverpool honours list   4
Introduction   5
Club telephone numbers   6
Foreword   9

NEW CAMPAIGN 10-33

Includes full profiles of the 2009/10 squad, a focus on Rafael Benitez and his coaching staff, a run-down of all Liverpool managers, the 2009 summer diary, key dates plus fixtures for the first team, reserves, Under-18s and ladies side.

THE 2008/09 SEASON 34-71

An in-depth review of the campaign, including news, quotes, results, six of the best of the season, appearances, goals and the player of the season. We also take a retrospective look at Sami Hyypia's central defensive partners throughout his Reds career, and focus on the seasons enjoyed by Liverpool reserves, Under-18s and ladies.

EUROPE 73-107

A full overview of the 2008/09 European season, with a complete record of the Reds' European results. The 1976/77 European Cup-winning campaign is revisited, along with a whole host of facts and statistics related to the club's – and players' – achievements in overseas competition.

PREMIER LEAGUE 108-123

Updated facts, figures and statistics concerning Liverpool's 17 seasons in the league – from team to player records.

THE FOOTBALL LEAGUE 124-133

Player, team and seasonal records from the club's league years 1893-1992.

DOMESTIC CUPS 134-153

The record of every competitive cup competition the Reds have competed in, with the FA Cup and League Cup player records also noted.

THE RECORDS 154-175

A compilation of Liverpool records including the complete first-team record, goalscoring and appearance record holders, notable landmarks, super subs, old/young Liverpool first-teamers, goalkeeping achievements, manager records and international Reds.

OPPOSITION 176-187

An in-depth guide to the teams who Liverpool FC will face in the Barclays Premier League in 2009/10.

ESSENTIALS 188-208

All the vital club information available at your fingertips – everything from ticket prices, Anfield details, club tours, the work of each department, store information and LFC media.

FOREWORD

The Guide is now acknowledged as the definitive annual publication about England's most successful club. This is the fifth such offering and as with the four previous editions, we hope that we have chronicled not only all of last season's achievements, but also continued to examine them in relation to previous accomplishments.

As all Liverpool FC supporters are aware, the club is so rich in honours and achievements that the present side, and succeeding ones, will find it extremely difficult to match their predecessors. However, as the Guide proves, it is very pleasing to note that last season the club did indeed set boundaries which can be compared with the past.

For many years now, we have been able to call upon Eric Doig for assistance in compiling statistics about the club, and this year is no exception. We see our role as updating records and making people aware of forthcoming additions. This includes the club, players and the manager. Statistics can of course be the mainstay of arguments and discussions about a topic, and we hope that the Guide will satisfy their demands.

We document the highlights of last season, naturally, which includes the comprehensive defeat of Real Madrid; our highest points tally in Premier League history; the double over Manchester United and our record against the 'top four', plus of course Rafael Benitez's impressive spell at the club. In all respects the club has continued to improve year on year, especially as regards points gained and goals scored, whilst Anfield is once again becoming a fortress where visitors were unable to exact maximum damage upon the Reds.

With the continued impact of the internet, supporters are able to access all kinds of information regarding their favourite team. However, the Guide is far more accessible and we will continue to provide updates in every aspect of the club and players.

We hope that older supporters are catered for as we have included results, scorers and records in all competitions, whilst for our younger readers and more serious stats buffs there is a comprehensive study of the Premier League. Once again, our aim is to provide an understanding of present and past achievements with everything supporters need to know about Liverpool FC.

Ged Rea & Dave Ball

THE SQUAD 2009/10

Stats correct before start of 2009/10 season

Diego Cavalieri – Squad number 1

Position	Goalkeeper
Born	Sao Paulo, Brazil
Age (at start of 09/10)	26
Birth date	01/12/82
Height	6ft 2ins
Other club	Palmeiras
Honours	2003 Brazilian Serie B, 2008 Sao Paulo State Championship
Liverpool debut	23/09/08 v Crewe Alexandra
Liverpool appearances	4
Liverpool goals	0
International caps	0

Peter Gulacsi - Squad number 42

Positions	Goalkeeper
Born	Glostrup, Denmark
Age (at start of 09/10)	19
Birth date	15/06/90
Height	6ft 2ins
Other club	Brondby
Honours	2007 FA Youth Cup
Liverpool debut	–
Liverpool appearances	–
Liverpool goals	–
International caps	0

David Martin

Position	Goalkeeper
Born	Romford
Age (at start of 09/10)	23
Birth date	22/01/86
Height	6ft 1ins
Other clubs	Milton Keynes Dons, Accrington Stanley, Leicester City
Honours	2006, 2007 FA Youth Cup, 2009 League One
Liverpool debut	–
Liverpool appearances	–
Liverpool goals	–
International caps	0

Pepe Reina – Squad number 25

Position	Goalkeeper
Born	Madrid, Spain
Age (at start of 09/10)	26
Birth date	31/08/82
Height	6ft 2ins
Other clubs	Barcelona, Villarreal
Honours	2004, 2005 UEFA Intertoto Cup, 2005 European Super Cup, 2006 FA Cup, 2006 FA Community Shield
Liverpool debut	13/07/05 v TNS
Liverpool appearances	207
Liverpool goals	0
International caps	16 (0 goals)
International honours	2008 Euro C'ships

Daniel Agger – Squad number 5

Position	Central Defence
Born	Hvidovre, Denmark
Age (at start of 09/10)	24
Birth date	12/12/84
Height	6ft 3ins
Other clubs	Rosenhoj, Brondby
Honours	2005 Danish League, 2005 Danish Cup, 2006 FA Comm. Shield
Liverpool debut	01/02/06 v Birmingham
Liverpool appearances	71 + 8 as substitute
Liverpool goals	6
International caps	27 (3 goals)

Fabio Aurelio – Squad number 12

Positions	Left Defence/ Midfield
Born	Sao Carlos, Brazil
Age (at start of 09/10)	29
Birth date	24/09/79
Height	5ft 8ins
Other clubs	Sao Paulo, Valencia
Honours	1998, 2000 Sao Paulo State C'ship, 2002, 2004 Spanish League, 2004 Euro. Super Cup, 2006 FA Community Shield
Liverpool debut	13/08/06 v Chelsea
Liverpool appearances	64 + 23 as sub.
Liverpool goals	4
International caps	0

Daniel Sanchez Ayala – Squad number 40

Position	Central Defence
Born	Seville, Spain
Age (at start of 09/10)	18
Birth date	07/11/90
Height	6ft 3ins
Other club	Seville
Liverpool debut	–
Liverpool appearances	–
Liverpool goals	–
International caps	0

Jamie Carragher – Squad number 23

Position	Central Defence
Born	Bootle, Liverpool
Age (at start of 09/10)	31
Birth date	28/01/78
Height	6ft 1ins
Honours	2001, 2006 FA Cup, 2001, 2003 Lge Cup, 2001 UEFA Cup, 2001, 2005 Euro. Super Cup, 2001, 2006 FA Comm. Shield, 2005 Champions Lge
Liverpool debut	08/01/97 v M'boro
Liverpool appearances	556 + 21 as substitute
Liverpool goals	5
International caps	34 (0 goals)

Stephen Darby – Squad number 32

Position	Right Defence
Born	Liverpool
Age (at start of 09/10)	20
Birth date	06/10/88
Height	5ft 8ins
Other clubs	–
Honours	FA Youth Cup 2006, 2007, 2008 FA Premier Reserve League
Liverpool debut	12/11/08 v Tottenham Hotspur
Liverpool appearances	0 + 2 as substitute
Liverpool goals	0
International caps	0

Philipp Degen – Squad number 27

Position	Right Defence
Born	Holstein, Switzerland
Age (at start of 09/10)	26
Birth date	15/02/83
Height	6ft 1ins
Other clubs	FC Basel, FC Aarau Borussia Dortmund
Honours	2002, 2004, 2005 Swiss League, 2003 Swiss Cup
Liverpool debut	23/09/08 v Crewe
Liverpool appearances	2 + 0 as substitute
Liverpool goals	0
International caps	31 (0 goals)

Andrea Dossena – Squad number 38

Position	Left Defence
Born	Lodi, Italy
Age (at start of 09/10)	27
Birth date	11/09/81
Height	5ft 11ins
Other clubs	Verona, Treviso, Udinese
Honours	–
Liverpool debut	13/08/08 v Standard Liege
Liverpool appearances	19 + 7 as substitute
Liverpool goals	2
International caps	10 (0 goals)

Emiliano Insua – Squad number 22

Position	Left Defence
Born	Buenos Aires, Argentina
Age (at start of 09/10)	20
Birth date	07/01/89
Height	5ft 8ins
Other club	Boca Juniors
Honours	2008 FA Premier Reserve League
Liverpool debut	28/04/07 v Portsmouth
Liverpool appearances	15 + 3 as substitute
Liverpool goals	0
International caps	0

Glen Johnson – Squad number 2

Position	Right Defence
Born	Greenwich
Age (at start of 09/10)	24
Birth date	23/08/84
Height	5ft 11ins
Other clubs	West Ham United, Millwall, Chelsea, Portsmouth
Honours	2005 FA Premier Lge, 2005 Lge Cup, 2008 FA Cup
Liverpool debut	-
Liverpool appearances	-
Liverpool goals	-
International caps	16 (0 goals)

Martin Kelly – Squad number 34

Position	Central Defence
Born	Whiston
Age (at start of 09/10)	19
Birth date	27/04/90
Height	6ft 3ins
Other club	Huddersfield Town
Honours	2008 FA Premier Reserve League
Liverpool debut	09/12/08 v PSV Eindhoven
Liverpool appearances	0 + 1 as substitute
Liverpool goals	0
International caps	0

Sotirios Kyrgiakos – Squad number 16

Position	Central Defence
Born	Trikala, Greece
Age (at start of 09/10)	30
Birth date	23/07/79
Height	6ft 3ins
Other clubs	Panathinaikos, Agios Nikolaos, Rangers, Eintracht Frankfurt, AEK Athens
Honours	2004 Greek Lge & Cup, 2005 Scottish League, 2005 Scottish Lge Cup
Liverpool debut	-
Liverpool appearances	-
Liverpool goals	-
International caps	50 (4 goals)

Martin Skrtel – Squad number 37

Position	Central Defence
Born	Handlova, Slovakia
Age (at start of 09/10)	24
Birth date	15/12/84
Height	6ft 3ins
Other clubs	FK AS Trencin, Zenit St. Petersburg
Honours	2007 Russian Premier League
Liverpool debut	21/01/08 v Aston Villa
Liverpool appearances	48 + 2 as substitute
Liverpool goals	0
International caps	32 (5 goals)

Alberto Aquilani – Squad number 4

Position	Central Midfield
Born	Rome, Italy
Age (at start of 09/10)	25
Birth date	07/07/84
Height	6ft 1ins
Other clubs	Roma, Triestina
Honours	2007, 2008 Italian Cup, 2007 Italian Super Cup
Liverpool debut	-
Liverpool appearances	-
Liverpool goals	-
International caps	11 (2 goals)

Yossi Benayoun – Squad number 15

Position	Midfield
Born	Dimona, Israel
Age (at start of 09/10)	29
Birth date	05/05/80
Height	5ft 8ins
Other clubs	Hapoel Be'er Sheva, Maccabi Haifa, Racing Santander, West Ham
Honours	2001, 2002 Israeli League
Liverpool debut	15/08/07 v Toulouse
Liverpool appearances	52 + 37 as substitute
Liverpool goals	20
International caps	73 (19 goals)

Steven Gerrard MBE – Squad number 8

Positions	Central/Right Midfield or Forward
Born	Whiston
Age (at start of 09/10)	29
Birth date	30/05/80
Height	6ft 0ins
Honours	2001, 2006 FA Cup, 2001, 2003 Lge Cup, 2001 UEFA Cup, 2001 European Super Cup, 2001, 2006 FA Community Shield, 2005 Champions League
Liverpool debut	29/11/98 v Blackburn Rovers
Liverpool appearances	441 + 42 as sub.
Liverpool goals	120
International caps	74 (14 goals)

Steven Irwin – Squad number 36

Positions	Defence/Midfield
Born	Liverpool
Age (at start of 09/10)	18
Birth date	29/09/90
Height	5ft 8ins
Other clubs	-
Honours	2007 FA Youth Cup
Liverpool debut	-
Liverpool appearances	-
Liverpool goals	-
International caps	0

Lucas Leiva – Squad number 21

Position	Central Midfield
Born	Dourados, Brazil
Age (at start of 09/10)	22
Birth date	09/01/87
Height	5ft 10ins
Other club	Gremio
Honours	2005 Brazilian Serie B, 2006, 2007 Rio Grande do Sul State Championship, 2008 FA Prem Res. Lge
Liverpool debut	28/08/07 v Toulouse
Liverpool appearances	40 + 31 as substitute
Liverpool goals	4
International caps	3 (0 goals)
International honours	2008 Olympics Bronze Medal

Javier Mascherano – Squad number 20

Position	Central Midfield
Born	San Lorenzo, Argentina
Age (at start of 09/10)	25
Birth date	08/06/84
Height	5ft 7ins
Other clubs	River Plate, Corinthians, West Ham
Honours	2004 Argentine Lge (Closing C'ship), 2005 Brazilian Lge
Liverpool debut	24/02/07 v Sheff Utd
Liverpool appearances	87 + 3 as substitute
Liverpool goals	1
International caps	49 (2 goals)
International honours	2004, 2008 Olympics Gold Medal

Damien Plessis – Squad number 28

Position	Central Midfield
Born	Neuville-aux-Bois, France
Age (at start of 09/10)	21
Birth date	05/03/88
Height	6ft 4ins
Other club	Lyon
Honours	2008 FA Premier Reserve League
Liverpool debut	05/04/08 v Arsenal
Liverpool appearances	4 + 1 as substitute
Liverpool goals	0
International caps	0

Albert Riera – Squad number 11

Position	Left Midfield
Born	Manacor, Spain
Age (at start of 09/10)	27
Birth date	15/04/82
Height	6ft 2ins
Other clubs	Real Mallorca, Bordeaux, Espanyol, Manchester City
Honours	2003 Spanish Cup
Liverpool debut	13/09/08 v Manchester United
Liverpool appearances	33 + 7 as substitute
Liverpool goals	5
International caps	14 (4 goals)

Jay Spearing – Squad number 26

Position	Central Midfield
Born	Wirral
Age (at start of 09/10)	20
Birth date	25/11/88
Height	5ft 6ins
Other clubs	–
Honours	2006, 2007 FA Youth Cup, 2008 FA Premier Reserve League
Liverpool debut	09/12/08 v PSV Eindhoven
Liverpool appearances	0 + 2 as substitute
Liverpool goals	0
International caps	0

Ryan Babel – Squad number 19

Position	Forward
Born	Amsterdam, Holland
Age (at start of 09/10)	22
Birth date	19/12/86
Height	6ft 0ins
Other club	Ajax
Honours	2005, 2006 Dutch Super Cup, 2006, 2007 Dutch Cup
Liverpool debut	11/08/07 v Aston Villa
Liverpool appearances	42 + 49 as substitute
Liverpool goals	14
International caps	34 (5 goals)

Nathan Eccleston – Squad number 39

Positions	Forward
Born	Manchester
Age (at start of 09/10)	18
Birth date	30/12/90
Height	5ft 10ins
Other clubs	–
Honours	2007 FA Youth Cup
Liverpool debut	–
Liverpool appearances	–
Liverpool goals	–
International caps	0

Nabil El Zhar – Squad number 31

Position	Forward
Born	Ales, France
Age (at start of 09/10)	22
Birth date	27/08/86
Height	5ft 6ins
Other clubs	Olympique Ales, Nimes Olympique, AS Saint-Etienne
Honours	2008 FA Premier Reserve League
Liverpool debut	29/11/06 v Portsmouth
Liverpool appearances	4 + 21 as substitute
Liverpool goals	1
International caps (Mor.)	8 (2 goals)

Dirk Kuyt – Squad number 18

Position	Forward
Born	Katwijk, Holland
Age (at start of 09/10)	29
Birth date	22/07/80
Height	6ft 0ins
Other clubs	FC Utrecht, Feyenoord
Honours	2003 Dutch Cup
Liverpool debut	26/08/06 v West Ham United
Liverpool appearances	122 + 25 as substitute
Liverpool goals	40
International caps	54 (13 goals)

David Ngog – Squad number 24

Position	Centre Forward
Born	Gennevilliers, France
Age (at start of 09/10)	20
Birth date	01/04/89
Height	6ft 3ins
Other club	Paris Saint-Germain
Honours	2008 French League Cup
Liverpool debut	31/08/08 v Aston Villa
Liverpool appearances	5 + 14 as substitute
Liverpool goals	3

Daniel Pacheco

Position	Forward
Born	Malaga, Spain
Age (at start of 09/10)	18
Birth date	05/01/91
Height	5ft 6ins
Other club	Barcelona
Honours	2008 FA Premier Reserve League
Liverpool debut	-
Liverpool appearances	-
Liverpool goals	-
International caps	0

Fernando Torres – Squad number 9

Position	Centre Forward
Born	Madrid, Spain
Age (at start of 09/10)	25
Birth date	20/03/84
Height	6ft 1ins
Other club	Atletico Madrid
Honours	2002 Spanish Second Division
Liverpool debut	11/08/07 v Aston Villa
Liverpool appearances	72 + 12
Liverpool goals	50
International caps	68 (23 goals)
International honours	2008 Euro C'ships

Andriy Voronin – Squad number 10

Position	Centre Forward
Born	Odessa, Ukraine
Age (at start of 09/10)	30
Birth date	21/07/79
Height	5ft 10ins
Other clubs	Borussia Moenchengladbach, Mainz, Cologne, Bayer Leverkusen, Hertha Berlin
Honours	-
Liverpool debut	11/08/07 v Aston Villa
Liverpool appearances	18 + 10 as substitute
Liverpool goals	6
International caps	58 (6 goals)

OTHER PLAYERS ON LOAN
2009/10

Ryan Flynn

Position	Midfield
Born	Falkirk
Age	20
Birth date	04/09/88
Height	5ft 10ins
Club	Falkirk
Loan spell	One year
Honours	2006, 2007 FA Youth Cup, 2008 Reserve Lge

Charles Itandje

Position	Goalkeeper
Born	Bobigny, France
Age	26
Birth date	02/11/82
Height	6ft 4ins
Club	Kavala
Loan spell	One year

Nikolay Mihaylov

Position	Goalkeeper
Born	Sofia, Bulgaria
Age	21
Birth date	28/06/88
Height	6ft 5ins
Club	FC Twente
Loan spell	One year

Krisztian Nemeth

Position	Forward
Born	Gyor, Hungary
Age	20
Birth date	05/01/89
Height	5ft 10ins
Club	AEK Athens
Loan spell	One year
Honours	2008 FA Premier Reserve Lge

Mikel San Jose

Position	Defence
Born	Pamplona, Spain
Age	20
Birth date	30/05/89
Height	6ft 0ins
Club	Athletic Bilbao
Loan spell	One year

Andras Simon

Position	Forward
Born	Salgotarjan, Hungary
Age	19
Birth date	30/03/90
Height	6ft 0ins
Club	Cordoba CF
Loan spell	One year

Loan Reds – Krisztian Nemeth (left) and Mikel San Jose

THE MANAGEMENT

Rafael Benitez – Manager

Appointed	16/06/04
Born	Madrid, Spain
Birth date	16/04/60
Other clubs managed	Real Valladolid, Osasuna, Extremadura, Tenerife, Valencia
Honours (senior manager)	2002, 2004 La Liga, 2004 UEFA Cup, 2005 Champ. Lge, 2005 E. Super Cup, 2006 FA Cup, 2006 FA Comm. Shield

Sammy Lee – Assistant-manager

Appointed	16/05/08
Born	Liverpool
Birth date	07/02/59
Coaching career	Liverpool, England, Bolton Wanderers
Clubs (player)	Liverpool, QPR, Osasuna, Southampton, Bolton
Honours (player)	1979, 1980, 1982 FA Charity Shield, 1981, 1984 European Cup, 1981, 1982, 1983, 1984 League Cup, 1982, 1983, 1984 Division One

Mauricio Pellegrino – First-team coach

Appointed	30/06/08
Born	Leones, Argentina
Birth date	05/10/71
Coaching career	Valencia youth
Clubs (player)	Velez Sarsfield, Barcelona, Velez Sarsfield, Valencia, Liverpool, Alaves
Honours (player)	1993, 1996, 1998 Clausura, 1994 Copa Libertadores, 1994 Intercont. Cup, 1995 Apertura, 1999, 2002, 2004 La Liga, 2004 UEFA Cup

BACKROOM STAFF
2009/10

Xavi Valero – GK coach

Appointed	July 2007
Born	Castellon de la Plana, Spain
Age	40
Birth date	12/03/69
Other clubs	Castellon, Mallorca, Logrones, Real Murcia, Cordoba, Wrexham

John Achterberg – GK coach

Appointed	June 2009
Born	Utrecht, Holland
Age	38
Birth date	08/07/71
Other clubs	NAC Breda, Eindhoven, Tranmere Rovers

Paco de Miguel – Fit. Coach

Appointed	2007
Born	Madrid, Spain
Age	36
Birth date	19/02/73
Other clubs	Atletico Madrid, Valencia

John McMahon – Res. coach

Appointed	April 2009
Born	Manchester
Age	59
Birth date	07/12/49
Other clubs	Preston, Southend Utd, Chesterfield, Crewe Alex., Tranmere Rov, Shrewsbury T.

Rob Price – Physiotherapist

Appointed	September 2005
Born	Oldham
Age	36
Birth date	31/10/72
Previous role	Football Association

Eduardo Macia – Chief scout

Appointed	June 2006
Born	Valencia, Spain
Age	35
Birth date	07/05/74
Other club	Valencia

THE LIVERPOOL MANAGERS
THE COMPLETE LIST 1892-2009

Rafael Benitez	June 2004-Present
Gerard Houllier	November 1998-May 2004
Roy Evans (joint manager with Gerard Houllier)	July 1998-November 1998
Roy Evans	January 1994-November 1998
Graeme Souness	April 1991-January 1994
Ronnie Moran (caretaker)	February 1991-April 1991
Kenny Dalglish	May 1985-February 1991
Joe Fagan	May 1983-May 1985
Bob Paisley	July 1974-May 1983
Bill Shankly	December 1959-July 1974
Phil Taylor	May 1956-November 1959
Don Welsh	March 1951-May 1956
George Kay	May 1936-February 1951
George Patterson	February 1928-May 1936
Matt McQueen	February 1923-February 1928
David Ashworth	December 1919-February 1923
Tom Watson	August 1896-May 1915
John McKenna	August 1892-August 1896

SUMMER DIARY 2009

A reminder of what went on and when during the summer months involving Liverpool FC.

JUNE

2 Pepe Reina, Alvaro Arbeloa, Xabi Alonso, Albert Riera and Fernando Torres are named in Spain's squad for the Confederations Cup.

5 Robbie Fowler reveals his dream to manage Liverpool.

6 Steven Gerrard sets up two goals in England's 4-0 World Cup qualifying defeat of Kazakhstan.

8 Shrewsbury Town assistant-manager John McMahon is appointed reserve-team coach.

10 Tranmere Rovers goalkeeper John Achterberg joins the Anfield coaching staff.
Dirk Kuyt and Ryan Babel help Holland to a 2-0 win over Norway, in the process becoming the first European country to qualify for the 2010 World Cup finals.
Fernando Torres and Albert Riera net in Spain's 6-0 stroll over Azerbaijan, while Steven Gerrard wins his 74th England cap in their victory over Andorra, by the same scoreline.
Liverpool legends Ian Callaghan and Gerry Byrne receive World Cup winners medals, having been part of England's 1966 squad, when only the first XI were awarded medals.

11 Former Liverpool forward Titi Camara takes over as coach of Guinea.

12 Goalkeeper Christopher Oldfield, defender Christopher Buchtmann, wingers David Amoo and Alex Kacaniklic and strikers Lauri Dalla Valle and Nathan Eccleston are promoted from the club Academy to Melwood to train with the reserves and first team.

14 Fernando Torres hits a hat-trick in Spain's 5-0 demolition of New Zealand in the Confederations Cup in South Africa.
David Ngog suffers disappointment as his France Under-20 side go down 1-0 to their Chilean counterparts in the final of the Toulon Tournament.

16 Former Liverpool favourite John Barnes lands the vacant managerial post at Tranmere Rovers, with another ex-Red, Jason McAteer, becoming his assistant.

17 The new Premier League fixtures pair Liverpool with Tottenham Hotspur on the opening day at White Hart Lane.
Hungarian prospect Zsolt Poloskei sees his loan deal extended for another season, having spent the entire 2008/09 campaign sidelined by injury.

19 Former chairman David Moores stands down from the board, although he retains his role as honorary life president.
Antonio Gomez Perez is appointed reserve-team coach, joining from Albacete.

20 Head of recruitment Malcolm Elias leaves the club's Academy.
The reserve side will play their home games at Tranmere Rovers next term.

22 Christian Purslow is named as the club's new managing director.

23 Rushden & Diamonds's striking prospect Aaron King joins the Reds on a two-year deal, with Cadiz midfielder Jesus Joaquin Fernandez following suit.

24 Spain, who included Fernando Torres, Xabi Alonso and Albert Riera in their side, suffer a shock 2-0 defeat to the USA in the Confederations Cup semi-final – their first defeat since 2006.

26 England full-back Glen Johnson becomes Liverpool's most expensive defender after completing his switch from Portsmouth on a four-year contract.

28 Xabi Alonso's extra-time free-kick earns Spain third place in the Confederations Cup, the European champions beating hosts South Africa 3-2.

JULY

1 Sebastian Leto and Paul Anderson officially leave the club, signing for Panathinaikos and Nottingham Forest respectively.

2 Fitness specialist Eduardo Garcia and sports therapist Ivan Ortega join the backroom staff from Spanish club Celta Vigo.

3 Kenny Dalglish's return to Liverpool FC is confirmed, being appointed to the dual role of Academy director and club ambassador.

SUMMER DIARY 2009

A reminder of what went on and when during the summer months involving Liverpool FC.

JULY

6   Yossi Benayoun signs a two-year contract extension.

7   The first-teamers not involved in international action during the summer return to Melwood to begin their pre-season preparations.

9   Skipper Steven Gerrard signs his new four-year contract with the Reds.
Fabio Aurelio will miss the start of the season having injured his knee during the close season – playing football with his children.
Former defender and reserve boss Gary Ablett is appointed Stockport County manager.

10   Jermaine Pennant joins Real Zaragoza, having been released at the end of the season.

11   Paris St Germain left-back Chris Mavinga, 18, signs for a nominal fee.
Nabil El Zhar signs a contract extension, until the summer of 2012.

15   Glen Johnson makes his Liverpool debut in the first team's first run-out of the summer, a 0-0 draw at Swiss outfit St Gallen.

19   Austrian side Rapid Vienna run out 1-0 winners in the Reds' latest pre-season friendly.

22   Thailand, under the guidance of Peter Reid, hold Liverpool to a 1-1 draw.
Germany Under-17 defender Stephen Sama, 16, pens a two-year deal with the Reds.

26   A 5-0 victory over Singapore ends the team's winless pre-season run at the end of their two-match Far East tour.

31   Alvaro Arbeloa praises the club after completing his move to Real Madrid.
Stephen Darby and Jay Spearing pen new deals, keeping them with the club until 2012.

AUGUST

2   The Reds go down 3-0 at Espanyol in a pre-season friendly.

4   Reserve striker Nathan Eccleston agrees a new three-year contract.

5   Andriy Voronin and David Ngog are on target in a 2-0 friendly win over FC Lyn.
Xabi Alonso thanks the Liverpool fans for their support after signing for Real Madrid.

8   Italy international midfielder Alberto Aquilani completes his move from AS Roma.
The Reds lose their final pre-season outing, going down 2-1 at home to Atletico Madrid.

10   Adam Hammill completes a permanent move to Barnsley.

11   A groin injury forces Steven Gerrard out of the England squad to face Holland.
Reserve striker Craig Lindfield, a member of the FA Youth Cup-winning sides of 2006 and 2007, is released.

12   Daniel Pacheco pens a new three-year deal.
Dirk Kuyt is on target as Holland and England draw 2-2 in Amsterdam.
Fernando Torres and Albert Riera net as Spain come back from two goals down to defeat Macedonia 3-2 in a friendly international.

15   Fernando Torres pens his new five-year contract.
Mikel San Jose returns to Athletic Bilbao on a season-long loan deal.

16   A Steven Gerrard penalty fails to prevent a 2-1 opening-day defeat at Tottenham.

17   The club skipper is nominated for UEFA's Club Footballer of the Year award.

19   Glen Johnson nets on his home debut as Liverpool cruise to a 4-0 victory over Stoke.

20   Prospects Peter Gulacsi and Krisztian Nemeth sign new deals.

21   Greece international defender Sotirios Kyrgiakos completes his move from AEK Athens.
Defender Robbie Threlfall joins Northampton Town on an initial one-month loan.

24   Aston Villa earn a shock 3-1 win at Anfield in the Barclays Premier League.

25   Hungarian duo Krisztian Nemeth and Andras Simon go out on loan for the season, to AEK Athens and Cordoba CF respectively.

27   The Reds are paired with Lyon, Fiorentina and Debrecen in the Champions League.

29   The Carling Cup third-round draw sees the club travel to Leeds United of League One.
A late Steven Gerrard strike ensures a 3-2 victory at 10-man Bolton Wanderers.

31   Goalkeeper Charles Itandje joins Greek club Kavala FC on loan for the season.

KEY DATES 2009/10

(Dates are subject to change)

August 2009

12	Holland v England, international friendly (Amsterdam)
15	Barclays Premier League kick-off
27	UEFA Champions League group stage draw
29	Carling Cup third-round draw

September 2009

1	Transfer window closes
5	England v Slovenia, international friendly (Wembley Stadium, London)
	Spain v Belgium, World Cup qualifier (Riazor, La Coruna)
	Argentina v Brazil, World Cup qualifier (Gigante de Arroyito, Rosario)
9	England v Croatia, World Cup qualifier (Wembley Stadium, London)
	Spain v Estonia, World Cup qualifier (Romano, Merida)
	Brazil v Chile, World Cup qualifier (Salvador De Bahia)
	Paraguay v Argentina (Defensores del Chaco, Asuncion)
15/16	UEFA Champions League group stage matchday 1
22/23	Carling Cup third round
26	Carling Cup fourth-round draw
29/30	UEFA Champions League group stage matchday 2

October 2009

10	Ukraine v England, World Cup qualifier (Dnipro Arena, Dnipropetrovsk)
	Armenia v Spain, World Cup qualifier (Hanrapetakan Stadium, Yerevan)
	Argentina v Peru, World Cup qualifier (El Monumental, Buenos Aires)
	Bolivia v Brazil, World Cup qualifier (Hernando Siles, La Paz)
14	England v Belarus, World Cup qualifier (Wembley Stadium, London)
	Bosnia-Herzegovina v Spain, World Cup qualifier (Sarajevo)
13	Uruguay v Argentina, World Cup qualifier (Estadio Centenario, Montevideo)
	Brazil v Venezuela, World Cup qualifier (TBC)
20/21	UEFA Champions League group stage matchday 3
27/28	Carling Cup fourth round
31	Carling Cup quarter-final draw

November 2009

3/4	UEFA Champions League group stage matchday 4
14	World Cup European Zone play-off, first leg
18	World Cup European Zone play-off, second leg
24/25	UEFA Champions League group stage matchday 5

December 2009

1/2	Carling Cup quarter-finals
2/9	Carling Cup semi-final draw
4	World Cup finals draw (Cape Town, South Africa)
8/9	UEFA Champions League group stage matchday 6
18	UEFA Champions League first knockout round draw
	Europa League last 32 and last 16 draw

KEY DATES 2009/10

(Dates are subject to change)

January 2010

1	Transfer window re-opens
2/3	FA Cup third round
5/6	Carling Cup semi-finals, first leg
19/20	Carling Cup semi-finals, second leg
23/24	FA Cup fourth round
31	Transfer window closes

February 2010

13/14	FA Cup fifth round
16/17/23/24	UEFA Champions League first knockout round, first leg
18	Europa League last 32, first leg
25	Europa League last 32, second leg
28	Carling Cup Final (Wembley Stadium, London)

March 2010

6/7	FA Cup quarter-finals
9/10/16/17	UEFA Champions League first knockout round, second leg
11	Europa League last 16, first leg
18	Europa League last 16, second leg
19	UEFA Champions League quarter-finals and semi-finals draw
	Europa League quarter-finals and semi-finals draw
30/31	UEFA Champions League quarter-finals, first leg

April 2010

1	Europa League quarter-finals, first leg
6/7	UEFA Champions League quarter-finals, second leg
8	Europa League quarter-finals, second leg
10/11	FA Cup semi-finals
20/21	UEFA Champions League semi-finals, first leg
22	Europa League semi-finals, first leg
27/28	UEFA Champions League semi-finals, second leg
29	Europa League semi-finals, second leg

May 2010

9	Barclays Premier League final day
12	Europa League Final (HSH Nordbank Arena, Hamburg, Germany)
15	FA Cup Final (Wembley Stadium, London)
22	UEFA Champions League Final (Santiago Bernabeu, Madrid, Spain)

June 2010

11	World Cup finals opening game, South Africa v TBC (Johannesburg, S. Africa)

July 2010

11	World Cup final (Johannesburg, S. Africa)

FIRST-TEAM FIXTURE LIST 2009/10

August 2009

16	Tottenham Hotspur	(A)	–	4pm
19	Stoke City	(H)	–	8pm
24	Aston Villa	(H)	–	8pm
29	Bolton Wanderers	(A)	–	3pm

September 2009

12	Burnley	(H)	–	3pm
16	Debrecen **(C. Lge Group E)**	(H)	–	7.45pm
19	West Ham United	(A)	–	5.30pm
22	Leeds United **(C. Cup 3)**	(A)	–	7.45pm
26	Hull City	(H)	–	3pm
29	Fiorentina **(C. Lge Group E)**	(A)	–	7.45pm

October 2009

4	Chelsea	(A)	–	4pm
17	Sunderland	(A)	–	3pm
20	Lyon **(C. Lge Group E)**	(H)	–	7.45pm
25	Manchester United	(H)	–	2pm
27/28	CARLING CUP 4			
31	Fulham	(A)	–	3pm

November 2009

4	Lyon **(C. Lge Group E)**	(A)	–	7.45pm
9	Birmingham City	(H)	–	8pm
21	Manchester City	(H)	–	12.45pm
24	Debrecen **(C. Lge Group E)**	(A)	–	7.45pm
29	Everton	(A)	–	1.30pm

December 2009

1/2	CARLING CUP QUARTER-FINALS			
5	Blackburn Rovers	(A)	–	3pm
9	Fiorentina **(C. Lge Group E)**	(H)	–	7.45pm
12	Arsenal	(H)	–	3pm
16	Wigan Athletic	(H)	–	8pm
19	Portsmouth	(A)	–	3pm
26	Wolverhampton Wanderers	(H)	–	3pm
28	Aston Villa	(A)	–	3pm

January 2010

2/3	FA CUP THIRD ROUND			
5/6	CARLING CUP SEMI-FINALS, FIRST LEG			
9	Tottenham Hotspur	(H)	–	3pm
16	Stoke City	(A)	–	3pm

FIRST-TEAM FIXTURE LIST 2009/10

January 2010

19/20	CARLING CUP SEMI-FINALS, SECOND LEG			
23/24	FA CUP FOURTH ROUND			
26	Wolverhampton Wanderers	(A)	–	8pm
30	Bolton Wanderers	(H)	–	3pm

February 2010

6	Everton	(H)	–	3pm
9	Arsenal	(A)	–	8pm
13/14	FA CUP FIFTH ROUND			
20	Manchester City	(A)	–	3pm
16/17/23/24	UEFA CHAMPIONS LEAGUE FIRST KNOCKOUT ROUND, FIRST LEG			
27	Blackburn Rovers	(H)	–	3pm
28	CARLING CUP FINAL			

March 2010

6	Wigan Athletic	(A)	–	3pm
6/7	FA CUP QUARTER-FINALS			
9/10/16/17	UEFA CHAMPIONS LEAGUE FIRST KNOCKOUT ROUND, SECOND LEG			
13	Portsmouth	(H)	–	3pm
20	Manchester United	(A)	–	3pm
27	Sunderland	(H)	–	3pm
30/31	UEFA CHAMPIONS LEAGUE QUARTER-FINALS, FIRST LEG			

April 2010

3	Birmingham City	(A)	–	3pm
6/7	UEFA CHAMPIONS LEAGUE QUARTER-FINALS, SECOND LEG			
10/11	FA CUP SEMI-FINALS			
11	Fulham	(H)	–	3pm
17	West Ham United	(H)	–	3pm
20/21	UEFA CHAMPIONS LEAGUE SEMI-FINALS, FIRST LEG			
24	Burnley	(A)	–	3pm
27/28	UEFA CHAMPIONS LEAGUE SEMI-FINALS, FIRST LEG			

May 2010

1	Chelsea	(H)	–	3pm
9	Hull City	(A)	–	3pm
12	EUROPA LEAGUE FINAL			
15	FA CUP FINAL			
22	UEFA CHAMPIONS LEAGUE FINAL			

Copyright © The FA Premier League Ltd and The Football League Ltd 2009.
Compiled in association with Atos Origin. All fixtures and kick off times subject to change.
Home UEFA Champions League matches kick off at 7.45pm.
FA Cup and Carling Cup kick off times to be confirmed.
All information correct at time of press - August 2009.

Please note all fixtures, kick-off times and dates are subject to change

FA PREMIER RESERVE LEAGUE NORTHERN SECTION FIXTURES 2009/10

AUGUST

27 Blackburn Rovers   (A)

SEPTEMBER

02 Bolton Wanderers   (H)
17 Manchester United   (H) - 7.30pm KO
29 Manchester City   (A)

OCTOBER

07 Burnley   (A)
20 Sunderland   (H)

NOVEMBER

03 Everton   (A)
10 Hull City   (H)
24 Wigan Athletic   (A)

DECEMBER

02 Blackburn Rovers   (H)

JANUARY

14 Manchester United   (A)
19 Manchester City   (H)

FEBRUARY

16 Burnley   (H)
23 Sunderland   (A)

MARCH

09 Everton   (H) - 7.30pm KO
23 Hull City   (A)
29 Bolton Wanderers   (A)

APRIL

06 Wigan Athletic   (H)

All fixtures 7pm,
subject to change.

Copyright © and Database Right 2009 The FA Premier League Ltd. All rights reserved. Compiled in association with Atos Origin.
All fixtures are subject to change.
Home fixtures to be played at Prenton Park, Tranmere Rovers FC, subject to change.
Please check on our website www.liverpoolfc.tv for up-to-date information on whether the match is still being played on the above scheduled date.

The Under-18s line up before the FA Youth Cup final, second leg against Arsenal, May 2009

FA PREMIER ACADEMY LEAGUE FIXTURES 2009/10

AUGUST
22 Fulham (A)
29 Leicester City (H)

SEPTEMBER
05 Nottingham Forest (A)
12 Barnsley (H)
19 Sunderland (A)
26 Manchester City (H)

OCTOBER
03 West Bromwich Albion (A)
10 Bolton Wanderers (H)
17 Blackburn Rovers (A)
31 Everton (H)

NOVEMBER
07 Crewe Alexandra (H)
14 Wolverhampton W. (A)
21 Manchester United (H)

DECEMBER
05 Stoke City (A)
12 Blackburn Rovers (H)

JANUARY
09 Everton (A)
16 Crewe Alexandra (A)
23 Wolverhampton W. (H)
30 Manchester United (A)

FEBRUARY
06 Stoke City (H)
20 Manchester City (A)
27 West Bromwich Albion (H)

MARCH
06 Bolton Wanderers (A)
13 Leeds United (H)
20 Derby County (H)
27 Huddersfield Town (A)

APRIL
17 Sheffield United (A)
24 Middlesbrough (H)

All fixtures 11am unless stated, subject to change.

FA YOUTH CUP DATES
R3   To be played by December 12
R4   To be played by January 16
R5   To be played by January 30
R6   To be played by February 13
S-F 1&2 To be played by March 6/March 20
F 1&2   To be confirmed

FA WOMEN'S PREMIER LEAGUE NORTH FIXTURES 2009/10

AUGUST
16 OOH Lincoln (H)
30 Luton Town (H)

SEPTEMBER
02 Preston North End (H)
06 Leeds City Vixens (A)
13 Sunderland (LC1) (A)
20 Newcastle United (A)
27 Derby County (H)
30 Preston North End (A)

OCTOBER
04 LEAGUE CUP SECOND ROUND
11 Sheffield Wednesday (H)
18 Curzon Ashton (A)
25 Aston Villa (H)

NOVEMBER
01 Manchester City (A)
08 OOH Lincoln (A)
15 Leicester City (H)
22 Luton Town (A)
29 Leeds City Vixens (H)

DECEMBER
06 Newcastle United (H)
13 FA CUP THIRD ROUND
20 Derby County (A)

JANUARY
10 FA CUP FOURTH ROUND
17 Sheffield Wednesday (A)
24 Curzon Ashton/FAC5 (H)
31 Aston Villa (A)

FEBRUARY
07 Manchester City (H)
14 FA CUP SIXTH ROUND

MARCH
14 FA CUP SEMI-FINAL

MAY
03 FA CUP FINAL

TBC Leicester City (A)

All fixtures 2pm unless stated, subject to change.

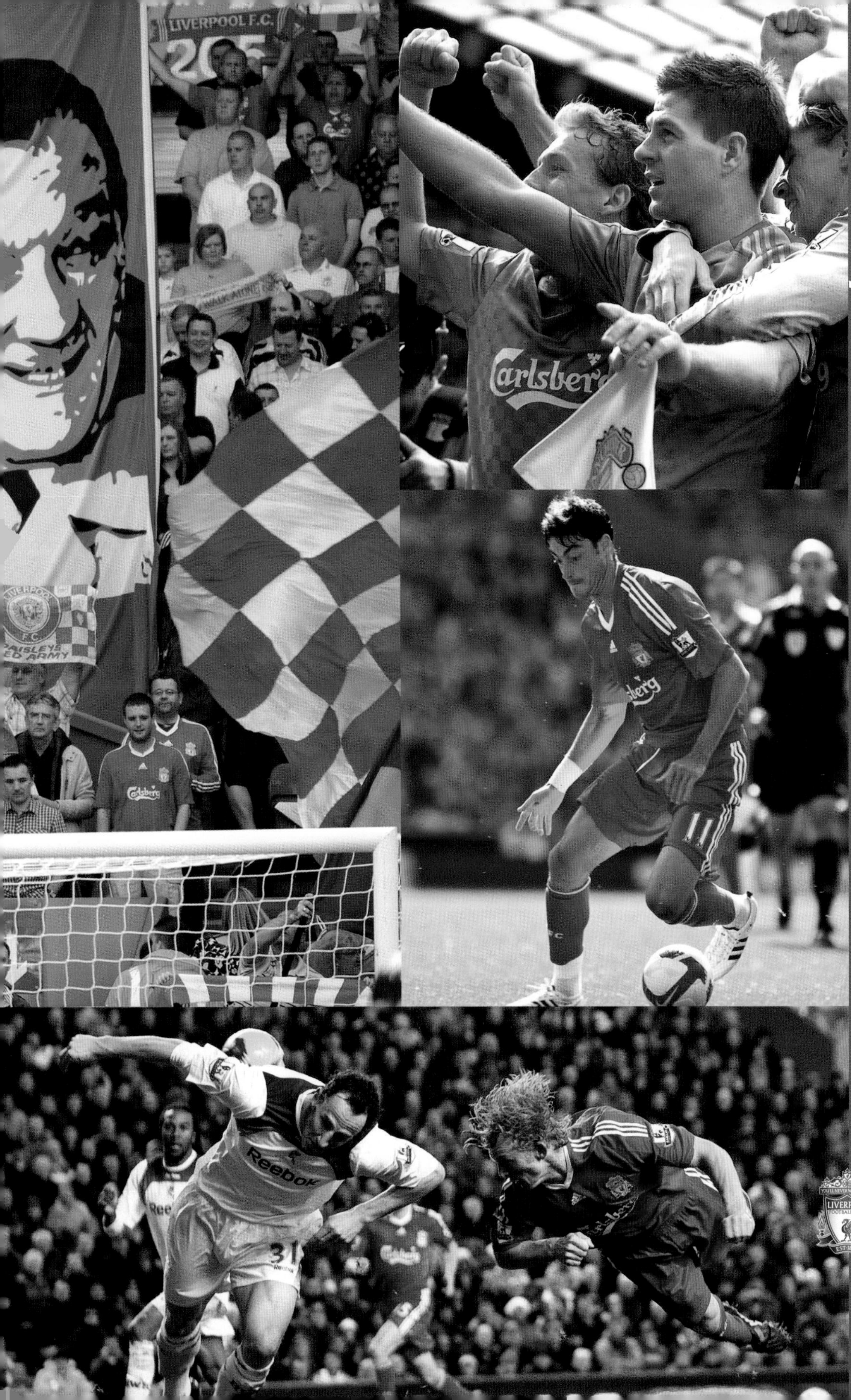

THE 2008/09 SEASON

WHAT HAPPENED WHEN?

August

1 Liverpool draw Standard Liege; new squad numbers are announced.

2 The Reds ease to a 4-0 win over Rangers at Ibrox.

5 Sebastian Leto is again denied a work permit; David Martin joins Leicester City on loan. The Reds beat Valerenga 4-1 in their latest pre-season workout.

6 Sebastian Leto joins Olympiakos on loan.

7 A late Andriy Voronin strike earns a 1-0 win over Lazio in the club's final pre-season clash.

12 Miki Roque agrees a season-long loan deal with Cartagena.

13 A 0-0 draw in Liege means the Reds are favourites to progress to the Champions League Group phase.

16 Fernando Torres' late goal earns victory at Sunderland on the opening day.

17 Andrea Dossena and Steven Gerrard earn international call-ups.

20 Eleven Liverpool players are on international duty, with Xabi Alonso (2) and Robbie Keane amongst the goals.

23 Pepe Reina, Jamie Carragher, Steven Gerrard and Fernando Torres are nominated for the UEFA European Club Footballer of the Year gong. Javier Mascherano helps Argentina to Olympic gold courtesy of a 1-0 defeat of Nigeria. Steven Gerrard's last-gasp winner secures a 2-1 victory over Middlesbrough.

27 Dirk Kuyt's late extra-time winner sees the Reds edge past Standard Liege 1-0 to qualify for the Champions League Group stage.

28 Atletico Madrid, Marseille and PSV Eindhoven are the Reds' group opponents.

30 Craig Lindfield extends his loan at Bournemouth; Liverpool land a home tie with Crewe in the League Cup.

31 The unbeaten record remains intact following a drab 0-0 draw at Aston Villa. Fernando Torres faces a spell on the sidelines after picking up a hamstring injury in the game.

Quotes of the month:

"My aim is to score more than last season, that is what I am working towards. I, at least, have to aim to equal last year's figure because it is very important to bring goals to the team."

Fernando Torres, aiming high

"...they have great players overall and looking at them now, you'd say they have an opportunity next season to challenge for the title. I think they can push forward and improve on their top-four finishes in recent seasons and Torres and Keane could give them that little edge."

Walter Smith, tipster

"He probably should have been here five or six years earlier."

Steven Gerrard on Robbie Keane

"We have to trust ourselves and believe we can do it. The squad has improved season after season and we have to believe this can be our year."

Pepe Reina, eyeing silverware

"If you'd asked me I'd be happy with two wins out of two in the league and making it through to the Champions League. We haven't given our best performances yet and maybe we have had a lot of luck, but one day your luck will run out and then we will have to perform really well to win."

Steven Gerrard, satisfied with opening month

AUGUST

THE GAMES

13	Standard Liege	A	0-0	
16	Sunderland	A	1-0	Torres 83
23	Middlesbrough	H	2-1	Carragher 86, Gerrard 90
27	Standard Liege	H	1-0 aet	Kuyt 118
31	Aston Villa	A	0-0	

WHERE THEY STOOD

1. Chelsea
2. **Liverpool**
3. Manchester City
4. Arsenal
5. West Ham United
6. Middlesbrough
7. Aston Villa

RAFA SAID. . .

'The team showed its winning mentality. This is the kind of determination we want to see.'

WHAT HAPPENED WHEN?

September

1   Albert Riera completes a deadline day move from Espanyol, with Steve Finnan moving in the other direction while young Hungarian goalkeeper Peter Gulasci completes a move from MTK Hungaria. Andriy Voronin joins Hertha Berlin on loan.

5   Young Hungarian midfielder Zsolt Poloskei joins the club's Academy on loan for the rest of the season.

6   Martin Skrtel and Yossi Benayoun net for their countries in the latest round of international matches.

9   Sami Hyypia is left out of Liverpool's Champions League squad, partly due to new UEFA regulations.

10   Xabi Alonso wins his 50th Spain cap in their 4-0 defeat of Armenia.

13   Ryan Babel's 77th-minute winner earns a 2-1 victory over Manchester United – the Reds' first in the league over Sir Alex Ferguson's side for four years – after the Red Devils had led early on.

17   Steven Gerrard's brace – the second a twice-taken penalty – earns a 2-1 win in Marseille in the Champions League Group opener.

20   Stoke City come away from Anfield with a goalless draw.

23   A weakened side progress in the League Cup, claiming a 2-1 win over Crewe.

27   Fernando Torres' double sees off Everton at Goodison. The Reds draw Tottenham away in round four of the League Cup.

Quotes of the month:

"As soon as I knew they were interested in me I knew there was only one club that I wanted to sign for and thankfully it has now happened."

Albert Riera, on his dream move

"As a manager, you have to analyse things properly, because you aren't a fan. You have a responsibility. You can't just say what people want to hear. The Premier League is becoming more and more difficult because so many people are spending money. La Liga is fantastic, but now the Premier League is better and more difficult."

Rafael Benitez, on competition

"The city will explode if we win the league, and I don't want it to happen when I'm retired. I'm 28 and realise the years are flying by. It seems like I only made my debut two or three months ago, I've enjoyed it that much. I want from 28 to 35 to be even better, and I feel my best years are ahead of me. I don't want to retire and have just Istanbul and a couple of FA Cups to remember. It will be a disaster, personally, if I don't win the league here."

Steven Gerrard, on title ambitions

"I think today is a game we can be really satisfied with because we were losing against a very good team. But we showed character and played very well in the second half, so this was very positive."

Rafael Benitez, post United victory

"It's a great result for us. Not just for the three points, but for the belief and confidence it will give us. We've just beaten the best side in Europe and a team we have a lot of respect for. It should do wonders for our confidence."

Jamie Carragher, likewise

SEPTEMBER

THE GAMES

13	Manchester United	H	2-1	Brown 27 (o.g.), Babel 77
16	Marseille	A	2-1	Gerrard 26, 32 (pen)
20	Stoke City	H	0-0	
23	Crewe Alexandra	H	2-1	Agger 15, Lucas 58
27	Everton	A	2-0	Torres 59, 62

WHERE THEY STOOD

1	Chelsea
2	Liverpool
3	Aston Villa
4	Arsenal
5	West Ham United
6	Hull City
7	Blackburn Rovers

RAFA SAID. . .

'The Premier League is becoming more difficult. La Liga is fantastic, but the Premier League is better and more difficult.'

WHAT HAPPENED WHEN?

October

1   Steven Gerrard notches his 100th Liverpool goal in the 3-1 victory over PSV Eindhoven, with Robbie Keane also breaking his duck for the club.

3   Former striker Dean Saunders is appointed manager of Wrexham.

5   A last-gasp Dirk Kuyt goal completes a fine comeback as Liverpool win 3-2 at Manchester City after being two-down at half-time. Fernando Torres' first of two goals was the club's 1,000th in the Barclays Premier League.

8   Martin Skrtel could be back in action by Christmas after being given the news the posterior cruciate ligament injury suffered at Manchester City does not now need an operation. Southend midfielder Medi Abalimba's trial with the Reds is extended.

11   The weekend internationals see Daniel Agger and Yossi Benayoun net penalties in wins for their national sides.

13   Stephane Henchoz confirms his retirement.

14   UEFA reveal that Liverpool's Champions League away clash at Atletico Madrid will be moved to a neutral venue 300km from the Spanish capital as punishment to the Spanish side due to crowd trouble at their last European game against Marseille.

15   Steven Gerrard opens the scoring in England's 3-1 win in Belarus. Yossi Benayoun and Robbie Keane also find the target during the midweek internationals.

17   Liverpool will now play in Madrid after all, after UEFA temporarily lift the stadium ban.

18   The Reds hit back from 2-1 down to defeat Wigan 3-2 thanks to Dirk Kuyt's double and Albert Riera's first goal for the club.

20   Fernando Torres and Steven Gerrard are amongst 30 players nominated for the Ballon D'Or.

22   A late Simao goal denies the Reds victory over Atletico Madrid in the Champions League.

26   The Reds go top after ending Chelsea's 86-match unbeaten league record at Stamford Bridge, Xabi Alonso's early goal securing a 1-0 win. It is also the club's best-ever start to a Barclays Premier League season.

28   Steven Gerrard and Fernando Torres are named in the Fifpro team of the year.

29   A late Steven Gerrard penalty maintains Liverpool's three-point advantage at the top following a 1-0 victory over Portsmouth.

Quotes of the month:

"The pain was unbearable. I thought that was the end for me. It hurts still, but things are getting better. I almost ripped the ligament fully – and if I had done that, I would have been out for eight months. But now it will be more like eight weeks if I am lucky."

Martin Skrtel, feared for the worst

"Chelsea were playing as well as anyone in Europe. To come and win should give our confidence a boost but we realise there's a long way to go. Their record was never going to go on forever, they were always going to lose at some point, I'm glad it was us who managed to beat them."

Jamie Carragher, post Chelsea

"I don't think you realise how big a club it is until you've played for them. I look back on it as probably the best time of my career. I loved every minute of it there. Nothing would give me greater satisfaction than to win, but for them to win the league."

Peter Crouch on Anfield return

OCTOBER

THE GAMES

1	PSV Eindhoven	H	3-1	Kuyt 5, Keane 34, Gerrard 76
5	Manchester City	A	3-2	Torres 55, 73, Kuyt 90
18	Wigan Athletic	H	3-2	Kuyt 37, 85, Riera 80
22	Atletico Madrid	A	1-1	Keane 14
26	Chelsea	A	1-0	Alonso 10
29	Portsmouth	H	1-0	Gerrard 76 (pen)

WHERE THEY STOOD

1	Liverpool
2	Chelsea
3	Arsenal
4	Aston Villa
5	Hull City
6	Manchester United
7	Portsmouth

RAFA SAID . . .

'He (Steven Gerrard) is one of the best offensive midfielders in the world and hopefully he will go on to score many for us.'

WHAT HAPPENED WHEN?

November

1   Liverpool's unbeaten Barclays Premier League record goes as a late goal earns Tottenham a 2-1 win at White Hart Lane.

4   A last-minute Steven Gerrard penalty earns the Reds a 1-1 draw with Atletico Madrid – and become favourites to progress to the Champions League knockout stages.

8   Rafael Benitez's side go back to the top of the Barclays Premier League after seeing off West Brom 3-0 – with Robbie Keane scoring twice, his first league goals for the club.

12   An under strength side bow out of the Carling Cup, going down 4-2 at holders Tottenham in round four – although Fernando Torres plays nearly an hour after a month out with a hamstring injury. Reserve-team captain Stephen Darby also makes his bow as a substitute.

15   Rafael Benitez is named the Manager of the Month for October.
        Bolton are defeated 2-0 at the Reebok, with Steven Gerrard and Dirk Kuyt on target.

19   Five Liverpool players earn caps as Spain defeat Chile 3-0 – sub Fernando Torres is given the captain's armband, and celebrates by scoring the second goal. Dirk Kuyt also nets in Holland's 3-1 defeat of Sweden. Javier Mascherano is named as the Argentina skipper in coach Diego Maradona's first game in charge, a 1-0 win over Scotland.

21   Steven Gerrard reveals his ambition to be at the club for the rest of his playing career.

22   A goalless draw at home to Fulham denies the Reds the chance to go back to the top of the Barclays Premier League.

23   Former defender Markus Babbel is confirmed as coach of German Bundesliga side FC Stuttgart.

26   Liverpool book their place in the last 16 of the Champions League after defeating Marseille 1-0 at Anfield. However, injuries to Fernando Torres and Fabio Aurelio could see the duo out for up to a month.

28   Ticket prices at Anfield and elsewhere are reduced (by £1 at Anfield) after the Government's decision to cut the rate of VAT. Youngster Ryan Flynn joins Wrexham on a month's loan.

Quotes of the month:

"If I had to choose anyone to win the Champions League then it would be Liverpool. They have great players like Fernando Torres, Steven Gerrard, Dirk Kuyt and Javier Mascherano, and they are difficult to play against. I can see them getting to the final in Rome."

Lionel Messi reveals his second choice

"It's how you come back from your setbacks that counts. This will be a test for us now. If you want to show you're championship contenders it's how you bounce back that matters."

Jamie Carragher takes positives from the first defeat of the season

"The Liverpool fans are one of the best in the world. When I'm out in the city they always come up to me to shake my hand and wish me all the best in my recovery. I just want to get back as quickly as possible to help the team win trophies and repay the supporters' faith in me."

Martin Skrtel, grateful for support

"Carragher is as important to Liverpool as Steven Gerrard. As a defender he is always there."

Gianfranco Zola, complementary of Liverpool's vice-captain

NOVEMBER

THE GAMES

1	Tottenham Hotspur	A	1-2	Kuyt 3
4	**Atletico Madrid**	**H**	**1-1**	Gerrard 90 (pen)
8	West Bromwich Alb.	H	3-0	Keane 34, 43, Arbeloa 90
12	**Tottenham Hotspur**	**A**	**2-4**	Plessis 49, Hyypia 63
15	Bolton Wanderers	A	2-0	Kuyt 28, Gerrard 73
22	Fulham	H	0-0	
26	**Marseille**	**H**	**1-0**	Gerrard 23

WHERE THEY STOOD

1. Chelsea
2. **Liverpool**
3. Manchester United
4. Arsenal
5. Aston Villa
6. Hull City
7. Everton

RAFA SAID . . .

'It means the team is playing well – you can't win Manager of the Month unless the team is winning.'

WHAT HAPPENED WHEN?

December

1 Liverpool are held to a frustrating goalless draw by West Ham at Anfield – although the Reds are now a point clear at the top of the Barclays Premier League. The match sees Sami Hyypia make his 454th appearance, moving him up to joint-20th with Ron Yeats in the club's all-time record appearance makers.

2 Fernando Torres is third in the Ballon d'Or voting, with Steven Gerrard 10th. The Reds' youngsters see off Leeds 2-1 to secure a place in round four of the FA Youth Cup.

5 Sami Hyypia is named as Finland's Player of the Year, the seventh time the defender has scooped the award.

6 Liverpool stay top after recording a 3-1 success at Blackburn Rovers.

9 The Reds finish top of group D after a youthful Liverpool side prove too strong for PSV Eindhoven, winning 3-1 in Holland. Three Academy players also came on with two of them, Spearing and Kelly, making their first-team debuts.

13 Results elsewhere mean the Reds are still top – after they are held to a 2-2 draw by Hull at Anfield, although the Tigers were two-up in the first half.

14 Rafael Benitez is admitted to hospital after suffering problems with a kidney stone.

16 Former midfielder Paul Ince is sacked by Blackburn Rovers, having only taken charge at Ewood Park in the summer.

19 Xabi Alonso's pre-draw wish comes true as Liverpool are paired to face Real Madrid in the Champions League.

21 With Rafael Benitez recovering at home from his operation, Sammy Lee leads the side to a useful 1-1 draw at Arsenal.

22 Chelsea's 0-0 draw at Everton means the Reds will be top of the Barclays Premier League at Christmas.

24 A hamstring injury rules Alvaro Arbeloa out of the Christmas matches.

26 Robbie Keane nets twice – taking his tally to three goals in two games – as Liverpool ease to a 3-0 win over Bolton Wanderers, which ends a run of three successive home league draws.

28 An inspired performance from Newcastle goalkeeper Shay Given fails to prevent the leaders running riot at St James's Park, Liverpool winning 5-1. Chelsea's 2-2 draw at Fulham also sees the Reds' lead rise to three points.

Quotes of the month:

"The 10 years seem to have gone by in a flash but there's an old saying that time flies when you're having fun, and that's exactly what I've had. It's been the best 10 years of my life and hopefully that will continue. There are still many more trophies I want to win before I hang my boots up."

Steven Gerrard, in reflective mood

"It's disappointing when you're not winning your home games because that is always what you want to do. But the positive thing is we've had three home games on the run and we've been poor in each one but still qualified for the last 16 of the Champions League and we're top of the league."

Jamie Carragher remaining positive

"We are a family club, it's one of the first things you recognize when you arrive. This is the best Liverpool team I've been involved in."

Dirk Kuyt, enjoying Liverpool life

"He's one of the best managers there is. Rafa is the type that when you finish a game as man of the match having scored three goals, he won't even mention it. Instead, he'll mention that you never used your left foot at a certain point! But Rafa does it right. When I need a pat on the back I get it. I have had lots of 'well dones' from him, but when I need a kick up the backside I get it too."

Steven Gerrard hails the boss

DECEMBER

THE GAMES

1	West Ham United	H	0-0	
6	Blackburn Rovers	A	3-1	Alonso 69, Benayoun 79, Gerrard 90
9	**PSV Eindhoven**	**A**	**3-1**	Babel 45, Riera 69, Ngog 77
13	Hull City	H	2-2	Gerrard 24, 32
21	Arsenal	A	1-1	Keane 42
26	Bolton Wanderers	H	3-0	Riera 26, Keane 53, 58
28	Newcastle United	A	5-1	Gerrard 31, 66, Hyypia 36, Babel 50, Alonso 77 (pen)

WHERE THEY STOOD

1	**Liverpool**
2	Chelsea
3	Manchester United
4	Aston Villa
5	Arsenal
6	Everton
7	Wigan Athletic

RAFA SAID . . .

'We are in a good position – some games we are playing well, some games not so well, there is plenty of room for improvement.'

WHAT HAPPENED WHEN?

January

3   Liverpool see off battling Preston North End in the FA Cup with a 2-0 win at Deepdale, the returning Fernando Torres clinching the tie late on.

4   Liverpool will meet Everton for the first time in the FA Cup for 18 years after the Merseyside clubs are paired together in the fourth round.

5   Double FA Youth Cup winner Robbie Threlfall joins Stockport County on loan.

6   Emiliano Insua and reserve defender Ronald Huth will miss the next month of club action due to the South American Under-20 Championships. Adam Hammill (Blackpool), Craig Lindfield (Bournemouth) and Godwin Antwi (Tranmere Rovers) all return from their respective loan spells.

7   German striker Marvin Pourie, an U18 regular, returns to his homeland to join Schalke.

8   Steven Gerrard is named the PFA Fans' Player of the Month for December.

10   The Reds are held to a 0-0 draw at Stoke City.

       Icelandic midfielder Victor Palsson, 17, is signed from Danish outfit AGF Arhus.

12   Fernando Torres is third and Steven Gerrard sixth in the FIFA World Player of the Year awards.

14   The club offer veteran defender Sami Hyypia a new one-year deal. The manager undergoes a third operation on his troublesome kidney stones.

18   Midfielder Alex Kacanaklic pens his first professional contract.

19   A late Tim Cahill header denies the Reds victory – and the chance to go back to the top of the Barclays Premier League – in the 209th Merseyside derby.

21   Jermaine Pennant joins Portsmouth on loan until the end of the season.

23   Reserve-team striker Jordy Brouwer joins RKC Waalwijk on loan for the rest of the season.

26   A second 1-1 derby draw, this time in the FA Cup, means the Reds must win at Goodison to earn a home last 16 spot against Aston Villa.

27   Strikers Krisztian Nemeth (Blackpool) and Craig Lindfield (Accrington Stanley) go out on loan for the rest of the campaign.

28   Wigan Athletic frustrate the Reds by earning a 1-1 draw after Yossi Benayoun had given Liverpool the lead.

Quotes of the month:

"The Newcastle game was one of my best performances. After the difficult game I had against Fulham I am improving a lot and I have got confidence. The supporters have been behind me and have tried to help me so I'm really happy. I always try to improve and try to take my chance."

Lucas Leiva, grateful for backing

"The players know that this is a fantastic opportunity. This season, from the beginning we were so good, we were scoring goals and winning games and everyone could see that it was an opportunity for us. We have created a lot of the expectation ourselves. But we are still in this position so everybody knows that we have to do our best."

Rafael Benitez rallies the troops

JANUARY

THE GAMES

3	Preston North End	A	2-0	Riera 25, Torres 90
10	Stoke City	A	0-0	
19	Everton	H	1-1	Gerrard 68
25	Everton	H	1-1	Gerrard 54
28	Wigan Athletic	A	1-1	Benayoun 41

WHERE THEY STOOD

1	Manchester United
2	Chelsea
3	Liverpool
4	Aston Villa
5	Arsenal
6	Everton
7	Wigan Athletic

RAFA SAID . . .

'We have had a good first half to the season...if we can do the same over the rest of the campaign then we will have a chance.'

WHAT HAPPENED WHEN?

February

1 Two late goals by Fernando Torres – his first at Anfield this season – see off 10-man Chelsea. Sami Hyypia returns to the Champions League squad.

2 Robbie Keane rejoins Tottenham Hotspur for a fee which could rise to £16m. Adam Hammill also signs for Barnsley on loan for three months, reserve keeper Peter Gulacsi moves on to Hereford United in a loan deal until the end of the season – while Ryan Flynn has his loan extended at Wrexham until April.

4 Philipp Degen is ruled out for a month with a metatarsal injury picked up for the reserves. Steven Gerrard is named PFA Fans' Player of the Month for the second successive month. The 10-man Reds fall in the FA Cup.

5 Steven Gerrard is ruled out for two weeks with a hamstring injury picked up against Everton.

6 Five players are named in the Spain squad to face England. Robbie Fowler joins Australian A-League side North Queensland Fury, signing a two-year deal.

7 Two late goals earn a 3-2 win at Portsmouth.

11 Andriy Voronin, on loan at Hertha Berlin, insists he would welcome a return to Anfield. Four of Liverpool's Spain contingent feature in the 2-0 win over England.

12 The club are seventh in the football rich list.

17 Godwin Antwi joins fellow reserve Peter Gulacsi at Hereford United on an emergency loan.

22 Dirk Kuyt's goal rescues a point in a 1-1 draw with Manchester City at Anfield, leaving the Reds seven points behind leaders Manchester United.

23 Steven Gerrard returns to the Liverpool squad to face Real Madrid – but a back injury leaves Daniel Agger on the sidelines.

25 Yossi Benayoun's late header gives the Reds an historic 1-0 victory in the Bernabeu against Real Madrid, in the first leg of their last 16 Champions League clash.

27 Chief executive Rick Parry will leave the club at the end of the season after 12 years at Anfield. Liverpool's U18 side reach the FA Youth Cup semi-finals after defeating Bolton Wanderers 4-2.

28 A shock 2-0 defeat at Middlesbrough dents Liverpool's Barclays Premier League title ambitions.

Quotes of the month:

"I am really pleased with my players because we deserved to win. When we were playing 11 against 11 I thought we the better team and then when they went down to 10 we had more control and we had more opportunities. We got what we deserved when we scored near the end and we deserved to win. We were better than them."

Rafael Benitez, post-Chelsea

"Sometimes good players cannot settle down in the team and when this happens you have to consider the situation and try to react quickly. I have to analyse things and try to look at the bigger picture and this means thinking of the club and the team and what is best for them."

Rafael Benitez on Robbie Keane's departure

"A lot of people said we needed to be in the title race at the end and be in with a fighting chance. We finished fourth last season, but we have overtaken Chelsea and Arsenal...it looks like it is going to be us and Manchester United for the title. Just by overtaking Chelsea and Arsenal in the challenge is an achievement in itself already so everyone should be proud of that."

Jamie Carragher on the title battle

"I'm very happy to have set up the goal. It's always pleasing when the free-kicks and set-pieces you've been practising in training work in a match."

Fabio Aurelio, after the Real Madrid match in Spain

FEBRUARY

THE GAMES

1	Chelsea	H	2-0	Torres 89, 90
4	Everton	A	0-1 aet	
7	Portsmouth	A	3-2	Aurelio 69, Kuyt 85, Torres 90
22	Manchester City	H	1-1	Kuyt 78
25	Real Madrid	A	1-0	Benayoun 82
28	Middlesbrough	A	0-2	

WHERE THEY STOOD

1	Manchester United
2	Chelsea
3	Liverpool
4	Aston Villa
5	Arsenal
6	Everton
7	Wigan Athletic

RAFA SAID . . .

'At this stage of the season the more players you have competing for positions the better the situation is.'

WHAT HAPPENED WHEN?

March

3   David Ngog scores his first Barclays Premier League goal for the club in a 2-0 victory over Sunderland.

6   Fernando Torres is confirmed as the PFA Fans' Player of the Month for February.

10   Liverpool complete a 5-0 aggregate triumph over Real Madrid at Anfield to reach the Champions League quarter-finals for the third successive season. Steven Gerrard scores twice in his 100th European outing for the Reds.

12   Philipp Degen's injury jinx continues, the Swiss defender pulling up with a suspected groin problem for the reserves.

14   Rafael Benitez celebrates his 100th league win as Liverpool boss as the Reds stun leaders Manchester United 4-1 at Old Trafford.

18   Manager Rafael Benitez agrees a new five-year contract, keeping him with the club until 2014.

20   The Reds draw Chelsea in the Champions League quarter-finals.

22   A minute's silence is observed before the 5-0 victory over Aston Villa, in tribute of club secretary Bryce Morrison, who passed away the previous day.

27   Martin Kelly joins Huddersfield Town on loan for the rest of the season.

28   Backroom staff Sammy Lee, Mauricio Pellegrino, Xavi Valero, Paco de Miguel and Eduardo Macia all agree contract extensions. Former Chief Scout Frank McParland also returns, to undertake a review of the running of the club's Academy.
Dirk Kuyt nets in Holland's 3-0 win over Scotland, one of 12 Liverpool players in international action.

Quotes of the month:

"The boss told me he needed someone to play in that position so I tried to do my best. I don't know if I was good or not but I tried to give the team as much as possible. It was a new experience."

Javier Mascherano, right-back against Sunderland

"I am awake at 4am designing a team. The selection? It's Javier Mascherano and 10 more."

New Argentina coach Diego Maradona

"I'm stuck for words. It's so different: the singing in the ground and the approach to the stadium. You walk through the area with all the houses and suddenly there it is, the stadium, you can't see it until it's on top of you – crowded with the fans, the noise, the passion. The atmosphere was incredible. It was a league game. I can't imagine what it's going to be like."

Raul, ahead of Real Madrid's Anfield visit

"Is he the best in the world? He might not get the attention of Messi and Ronaldo but I think he just might be. If you don't have a player like Steven Gerrard, who is the engine room, it can affect the team. He has great passing ability, can tackle and scores goals, but most importantly he gives the players confidence and belief. You can't learn that – players like him are born with that presence."

Zinedine Zidane, in praise of Liverpool's skipper

"It was magnificent – a great team performance. From the back we worked very hard, showed great character coming from a goal down and it was a magnificent win. I think it was comfortable. Obviously they had a man sent off but even when it was 11 v 11 we were men today and it was a very comfortable win. It's not very often you see Manchester United beaten 4-1 at home."

Steven Gerrard, post-United

"How do you look after Torres? I am not too sure. I think you've got to give yourself at least 10 yards head-start."

Luke Young, sounding an ominous admission

MARCH

THE GAMES

3	Sunderland	H	2-0	Ngog 52, Benayoun 65
10	**Real Madrid**	**H**	**4-0**	Torres 16, Gerrard 28 (pen), 47, Dossena 88
14	Manchester United	A	4-1	Torres 28, Gerrard 44 (pen), Aurelio 77, Dossena 90
22	Aston Villa	H	5-0	Kuyt 8, Riera 33, Gerrard 39 (pen), 50, 65 (pen)

WHERE THEY STOOD

1 Manchester United
2 **Liverpool**
3 Chelsea
4 Aston Villa
5 Arsenal
6 Everton
7 Wigan Athletic

RAFA SAID . . .

'My heart is with Liverpool Football Club, so I'm delighted to sign this new deal.'

WHAT HAPPENED WHEN?

April

1   Steven Gerrard wins his 72nd cap in England's 2-1 victory over Ukraine in the World Cup qualifier at Wembley.

3   Skipper Gerrard agrees a two-year extension to his current deal, keeping him with the Reds until 2013. Dirk Kuyt follows suit, his new contract lasting until 2012.

4   Liverpool go top of the Barclays Premier League – for a day at least – after Yossi Benayoun's last-minute winner earns a vital 1-0 win at Fulham.

8   The Reds surrender an early lead to go down to a 3-1 home defeat in the first leg of the Champions League quarter-final at the hands of Chelsea.

11   A potential goal of the season from Fernando Torres inspires Liverpool to a 4-0 stroll over Blackburn Rovers.

12   The Fields of Anfield Road, released for the 20th anniversary of Hillsborough, enters the UK Top 40 chart at No. 16 – it peaks at No. 14 a week later.

14   Liverpool scare Chelsea by levelling on aggregate, before bowing out of the Champions League 7-5 overall, after an amazing 4-4 draw at Stamford Bridge.

15   Steven Gerrard is the only non-Manchester United player named on the shortlist for the PFA Player of the Year award.

        A two-minute silence is observed in Liverpool at 3.06pm – the time play was halted at Hillsborough when 96 Reds' fans lost their lives attending the 1989 FA Cup semi-final.

21   Yossi Benayoun's stoppage-time strike rescues a point from another 4-4 thriller, this time against Arsenal at Anfield.

23   The club announce price freezes for 2009/10 tickets.

24   A 6-1 aggregate success over Birmingham City Under-18s earns the club's youth side a place in the FA Youth Cup final for a third time in four years.

25   Defender Jack Hobbs agrees to join Leicester City on a permanent deal.

        Dirk Kuyt scores twice in his 100th Barclays Premier League game in a 3-1 victory at Hull City.

26   Steven Gerrard and Fernando Torres are included in the PFA Team of the Year.

27   The reserves win the Liverpool Senior Cup for the 39th time, beating Waterloo Dock 1-0.

Quotes of the month:

"Liverpool are the hardest team to play against in Europe. Benitez is a great coach. He has a well organised defence and the perfect counter-attack. To play against them is always dangerous."

Carlo Ancelotti, impressed by the Reds

"I have said as long as the club wanted me then I would stay. I've been a fan all my life and it'll be fantastic to look back and say I have been with Liverpool all the way through."

Steven Gerrard, delighted with new deal

"He is the best striker in the world. The goals that he scores are just unbelievable. Look at the first one. It was incredible. He makes it look so simple too. It's always easier for us when he is playing."

Yossi Benayoun hails Torres' first goal against Blackburn

"I would love to remain at Liverpool for many seasons to come. I feel at home here. The club has been brilliant with me and I owe the fans a lot. They took to me as if I was one of their own. They treat me in the same way they do Gerrard or Carragher...it is unbelievable."

Fernando Torres, enjoying life

"It was typical English football, with a high tempo, good skill, good chances and an amazing atmosphere at Anfield. I must say that with the crowd there, it's like you're 11 men playing against one big family. It's not like their supporters have just come to watch the team, it's as if you are playing them as well!"

Andrei Arshavin, after his four goals for Arsenal in the 4-4 draw

APRIL

THE GAMES

4	Fulham	A	1-0	Benayoun 90
8	**Chelsea**	**H**	**1-3**	Torres 6
11	Blackburn Rovers	H	4-0	Torres 5, 33, Agger 83, Ngog 90
14	**Chelsea**	**A**	**4-4**	Aurelio 19, Alonso 28 (pen), Lucas 81, Kuyt 82
21	Arsenal	H	4-4	Torres 49, 72, Benayoun 56, 90
25	Hull City	A	3-1	Alonso 45, Kuyt 63, 89

WHERE THEY STOOD

1	Manchester United
2	**Liverpool**
3	Chelsea
4	Arsenal
5	Aston Villa
6	Everton
7	Fulham

RAFA SAID . . .

'The players have done a fantastic job and the fans will be really pleased with the team.'

WHAT HAPPENED WHEN?

May

3   A 3-0 win over Newcastle United maintains Liverpool's faint title bid.

5   It is confirmed that Sami Hyypia will leave at the end of the season, having agreed a two-year deal with Bayer Leverkusen.

9   A Steven Gerrard goal after only 76 seconds sets Liverpool on the way to a 3-0 win at West Ham.

12   It is confirmed that Academy director Piet Hamberg will leave the club at the end of the season.

13   Skipper Steven Gerrard is announced as the winner of the prestigious Football Writers' Player of the Year award.

17   The 2-0 victory at West Brom confirms the Baggies' relegation from the top flight and although Manchester United are confirmed as champions, the Reds have beaten their best-ever Barclays Premier League points haul, while equalling a 104-year-old club record for away wins in a season – 13.

24   Sami Hyypia is given an emotional send off at Anfield. He dons the captain's armband in the 3-1 defeat of Tottenham Hotspur, coming on for the last five minutes for his final Liverpool first-team appearance. The three points takes the Reds' tally for the season to 86, and sees them end the league campaign unbeaten at home.

26   Liverpool's youth side go down 2-1 at Anfield, 6-2 on aggregate to their Arsenal counterparts in the FA Youth Cup final.

28   Reserve-team boss Gary Ablett and youth coaches Hugh McAuley, Dave Shannon and Paul Lever will leave the club at the end of their contracts in the summer.

29   Fernando Torres extends his contract with the club until the summer of 2014.

Quotes of the month:

"You should have stayed on the telly!"

     The Kop directs a chant towards Newcastle United caretaker-manager Alan Shearer – the Match of the Day theme followed soon after

"I'm not a player who blames other people for my mistakes, but before the game Carra said I was due a penalty miss so this was his fault for jinxing it!"

     Steven Gerrard 'blames' Jamie Carragher for his penalty miss against West Ham

"It's important that going into next season we both try and stay fit to give Liverpool the best chance of being successful. The pair of us feel that if we are both fit and in top form then we can cause defenders and teams problems. I'm sure you would see a lot of goals from us."

     Steven Gerrard reflecting on his on-field partnership with Fernando Torres

"I think we have taken a big step this season, a really big step. Our job now is to continue to work hard and to improve because we have shown that we can win against the biggest teams."

     Javier Mascherano, eyeing future success

"It's fully deserved – and not just in terms of England, but for the whole world. This season he has been superb – our best player, the best player in England and the best player in the world."

     Pepe Reina hails the Football Writers' Player of the Year

"I am really pleased for him but a little bit sad because we're losing a fantastic professional, a good player and a good person too. I told him before the game I wanted to wait until the last minute, but the fans were pushing. At the end it was better because he almost scored. I was thinking about him coming on in the last minute and all the fans applauding him until the end. It has been 10 years and he's an idol here with the fans. Everyone loves him because he's been so good."

     Rafael Benitez pays tribute to Sami Hyypia

MAY

THE GAMES

3	Newcastle United	H	3-0	Benayoun 22, Kuyt 28, Lucas 87
9	West Ham United	A	3-0	Gerrard 2, 38, Babel 84
17	West Bromwich Alb	A	2-0	Gerrard 28, Kuyt 63
24	Tottenham Hotspur	H	3-1	Torres 31, Hutton 64 (o.g.), Benayoun 81

WHERE THEY FINISHED

1	Manchester United
2	**Liverpool**
3	Chelsea
4	Arsenal
5	Everton
6	Aston Villa
7	Fulham

RAFA SAID . . .

'I am pleased because we have been more consistent. It's very positive and good for the future.'

■ Game played
■ Substituted player
■ Unused sub

1 Goal scored
■ Used Sub
■ Substituted sub

2008/09

BARCLAYS PREMIER LEAGUE

Players (columns 1–25):
1. Diego Cavalieri
2. Andrea Dossena
3. Sami Hyypia
4. Daniel Agger
5. Robbie Keane
6. Steven Gerrard
7. Fernando Torres
8. Albert Riera
9. Fabio Aurelio
10. Xabi Alonso
11. Yossi Benayoun
12. Jermaine Pennant
13. Alvaro Arbeloa
14. Dirk Kuyt
15. Ryan Babel
16. Javier Mascherano
17. Lucas
18. Emiliano Insua
19. Jamie Carragher
20. David Ngog
21. Pepe Reina

DATE	OPPONENTS		RES	ATT
Wed 13 Aug	Standard Liege (CL Q3 1st)	A	0-0	25,000
Sat 16 Aug	Sunderland	A	1-0	43,259
Sat 23 Aug	Middlesbrough	H	2-1	43,168
Wed 27 Aug	Standard Liege (CL Q3 2nd)	H	1-0^	43,889
Sun 31 Aug	Aston Villa	A	0-0	41,647
Sat 13 Sep	Manchester United	H	2-1*	44,192
Tue 16 Sep	Marseille (CL match 1)	A	2-1	45,000
Sat 20 Sep	Stoke City	H	0-0	43,931
Tue 23 Sep	Crewe (Carling Cup Rd 3)	H	2-1	28,591
Sat 27 Sep	Everton	A	2-0	39,574
Wed 01 Oct	PSV (CL match 2)	H	3-1	41,097
Sun 05 Oct	Manchester City	A	3-2	47,280
Sat 18 Oct	Wigan Athletic	H	3-2	43,868
Wed 22 Oct	Atletico Madrid (CL match 3)	A	1-1	48,750
Sun 26 Oct	Chelsea	A	1-0	41,705
Wed 29 Oct	Portsmouth	H	1-0	43,378
Sat 01 Nov	Tottenham Hotspur	A	1-2	36,183
Tue 04 Nov	Atletico Madrid (CL match 4)	H	1-1	42,010
Sat 08 Nov	West Bromwich Albion	H	3-0	43,451
Wed 12 Nov	Tottenham (Carling Cup 4)	A	2-4	33,242
Sat 15 Nov	Bolton Wanderers	A	2-0	24,893
Sat 22 Nov	Fulham	H	0-0	43,589
Wed 26 Nov	Marseille (CL match 5)	H	1-0	40,024
Mon 01 Dec	West Ham United	H	0-0	41,169
Sat 06 Dec	Blackburn Rovers	A	3-1	26,920
Tue 09 Dec	PSV (CL match 6)	A	3-1	35,000
Sat 13 Dec	Hull City	H	2-2	43,835
Sun 21 Dec	Arsenal	A	1-1	60,094
Fri 26 Dec	Bolton Wanderers	H	3-0	43,548
Sun 28 Dec	Newcastle United	A	5-1	52,114
Sat 03 Jan	Preston (FA Cup 3rd)	A	2-0	23,046
Sat 10 Jan	Stoke City	A	0-0	27,500
Mon 19 Jan	Everton	H	1-1	44,382
Sun 25 Jan	Everton (FA Cup 4th)	H	1-1	43,524
Wed 28 Jan	Wigan Athletic	A	1-1	21,237
Sun 01 Feb	Chelsea	H	2-0	44,174
Wed 04 Feb	Everton (FA Cup 4th replay)	A	0-1^	37,918
Sat 07 Feb	Portsmouth	A	3-2	20,524
Sun 22 Feb	Manchester City	H	1-1	44,259
Wed 25 Feb	Real Madrid (CL last 16 1st)	A	1-0	85,000
Sat 28 Feb	Middlesbrough	A	0-2	33,724
Tue 03 Mar	Sunderland	H	2-0	41,587
Tue 10 Mar	Real Madrid (CL last 16 2nd)	H	4-0	42,550
Sat 14 Mar	Manchester United	A	4-1	75,569
Sun 22 Mar	Aston Villa	H	5-0	44,131
Sat 04 Apr	Fulham	A	1-0	25,661
Wed 08 Apr	Chelsea (CL QF 1st leg)	H	1-3	42,543
Sat 11 Apr	Blackburn Rovers	H	4-0	43,466
Tue 14 Apr	Chelsea (CL QF 2nd leg)	A	4-4	38,286
Tue 21 Apr	Arsenal	H	4-4	44,424
Sat 25 Apr	Hull City	A	3-1	24,942
Sun 03 May	Newcastle United	H	3-0	44,121
Sat 09 May	West Ham United	A	3-0	34,951
Sun 17 May	West Bromwich Albion	A	2-0	26,138
Sun 24 May	Tottenham Hotspur	H	3-1*	43,937

^ after extra-time
* Own goal v Man Utd (Brown)
* Own goal v Tottenham (Hutton)

	28	29	30	31	32	33	34	36	37	38	39	41	42	43
Damien Plessis														
Charles Itandje														
Nabil El Zhar														
Stephen Darby														
Martin Kelly														
Steven Irwin														
Martin Skrtel														
Craig Lindfield														
Nathan Eccleston														
Martin Hansen														
Peter Gulacsi														
Hakan Duyan														
Andriy Voronin														

FINAL TABLE

BARCLAYS PREMIER LEAGUE   **2008/09**

	Team	Pd	HOME					AWAY					Pts	GD
			W	D	L	F	A	W	D	L	F	A		
1	Man Utd	38	16	2	1	43	13	12	4	3	25	11	90	+44
2	**Liverpool**	**38**	**12**	**7**	**0**	**41**	**13**	**13**	**4**	**2**	**36**	**14**	**86**	**+50**
3	Chelsea	38	11	6	2	33	12	14	2	3	35	12	83	+44
4	Arsenal	38	11	5	3	31	16	9	7	3	37	21	72	+31
5	Everton	38	8	6	5	31	20	9	6	4	24	17	63	+18
6	Aston Villa	38	7	9	3	27	21	10	2	7	27	27	62	+6
7	Fulham	38	11	3	5	28	16	3	8	8	11	18	53	+5
8	Tottenham	38	10	5	4	21	10	4	4	11	24	35	51	0
9	West Han	38	9	2	8	23	22	5	7	7	19	23	51	-3
10	Man City	38	13	0	6	40	18	2	5	12	18	32	50	+8
11	Wigan	38	8	5	6	17	18	4	4	11	17	27	45	-11
12	Stoke City	38	10	5	4	22	15	2	4	13	16	40	45	-17
13	Bolton	38	7	5	7	21	21	4	3	12	20	32	41	-12
14	Portsmouth	38	8	3	8	26	29	2	8	9	12	28	41	-19
15	Blackburn	38	6	7	6	22	23	4	4	11	18	37	41	-20
16	Sunderland	38	6	3	10	21	25	3	6	10	13	29	36	-20
17	Hull City	38	3	5	11	18	36	5	6	8	21	28	35	-25
18	Newcastle	38	5	7	7	24	29	2	6	11	16	30	34	-19
19	Middlesbro	38	5	9	5	17	20	2	2	15	11	37	32	-29
20	West Brom	38	7	3	9	26	33	1	5	13	10	34	32	-31

Sami farewell – The players salute Hyypia on the 08/09 final day

6 Villa thriller

Although Aston Villa's Champions League ambitions had all but died after a bright first half of the season, Liverpool produced another five-goal show, with Steven Gerrard hitting a hat-trick. Amazingly, it took the Reds' goal tally to 13 in three games.

Torres double

A third Merseyside derby victory in a row was achieved back in September. Fernando Torres again showed his class against a sorry Everton side in the Goodison sunshine.

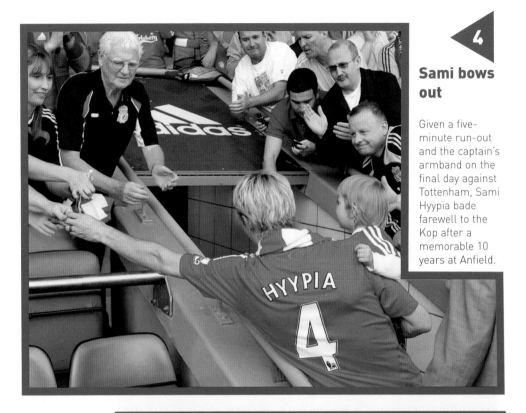

4

Sami bows out

Given a five-minute run-out and the captain's armband on the final day against Tottenham, Sami Hyypia bade farewell to the Kop after a memorable 10 years at Anfield.

3

Xabi ends Bridge run

Xabi Alonso's early deflected strike at Chelsea secured a crucial league success against one of the Reds' title rivals. It also inflicted a first home defeat on the London Blues since February 2004 – a run of 86 games unbeaten.

2

Madrid marvels

A deserved one-goal win in Madrid, a memorable 4-0 victory at Anfield. Liverpool totally outclassed Real in the last-16 of the Champions League, with Gerrard netting a double in the second leg.

1

United double

Always a welcome occurrence in a Liverpool season, a double over Manchester United. The 2-1 win at Anfield was enjoyable, but it was the 4-1 demoltion of United at Old Trafford that was the most memorable moment – the Reds' biggest win at United since 1936.

PLAYER STATISTICS 2008/2009

PLAYER	PLAYED	SUBSTITUTED	SUB NOT USED	GOALS
Cavalieri	4	0	51	0
Dossena	19 + 7	5	23	2
Hyypia	15 + 4	0	17	2
Agger	23 + 3	0	18	2
Keane	23 + 5	18	5	7
Gerrard	41 + 3	16	2	24
Torres	32 + 6	16	1	17
Voronin	0	0	1	0
Riera	33 + 7	27	7	5
Aurelio	27 + 6	4	5	3
Alonso	40 + 7	7	4	5
Benayoun	26 + 16	13	7	9
Pennant	3 + 1	1	3	0
Arbeloa	43	5	2	1
Kuyt	48 + 3	15	0	15
Babel	13 + 29	4	6	4
Mascherano	37 + 1	13	7	0
Lucas	20 + 19	2	9	3
Insua	11 + 2	0	6	0
Carragher	53 + 1	2	1	1
Ngog	5 + 14	3	16	3
Reina	51	0	2	0
Spearing	0 + 2	0	2	0
Degen	2	2	5	0
Plessis	4 + 1	2	3	1
El Zhar	3 + 16	2	10	0
Darby	0 + 2	0	4	0
Kelly	0 + 1	0	2	0
Skrtel	29 + 1	0	7	0
Gulacsi	0	0	2	0

Dirk Kuyt – Busiest of the outfield players during 2008/09

MINUTES ON PITCH 2008/2009

PLAYER	LEAGUE	FA CUP	LEAGUE CUP	CHAMP. LEAGUE	TOTAL
Cavalieri	0	90	180	90	360
Dossena	1040	210	90	427	1767
Hyypia	1093	90	180	0	1363
Agger	1366	90	180	450	2086
Keane	1260	73	3	442	1778
Gerrard	2630	196	0	699	3525
Torres	1731	208	79	768	2786
Riera	1895	185	0	560	2640
Aurelio	1737	7	0	690	2434
Alonso	2562	255	24	885	3726
Benayoun	1890	104	0	513	2507
Pennant	157	0	90	0	247
Arbeloa	2578	210	0	1084	3872
Kuyt	3179	210	0	951	4340
Babel	838	184	180	442	1644
Mascherano	2308	213	0	685	3206
Lucas	1286	121	180	429	2016
Insua	846	90	125	0	1061
Carragher	3401	300	17	1101	4819
Ngog	314	0	156	119	589
Reina	3420	210	0	1020	4650
Spearing	0	0	0	31	31
Degen	0	0	157	0	157
Plessis	45	0	156	91	292
El Zhar	238	0	177	45	460
Darby	0	0	6	21	27
Kelly	0	0	0	9	9
Skrtel	1810	210	0	660	2680

PLAYER GOALS 2008/2009 SEASON

PLAYER	ALL COMPETITIONS			
	1ST HALF	2ND HALF	EXTRA TIME	TOTAL
Gerrard	12	12	0	24
Torres	6	11	0	17
Kuyt	6	8	1	15
Benayoun	2	7	0	9
Keane	5	2	0	7
Alonso	3	2	0	5
Riera	3	2	0	5
Babel	1	3	0	4
Aurelio	1	2	0	3
Lucas	0	3	0	3
Ngog	0	3	0	3
Agger	1	1	0	2
Dossena	0	2	0	2
Hyypia	1	1	0	2
Own Goals	1	1	0	2
Arbeloa	0	1	0	1
Carragher	0	1	0	1
Plessis	0	1	0	1
TOTAL	42	63	1	106

APPEARANCES & GOALS FOR LIVERPOOL

AT END OF 2008/09 SEASON - CURRENT SQUAD ONLY (AT START OF 2009/10)

L'POOL	LGE GMS	LGE GLS	FA GMS	FA GLS	L. CUP GMS	L. CUP GLS	EURO GMS (inc Spr Cup)	EURO GLS	OTHER GMS (inc C. Shield & C. World)	OTHER GLS	L'POOL GMS	GLS
Cavalieri	0	0	1	0	2	0	1	0	0	0	4	0
Dossena	16	1	2	0	1	0	7	1	0	0	26	2
Agger	54	3	2	0	4	2	18	1	1	0	79	6
Gerrard	333	71	26	9	19	7	101	32	4	1	483	120
Torres	57	38	4	1	3	3	20	8	0	0	84	50
Voronin	19	5	1	0	1	0	7	1	0	0	28	6
Riera	28	3	3	1	0	0	9	1	0	0	40	5
Aurelio	57	3	3	0	4	0	22	1	1	0	87	4
Benayoun	62	4	4	3	3	1	20	4	0	0	89	20
Kuyt	104	27	7	2	2	0	34	11	0	0	147	40
Babel	57	7	7	1	4	0	23	6	0	0	91	14
Mascherano	59	1	5	0	1	0	25	0	0	0	90	1
Lucas	43	1	6	1	5	1	17	1	0	0	71	4
Insua	15	0	1	0	2	0	0	0	0	0	18	0
Carragher	398	4	32	0	27	0	116	1	4	0	577	5
Ngog	14	2	0	0	2	0	3	1	0	0	19	3
Reina	144	0	7	0	1	0	52	0	3	0	207	0
Spearing	0	0	0	0	0	0	2	0	0	0	2	0
Degen	0	0	0	0	2	0	0	0	0	0	2	0
Plessis	3	0	0	0	2	1	2	0	0	0	7	1
Itandje	0	0	4	0	3	0	0	0	0	0	7	0
El Zhar	18	0	1	0	4	1	2	0	0	0	25	1
Darby	0	0	0	0	1	0	1	0	0	0	2	0
Kelly	0	0	0	0	0	0	1	0	0	0	1	0
Skrtel	35	0	3	0	0	0	12	0	0	0	50	0

FEWEST LEAGUE DEFEATS IN ENGLAND

2008/09 SEASON

CLUB	DEFEATS	DIVISION	FINAL POSITION
Liverpool	2	Premier League	2nd
Leicester City	4	League One	1st
Manchester United	4	Premier League	1st
Chelsea	5	Premier League	3rd
Arsenal	6	Premier League	4th
Brentford	7	League Two	1st
Wycombe Wanderers	8	League Two	3rd
Birmingham City	9	Championship	2nd
Everton	9	Premier League	5th
Peterborough United	9	League One	2nd

LFC MAGAZINE AWARDS 2008/09

LFC Magazine writers were divided in their opinions on which player should be voted the club's Player of the Season. Football Writers' Player of the Year Steven Gerrard garnered two votes, while there were also two votes for Xabi Alonso, who enjoyed arguably his finest season in a red shirt. Gerrard netted a best-ever 24 goals, while also reaching the landmark tally of 100 Liverpool goals and European appearances. But his Spanish team-mate also produced some outstanding displays, his five goals including the winner which ended Chelsea's 86-match unbeaten run at Stamford Bridge.

Steven Gerrard featured prominently in the running for Goal of the Season, landing 2nd and 3rd place with his strikes against Marseille – the first goal, his curling effort from long range – and Real Madrid – the second goal from Ryan Babel's cross. But it was Fernando Torres who scooped this particular accolade, for his stunning swivel and volley against Blackburn Rovers at Anfield.

There was one clear winner in the category Match of the Season. The victor? The 4-1 victory at Manchester United.

Steven Gerrard and Xabi Alonso – Players of the season

SAMI HYYPIA'S CENTRE-BACK PARTNERS

With Sami Hyypia leaving at the end of the 2008/09 campaign after 10 years' loyal service, we look back on the players the Finland central defender partnered during his time at Anfield.

DANIEL AGGER

COMPETITION	P	W	D	L	FOR	AG	CLEAN SHEETS	%W	%CLEAN SHEETS
League	10	8	2	0	26	4	6	80	60
FA Cup	1	1	0	0	2	0	1	100	100
League Cup	2	1	0	1	4	5	0	50	0
Europe	3	2	1	0	6	1	2	67	67
TOTAL	16	12	3	1	38	10	9	75	56

ALVARO ARBELOA

COMPETITION	P	W	D	L	FOR	AG	CLEAN SHEETS	%W	%CLEAN SHEETS
League	1	1	0	0	3	2	0	100	0
TOTAL	1	1	0	0	3	2	0	100	0

MARKUS BABBEL

COMPETITION	P	W	D	L	FOR	AG	CLEAN SHEETS	%W	%CLEAN SHEETS
League	6	4	1	1	16	6	3	67	50
FA Cup	1	1	0	0	4	2	0	100	0
Europe	3	1	2	0	5	4	1	33	33
TOTAL	10	6	3	1	25	12	4	60	40

IGOR BISCAN

COMPETITION	P	W	D	L	FOR	AG	CLEAN SHEETS	%W	%CLEAN SHEETS
League	25	12	6	7	41	27	9	48	36
FA Cup	1	1	0	0	2	0	1	100	100
Europe	5	2	2	1	7	4	2	40	40
TOTAL	31	15	8	8	50	31	12	48	39

JAMIE CARRAGHER

COMPETITION	P	W	D	L	FOR	AG	CLEAN SHEETS	%W	%CLEAN SHEETS
League	107	59	23	25	164	94	44	55	41
FA Cup	9	7	1	1	27	11	3	78	33
League Cup	2	0	0	2	3	5	0	0	0
Europe	37	25	7	5	68	20	20	50	54
World Club C'ship	2	1	0	1	3	1	1	50	50
TOTAL	157	92	31	34	265	131	68	59	43

SALIF DIAO

COMPETITION	P	W	D	L	FOR	AG	CLEAN SHEETS	%W	%CLEAN SHEETS
League	1	0	1	0	2	2	0	0	0
Europe	1	0	0	1	0	2	0	0	0
TOTAL	2	0	1	1	2	4	0	0	0

SAMI HYYPIA'S CENTRE-BACK PARTNERS

STEPHANE HENCHOZ

COMPETITION	P	W	D	L	FOR	AG	CLEAN SHEETS	%W	%CLEAN SHEETS
League	124	63	36	25	187	104	54	51	44
FA Cup	14	9	1	4	22	11	5	64	36
League Cup	12	9	0	3	34	14	5	75	42
Europe	32	18	11	3	50	22	20	56	63
FA Community Shield	2	1	0	1	2	2	0	50	0
TOTAL	184	100	48	36	295	153	84	54	46

JOSEMI

COMPETITION	P	W	D	L	FOR	AG	CLEAN SHEETS	%W	%CLEAN SHEETS
Europe	1	0	0	1	0	1	0	0	0
TOTAL	1	0	0	1	0	1	0	0	0

GABRIEL PALETTA

COMPETITION	P	W	D	L	FOR	AG	CLEAN SHEETS	%W	%CLEAN SHEETS
League	2	0	0	2	1	3	0	0	0
League Cup	1	0	0	1	3	6	0	0	0
TOTAL	3	0	0	3	4	9	0	0	0

MAURICIO PELLEGRINO

COMPETITION	P	W	D	L	FOR	AG	CLEAN SHEETS	%W	%CLEAN SHEETS
League	2	0	0	2	0	3	0	0	0
TOTAL	2	0	0	2	0	3	0	0	0

MARTIN SKRTEL

COMPETITION	P	W	D	L	FOR	AG	CLEAN SHEETS	%W	%CLEAN SHEETS
League	8	5	3	0	16	5	4	63	50
FA Cup	1	1	0	0	5	2	0	100	0
Europe	3	2	1	0	6	3	1	67	33
TOTAL	12	8	4	0	27	10	5	67	42

DJIMI TRAORE

COMPETITION	P	W	D	L	FOR	AG	CLEAN SHEETS	%W	%CLEAN SHEETS
League	16	9	1	6	28	17	7	56	44
FA Cup	1	0	1	0	0	0	1	0	100
League Cup	1	1	0	0	5	1	0	100	0
Europe	6	2	2	2	11	9	0	33	0
TOTAL	24	12	4	8	44	27	8	50	33

ZAK WHITBREAD

COMPETITION	P	W	D	L	FOR	AG	CLEAN SHEETS	%W	%CLEAN SHEETS
FA Cup	1	0	0	1	0	1	0	0	0
League Cup	1	0	0	1	1	2	0	0	0
Europe	1	1	0	0	2	0	1	100	100
TOTAL	3	1	0	2	3	3	1	33	33

RESERVES 2008/09

SEASON REVIEW

After the success of 2007/08, when the side finished as national champions, the campaign was much more difficult in what would prove Gary Ablett's last season in charge of the second string. The youthful squad struggled for form early on, losing five of their first eight games, while a pre-season injury to the previous year's top scorer Krisztian Nemeth was a big blow. The Hungarian did come back to fitness in the latter half of the season, and hit the winner in the final as Liverpool made up for Liverpool Senior Cup disappointment in 2008 by clinching the trophy for the 39th time in the club's history. Jay Spearing scooped LFC Magazine's reserve player of the year. The 2009/10 season will see the side led by John McMahon. Brother of Liverpool legend Steve, John spent eight years on the Tranmere Rovers coaching staff before joining Shrewsbury Town as assistant-manager in the summer of 2006. One other major change is that Tranmere's 16,567-capacity Prenton Park ground will host the Reserves' home games.

2008/09 STATISTICS

RES. LGE & CUP APPS. & GOALS 2008/09

	Appearances	Goals
David Amoo	2	0
Godwin Antwi	5	0
Daniel Ayala	7	0
Dean Bouzanis	8	0
Jordy Brouwer	8	2
Gerardo Bruna	16	2
Ryan Crowther	9	0
Lauri Dalla Valle	2	0
Stephen Darby	18	0
Philipp Degen	5	1
Francisco Duran	4	0
Nathan Eccleston	1	0
Nabil El Zhar	7	2
Vitor Flora	8	3
Ryan Flynn	2	0
Peter Gulacsi	8	0
Martin Hansen	7	0
Ronald Huth	9	0
Emiliano Insua	10	0
Steven Irwin	9	0
Alex Kacaniklic	1	0
Martin Kelly	9	1
Gary Mackay-Steven	5	0
Emmanuel Mendy	13	0
Krisztian Nemeth	11	2
David Ngog	6	3
Daniel Pacheco	21	5
Victor Palsson	11	1
Jermaine Pennant	1	0
Damien Plessis	18	2
Nikola Saric	1	0
Mikel San Jose	20	1
Michael Scott	1	0
Andras Simon	14	1
Jay Spearing	17	4
Robbie Threlfall	1	0
Vincent Weijl	16	2

RESERVES LEAGUE RESULTS 2008/09

			Result
02.09.08	Middlesbrough	A	1-0
17.09.08	Sunderland	A	1-2
07.10.08	Manchester City	A	0-1
14.10.08	Everton	H	2-3
03.11.08	Manchester City	H	1-2
18.11.08	Wigan Athletic	H	1-0
24.11.08	Newcastle United	A	1-1
04.12.08	Blackburn Rovers	A	0-1
10.12.08	Bolton Wanderers	A	1-2
16.12.08	Hull City	H	0-0
20.01.09	Middlesbrough	H	2-0
29.01.09	Manchester United	A	0-0
17.02.09	Everton	A	1-1
12.03.09	Manchester United	H	2-2
17.03.09	Wigan Athletic	A	2-2
02.04.09	Sunderland	H	0-2
06.04.09	Blackburn Rovers	A	1-1
20.04.09	Bolton Wanderers	H	3-4
23.04.09	Hull City	A	2-1
29.04.09	Newcastle United	H	5-1

BARCLAYS PREMIERSHIP RESERVE LEAGUE NORTH — RESERVES LEAGUE NORTH TABLE 2008/09

		Pld	W	D	L	F	A	Pts
1	Sunderland	20	13	4	3	33	13	43
2	Man Utd	20	10	6	4	35	19	36
3	Blackburn	20	9	6	5	30	19	33
4	Newcastle	20	9	5	6	34	30	32
5	Man City	20	10	0	10	32	29	30
6	Wigan Ath.	20	7	3	10	25	36	24
7	**Liverpool**	**20**	**5**	**7**	**8**	**26**	**26**	**22**
8	Everton	20	5	7	8	19	25	22
9	Hull City	20	6	4	10	22	36	22
10	Middlesbro	20	6	3	11	26	33	21
11	Bolton Wan.	20	6	3	11	22	38	21

RESERVES/ACADEMY CUP RESULTS 2008/09

LIVERPOOL IN THE LIVERPOOL SENIOR CUP 2008/09

Quarter-final

24th February 2009
Formby 0-3 Liverpool   (Altcar Road, Formby)
Liverpool goalscorers: Simon (20), Kelly (57), Flora (60)

Semi-final

24th March 2009
Southport 0-3 Liverpool (aet)   (Haig Avenue, Southport)
Liverpool goalscorers: Thornton (92, o.g.), Pacheco (99), Spearing (113)

Final

27th April 2009
Waterloo Dock 0-1 Liverpool   (The Arriva Stadium, Crosby)
Liverpool goalscorer: Nemeth (76)

LIVERPOOL IN THE FA YOUTH CUP 2008/09

Round 3

2nd December 2008
Leeds United 1-2 Liverpool   (Elland Road)
Liverpool goalscorers: Ince (14), Dalla Valle (59)

Round 4

15th January 2009
Bristol Rovers 2-2 Liverpool (aet)   (Memorial Stadium)
Liverpool win 4-2 on penalties
Liverpool goalscorers: Dalla Valle (54, 92)

Round 5

5th February 2009
Liverpool 1-0 Chelsea   (Anfield)
Liverpool goalscorer: Amoo (17)

Quarter-final

27th February 2009
Liverpool 4-2 Bolton Wanderers   (Anfield)
Liverpool goalscorers: Eccleston (25), Amoo (31), Irwin (42, 78)

Semi-final, 1st leg

16th April 2009
Birmingham City 0-3 Liverpool   (St Andrew's)
Liverpool goalscorers: Dalla Valle (12, 28), Amoo (24)

Semi-final, 2nd leg

24th April 2009
Liverpool 3-1 Birmingham City   (Anfield)
Liverpool goalscorers: Dalla Valle (17, 57), Kacaniklic (53)

Final, 1st leg

22nd May 2009
Arsenal 4-1 Liverpool   (Emirates Stadium)
Liverpool goalscorer: Kacaniklic (36)
Team: Bouzanis, Clair, Buchtmann, Ayala, Kennedy, Wisdom, Amoo, Irwin, Dalla Valle (Robinson 80), Ince, Kacaniklic (Eccleston 63).

Final, 2nd leg

22nd May 2009
Liverpool 1-2 Arsenal   (Anfield)
Liverpool goalscorer: Dalla Valle (51)
Team: Bouzanis, Robinson, Ayala, Kennedy, Irwin, Kacaniklic (Eccleston 45), Amoo, Buchtmann (Cooper 84), Wisdom (Roberts 84) Dalla Valle, Ince.

THE ACADEMY 2008/09

SEASON REVIEW

A third FA Youth Cup final in only four seasons was the highlight of the Under-18s season. Although Arsenal's youngsters proved too strong in the final, there was enough promise in their efforts to encourage the coaching staff. The side averaged an impressive two goals a game in their league programme, as they went one better than the 2007/08 squad in finishing fourth. LFC Magazine U18 player of the year Lauri Dalla Valle finished as top scorer, netting 12 goals in the league in his total of 19, while David Amoo hit 12 (nine in the league).

2008/09 STATISTICS

U18s APPEARANCES & GOALS 2008/09

	Appearances	Goals
Astrit Ajdarevic	8	2
David Amoo	31	12
Daniel Ayala	5	0
Dean Bouzanis	15	0
Christopher Buchtmann	19	0
Deale Chamberlain	5	0
Karl Clair	8	1
Conor Coady	9	0
Alex Cooper	14	0
Lauri Dalla Valle	26	19
Adam Dawson	5	1
Hakan Duyan	1	0
Nathan Eccleston	17	6
James Ellison	15	5
John Flanaghan	6	1

U18s APPEARANCES & GOALS 2008/09

	Appearances	Goals
Martin Hansen	10	0
Thomas Ince	27	3
Steven Irwin	10	2
Alex Kacaniklic	22	3
Joe Kennedy	28	4
Jack Metcalf	13	0
Shane O'Connor	9	0
Chris Oldfield	4	0
Adam Pepper	28	3
Marvin Pourie	12	7
Michael Roberts	18	0
Jack Robinson	6	1
Michael Scott	18	0
Andre Wisdom	26	0

U18s LEAGUE & YOUTH CUP RESULTS 08/09

			Result
23.08.08	Crystal Palace	H	4-3
30.08.08	Coventry City	A	0-2
06.09.08	Nottingham Forest	H	2-0
13.09.08	Newcastle United	H	3-2
20.09.08	Sheffield Wednesday	A	3-0
27.09.08	Crewe Alexandra	A	3-1
04.10.08	Wolves	H	4-2
11.10.08	Blackburn Rovers	A	0-4
18.10.08	Manchester United	A	2-2
01.11.08	Bolton Wanderers	H	5-0
08.11.08	Manchester City	A	1-4
15.11.08	Everton	H	2-0
22.11.08	Stoke City	A	2-2
02.12.08	Leeds United (FAYC3)	A	2-1
06.12.08	West Bromwich Albion	H	3-0
13.12.08	Manchester United	H	1-3
15.01.09	Bristol Rovers (FAYC4)	A	2-2*
24.01.09	Manchester City	H	1-1
31.01.09	Everton	A	2-3
05.02.09	Chelsea (FAYC5)	H	1-0
14.02.09	West Bromwich Albion	A	0-4
21.02.09	Crewe Alexandra	H	3-1
27.02.09	Bolton W (FAYCQF)	H	4-2
07.03.09	Wolves	A	0-1
14.03.09	Blackburn Rovers	H	2-2
21.03.09	Leeds United	A	1-3

U18s LEAGUE & YOUTH CUP RESULTS 08/09

			Result
28.03.09	Huddersfield Town	A	3-3
04.04.09	Stoke City	H	2-1
16.04.09	Birmingham (FAYCSF1)	A	3-0
24.04.09	Birmingham (FAYCSF2)	H	3-1
12.05.09	Sheffield United	H	5-0
16.05.09	Bolton Wanderers	A	0-3
22.05.09	Arsenal (FAYCF1)	A	1-4
26.05.09	Arsenal (FAYCF2)	H	1-2

* Liverpool won 4-2 on penalties

FA PREMIER ACADEMY 2008/09 GROUP C

	P	W	D	L	F	A	Pts
1 Man City	28	22	6	0	88	33	72
2 Man Utd	28	15	8	5	65	34	53
3 West Brom	28	13	5	10	55	37	44
4 Liverpool	**28**	**13**	**5**	**10**	**56**	**49**	**44**
5 Everton	28	11	8	9	49	39	41
6 Stoke City	28	11	7	10	30	41	40
7 Wolves	28	10	9	9	36	39	39
8 Crewe Alex.	28	11	5	12	54	53	38
9 Blackburn	28	8	6	14	36	50	30
10 Bolton W.	28	7	2	19	28	57	23

LIVERPOOL LADIES 2008/09

SEASON REVIEW

Led by Robbie Johnson and his assistant Graeme Hurst, the girls will be looking to bounce back to the Premier League at the first attempt after a disappointing campaign which saw the side drop out of the top flight after a two-year spell at this level. A run of one draw and eight defeats from their first nine league games proved too much to recover.

The cups provided little cheer either, with the Reds thrown out of the FA Cup having inadvertently fielded a suspended player in their tie with Nottingham Forest. The same opposition also knocked them out of the Premier League Cup.

The squad look in good shape to achieve promotion, managing to keep hold of most of their key players for the Northern Division season. These include last season's top scorer Cheryl Foster, defender Jo Traynor and twins Kelly and Vicky Jones. They will again play their home fixtures at Skelmersdale United FC. For more on the team, log on to **www.liverpoolladiesfc.co.uk**

2008/09 STATISTICS

LADIES LEAGUE & CUP RESULTS 2008/09

Date	Opponent		Result
17.08.08	Chelsea	A	0-5
24.08.08	Arsenal	H	2-11
27.08.08	Everton	H	1-2
31.08.08	Bristol Academy	A	0-6
07.09.08	Fulham	H	2-2
14.09.08	Nottingham F. (LC1)	A	2-4
17.09.08	Blackburn Rovers	H	1-2
21.09.08	Nottingham Forest	A	2-2
28.09.08	Doncaster Rovers Bel.	H	2-5
12.10.08	Leeds Carnegie	A	1-4
19.10.08	Birmingham City	A	1-0
22.10.08	Everton	A	0-5
06.11.08	Blackburn Rovers	A	1-0
16.11.08	Mossley Hill (CCQF)	H	3-2
23.11.08	Arsenal	A	0-2
14.12.08	Birmingham City	H	2-3
04.01.09	Nottingham F. (FAC3)	A	1-0*
15.02.09	Chelsea	H	1-1
22.02.09	Nottingham Forest	H	1-2
25.02.09	Everton (CCSF)	A	0-1
01.03.09	Leeds Carnegie	H	1-3
15.03.09	Watford	A	3-0
22.03.09	Watford	H	0-1
29.03.09	Bristol Academy	H	2-3
05.04.09	Fulham	A	2-2
21.03.09	Leeds United	A	1-3

* Liverpool disqualified from competition

FA WOMEN'S PREMIER LEAGUE 2008/09

	P	W	D	L	F	A	Pts
1 Arsenal	22	20	1	1	89	14	61
2 Everton	22	20	1	1	68	10	61
3 Chelsea	22	16	2	4	55	23	50
4 Doncaster	22	9	6	7	43	36	33
5 Birmingham	22	10	3	9	39	43	33
6 Leeds Carn.	22	8	4	10	32	40	28
7 Watford	22	7	4	11	31	40	25
8 Bristol Ac.	22	5	8	9	39	49	23
9 Blackburn	22	5	3	14	27	52	18
10 Notts. For.	22	5	2	15	25	59	17
11 Liverpool	**22**	**4**	**4**	**14**	**28**	**63**	**16**
12 Fulham	22	1	6	15	17	64	9

2009/10 SQUAD LIST

Anisha Bateman
Carmel Bennett
Emily Brown
Sam Chappell
Caroline Charlton
Georgie Donnelly
Amie Flemming
Cheryl Foster
Alicia Hardacre
Aly Hastie
Madeline Hills
Kelly Jones
Sophie Jones
Vicky Jones (captain)
Sophia Riccio
Jo Rutherford
Natalie Sage
Jenny Toole
Jo Traynor
Hannah Williams
Katie Williams

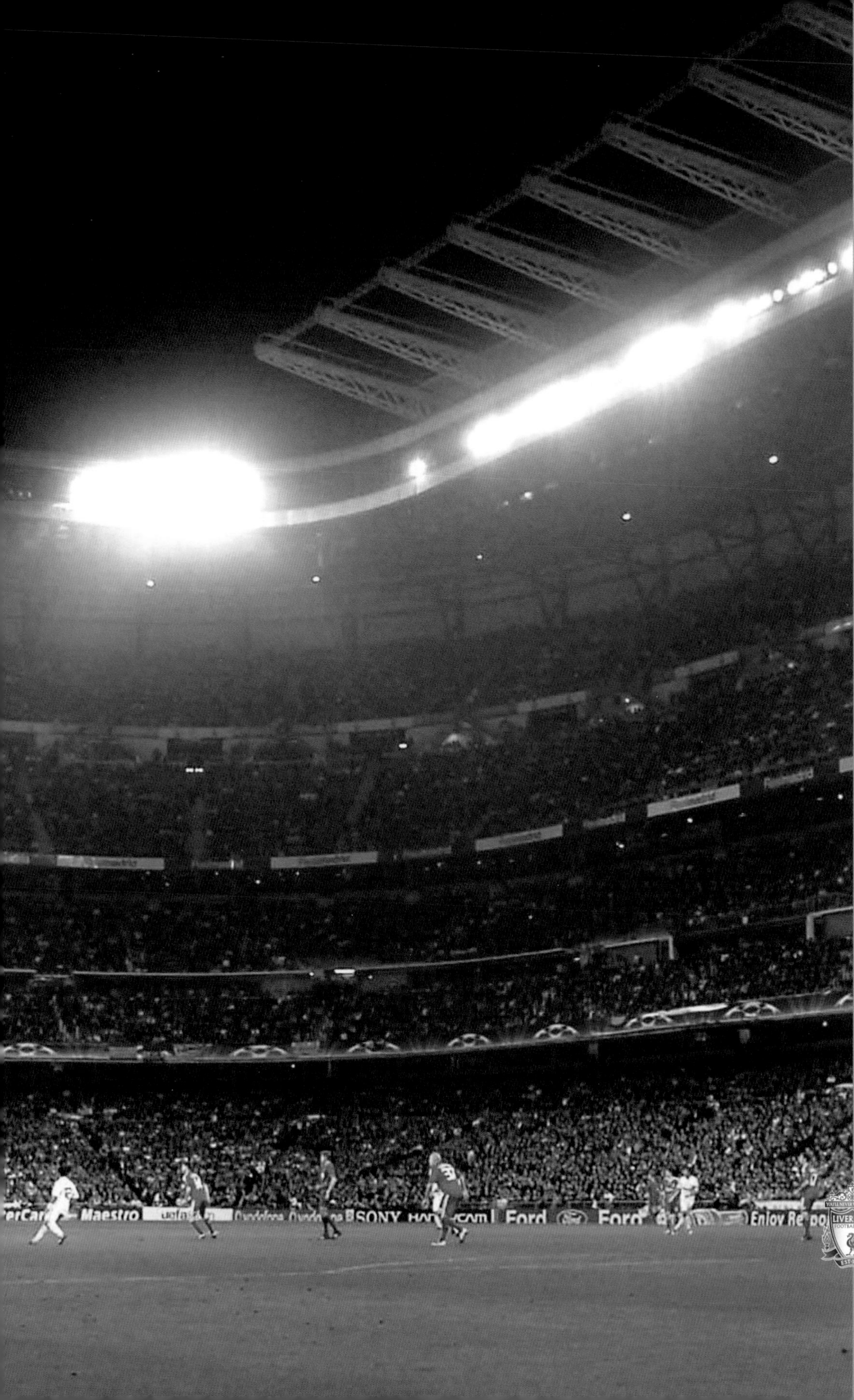
Maestro
SONY
Ford
Ford

Team line-ups

Standard Liege (4-4-2):

Mbokani   De Camargo

Witsel   Fellaini   Defour   Dalmat

Dante   Camozzato
Sarr   Mikulic

Aragon

Subs: Nicaise (Mikulic) 90
Subs not used: De Vriendt, Goreux, Toamba,
Benko, Ingrao, Dembele

Liverpool (4-4-2):

Keane   Torres

Benayoun   Plessis   Alonso   Kuyt

Dossena   Agger   Carragher   Arbeloa

Reina

Subs: Gerrard (Keane) 67, El Zhar (Kuyt) 83
Subs not used: Cavalieri, Hyypia, Voronin,
Pennant, Insua

STANDARD LIEGE   0
LIVERPOOL   0

UEFA Champions League
Third Qualifying Round, 1st Leg
Maurice Dufrasne
Wednesday August 13, 2008.
Attendance: 25,000

Bookings: Camozzato, Mikulic
(Standard Liege), Alonso (Liverpool)
Referee: Tom Ovrebo (Norway)

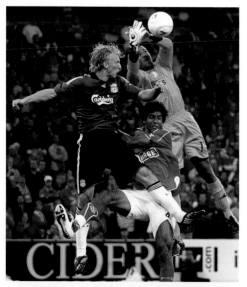

Team line-ups

Liverpool (4-4-2):

Keane Torres

Benayoun Alonso Gerrard Kuyt

Aurelio Skrtel Carragher Arbeloa

Reina

Subs: Babel (Benayoun) 61, El Zhar (Keane) 83, Plessis (Torres) 120
Subs not used: Cavalieri, Dossena, Agger, Spearing

Standard Liege (4-4-2)

Mbokani De Camargo

Witsel Fellaini Defour Dalmat

Dante Sarr Onyewu Camozzato

Aragon

Subs: Jovanovic (Dalmat) 86, Toamba (De Camargo) 101, Nicaise (Defour) 118
Subs not used: De Vriendt, Goreux, Mikulic, Ingrao

LIVERPOOL   1
STANDARD LIEGE   0
after extra time

UEFA Champions League
Third Qualifying Round, 2nd Leg
Wednesday August 27, 2008.
Attendance: 43,889

Goal: Kuyt (118)
Bookings: Sarr, De Camargo, Dante (Standard Liege)
Referee: Massimo Busacca (Switzerland)

Team line-ups

Marseille (4-1-3-2):

Niang
Ben Arfa

Kone

Cheyrou
Cana

M'Bami

Taiwo
Hilton
Zubar
Bonnart

Mandanda

Subs: Valbuena (M'Bami) 41, Ziani (Ben Arfa) 57, Samassa (Kone) 75
Subs not used: Riou, Zenden, Kabore, Erbate

Liverpool (4-4-1-1):

Torres

Gerrard

Babel
Mascherano
Lucas
Kuyt

Dossena
Skrtel
Carragher
Arbeloa

Reina

Subs: Riera (Torres) 65, Benayoun (Gerrard) 69, Keane (Kuyt) 86
Subs not used: Cavalieri, Agger, Alonso, Degen

MARSEILLE 1
LIVERPOOL 2

UEFA Champions League
Group D game 1
Tuesday September 16, 2008.
Attendance: 45,000

Goals: Cana (23), Gerrard (26, 32 pen)
Bookings: Zubar (Marseille), Skrtel, Lucas (Liverpool)
Referee: Konrad Plautz (Austria)

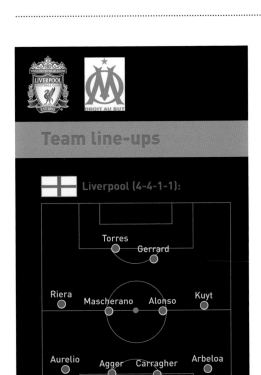

Team line-ups

Liverpool (4-4-1-1):

Torres
Gerrard

Riera Mascherano Alonso Kuyt

Aurelio Agger Carragher Arbeloa

Reina

Subs: Dossena (Aurelio) 46, Benayoun (Riera) 64, Lucas (Kuyt) 85
Subs not used: Cavalieri, Keane, Babel, Kelly

Marseille (4-3-3):

Niang

Ben Arfa Kone

Cheyrou Cana Ziani

Taiwo Hilton Zubar Bonnart

Mandanda

Subs: Valbuena (Kone) 78, Samassa (Bonnart) 89
Subs not used: Riou, Rodriguez, Zenden, Kabore, Grandin

LIVERPOOL 1
MARSEILLE 0

UEFA Champions League
Group D game 5
Wednesday November 26, 2008.
Attendance: 40,024

Goal: Gerrard (23)
Bookings: Mascherano (Liverpool), Niang (Marseille)
Referee: Olegario Benquerenca (Portugal)

Team line-ups

Liverpool (4-4-2):

Torres
Keane

Riera
Alonso
Gerrard
Kuyt

Aurelio
Skrtel
Carragher
Arbeloa

Reina

Subs: Benayoun (Riera) 68, Lucas (Keane) 76, Babel (Gerrard) 82
Subs not used: Cavalieri, Dossena, Agger, Mascherano

PSV Eindhoven (5-4-1):

Amrabat

Bakkal
Culina
Mendez
Wuytens

Brechet
Salcido
Marcellis
Simons
Kromkamp

Isaksson

Subs: Pieters (Brechet) 46, Koevermans (Wuytens) 60, Dzsudzsak (Mendez) 76
Subs not used: Cassio, Rodriguez, Zonneveld, Nijland

LIVERPOOL 3
PSV EINDHOVEN 1

UEFA Champions League
Group D game 2
Wednesday October 1, 2008.
Attendance: 41,097

Goals: Kuyt (4), Keane (34), Gerrard (76), Koevermans (78)
Booking: Marcellis(PSV Eindhoven)
Referee: Felix Brych (Germany)

Team line-ups

PSV Eindhoven (4-4-2):

Lazovic Amrabat

Bakkal   Mendez
      Dzsudzsak Simons

Salcido   Culina
      Brechet Marcellis

Isaksson

Subs: Koevermans (Amrabat) 72, Manco (Mendez) 80, Nijland (Bakkal) 83
Subs not used: Cassio, Rodriguez, Pieters, Wuytens

Liverpool (4-4-2):

Ngog   Keane

Riera   Babel
      Mascherano Lucas

Dossena Agger Carragher Arbeloa

Cavalieri

Subs: Darby (Arbeloa) 69, Spearing (Riera) 76, Kelly (Carragher) 81
Subs not used: Reina, Gerrard, Alonso, Benayoun

PSV EINDHOVEN   1
LIVERPOOL   3

UEFA Champions League
Group D game 6
Tuesday December 9, 2008.
Attendance: 35,000

Goals: Lazovic (36), Babel (45), Riera (69), Ngog (77)
Bookings: Simons, Mendez (PSV Eindhoven), Riera, Arbeloa, Dossena (Liverpool)
Referee: Nikolai Ivanov (Russia)

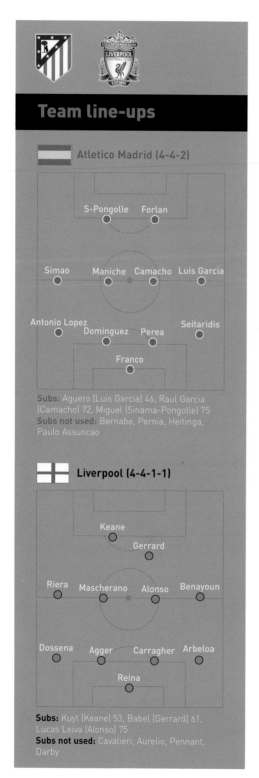

Team line-ups

Atletico Madrid (4-4-2)

S-Pongolle   Forlan

Simao   Maniche   Camacho   Luis Garcia

Antonio Lopez   Dominguez   Perea   Seitaridis

Franco

Subs: Aguero (Luis Garcia) 46, Raul Garcia (Camacho) 72, Miguel (Sinama-Pongolle) 75
Subs not used: Bernabe, Pernia, Heitinga, Paulo Assuncao

Liverpool (4-4-1-1)

Keane

Gerrard

Riera   Mascherano   Alonso   Benayoun

Dossena   Agger   Carragher   Arbeloa

Reina

Subs: Kuyt (Keane) 53, Babel (Gerrard) 61, Lucas Leiva (Alonso) 75
Subs not used: Cavalieri, Aurelio, Pennant, Darby

ATLETICO MADRID   1
LIVERPOOL   1

**UEFA Champions League
Group D game 3**
Wednesday October 22, 2008.
Attendance: 48,769

Goals: Keane (14), Simao (83)
Bookings: Maniche (Atletico Madrid), Riera, Arbeloa (Liverpool)
Referee: Claus Bo Larsen (Denmark)

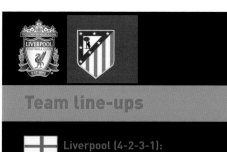

Team line-ups

Liverpool (4-2-3-1):

Keane

Riera　Gerrard　Kuyt

Mascherano　Alonso

Aurelio　Agger　Carragher　Arbeloa

Reina

Subs: Babel (Riera) 61, Ngog (Keane) 71, Lucas Leiva (Mascherano) 77
Subs not used: Cavalieri, Dossena, Benayoun, Degen

Atletico Madrid (4-5-1):

Forlan

Maxi

Simao　Raul Garcia

Maniche　Assuncao

Pernia　Antonio Lopez

Heitinga　Perea

Franco

Subs: Aguero (Forlan) 71, Luis Garcia (Simao) 90
Subs not used: Coupet, Sinama-Pongolle, Banega, Pablo, Camacho

LIVERPOOL　　　　　1
ATLETICO MADRID　 1

UEFA Champions League
Group D game 4
Tuesday November 4, 2008.
Attendance: 42,010

Goals: Maxi (37), Gerrard (90 pen)
Bookings: Maniche, Perea, Heitinga, Pernia, Aguero (Atletico Madrid)
Referee: Martin Hansson (Sweden)

Team line-ups

Real Madrid (4-2-2-2)

Raul Higuain

Robben Marcelo

Gago Diarra

Heinze Sergio Ramos
Cannavaro Pepe

Casillas

Sub: Guti (Marcelo) 46
Subs not used: Dudek, Saviola, Sneijder, Metzelder, Miguel Torres, Van der Vaart

Liverpool (4-2-3-1)

Torres

Kuyt
Riera Benayoun

Mascherano Alonso

Aurelio Skrtel Carragher Arbeloa

Reina

Subs: Babel (Torres) 61, Gerrard (Riera) 88, Lucas Leiva (Kuyt) 90
Subs not used: Cavalieri, Dossena, Hyypia, Ngog

REAL MADRID   0
LIVERPOOL   1

UEFA Champions League
First knockout round, 1st Leg
Wednesday February 25, 2009.
Attendance: 85,000

Goal: Benayoun (82)
Bookings: Cannavaro, Gago (Real Madrid), Torres, Mascherano, Riera (Liverpool)
Referee: Roberto Rosetti (Italy)

Team line-ups

Liverpool (4-2-3-1):

Torres

Gerrard

Babel   Kuyt

Mascherano   Alonso

Aurelio   Skrtel   Carragher   Arbeloa

Reina

Subs: Lucas Leiva (Alonso) 60, Spearing (Gerrard) 73, Dossena (Torres) 84
Subs not used: Cavalieri, Hyypia, Ngog, Kelly

Real Madrid (4-2-2-2):

Raul   Higuain

Robben   Sneijder

Diarra   Gago

Heinze   Cannavaro   Pepe   Sergio Ramos

Casillas

Subs: Marcelo (Robben) 46, Van der Vaart (Cannavaro) 64, Guti (Gago) 77
Subs not used: Dudek, Saviola, Metzelder, Miguel Torres

LIVERPOOL 4
REAL MADRID 0

**UEFA Champions League
First knockout round, 2nd Leg**
Tuesday March 10, 2009.
Attendance: 42,550

Goals: Torres (16), Gerrard (28 pen, 47), Dossena (88)
Bookings: Gerrard, Mascherano, Dossena (Liverpool), Pepe, Heinze, Marcelo (Real Madrid)
Referee: Frank De Bleeckere (Belgium)

Team line-ups

Liverpool (4-4-1-1)

Torres
Gerrard
Riera Lucas Alonso Kuyt
Aurelio Skrtel Carragher Arbeloa
Reina

Subs: Benayoun (Riera) 67, Dossena (Aurelio) 75, Babel (Lucas Leiva) 79
Subs not used: Cavalieri, Hyypia, Agger, Ngog

Chelsea (4-3-3)

Drogba
Malouda Kalou
Lampard
Ballack Essien
A. Cole Alex Terry Ivanovic
Cech

Sub: Anelka (Drogba) 79
Subs not used: Hilario, Carvalho, Belletti, Mancienne, Mikel, Deco

LIVERPOOL 1
CHELSEA 3

UEFA Champions League
Quarter-final, 1st Leg
Wednesday April 8, 2009.
Attendance: 42,543

Goals: Torres (6), Ivanovic (39, 62), Drogba (67)
Bookings: Aurelio (Liverpool), Kalou, Terry (Chelsea)
Referee: Claus Bo Larsen (Denmark)

Team line-ups

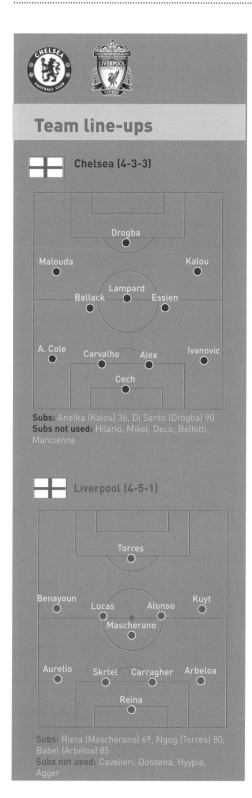

Chelsea (4-3-3)

Drogba

Malouda
Kalou

Lampard
Ballack   Essien

A. Cole
Carvalho   Alex   Ivanovic

Cech

Subs: Anelka (Kalou) 36, Di Santo (Drogba) 90
Subs not used: Hilario, Mikel, Deco, Belletti, Mancienne

Liverpool (4-5-1)

Torres

Benayoun
Kuyt
Lucas   Alonso
Mascherano

Aurelio   Skrtel   Carragher   Arbeloa

Reina

Subs: Riera (Mascherano) 69, Ngog (Torres) 80, Babel (Arbeloa) 85
Subs not used: Cavalieri, Dossena, Hyypia, Agger

CHELSEA 4
LIVERPOOL 4

UEFA Champions League
Quarter-final, 2nd Leg
Tuesday April 14, 2009.
Attendance: 38,286

Goals: Aurelio (19), Alonso (28 pen), Drogba (52), Alex (57), Lampard (76, 89), Lucas Leiva (81), Kuyt (82)
Bookings: Ivanovic, Carvalho, A. Cole (Chelsea), Benayoun, Arbeloa (Liverpool)
Referee: Luis Medina Cantalejo (Spain)

EUROPEAN/WORLD ROLL OF HONOUR

EUROPEAN CHAMPIONS CUP/UEFA CHAMPIONS LEAGUE

WINNERS
1976/1977, 1977/1978, 1980/1981, 1983/1984, 2004/2005

RUNNERS-UP
1984/1985, 2006/2007

SEMI-FINALISTS
1964/65, 2007/08

INTER-CITIES FAIRS CUP/UEFA CUP

WINNERS
1972/1973, 1975/1976, 2000/2001

SEMI-FINALISTS
1970/71

EUROPEAN CUP WINNERS' CUP

RUNNERS-UP
1965/1966

SEMI-FINALISTS
1996/97

UEFA SUPER CUP

WINNERS
1977, 2001, 2005

RUNNERS-UP
1978, 1985

INTERCONTINENTAL CUP/FIFA CLUB WORLD CUP

RUNNERS-UP
1981, 1984, 2005

LIVERPOOL'S RESULTS IN EUROPEAN COMPETITION

Season	Round	Venue	Opponents	Opponent Country	Score	Scorers	Att
1964/65	**EUROPEAN CUP**		**(WINNERS – INTER MILAN)**				
17th Aug	1 Leg 1	(a)	Reykjavik	Ice	5-0	Wallace 2, Hunt 2, Chisnall	10,000
14th Sept	1 Leg 2	(h)	Reykjavik	"	6-1	Byrne, St John 2, Hunt, Graham, Stevenson	32,957
25th Nov	2 Leg 1	(h)	Anderlecht	Bel	3-0	St John, Hunt, Yeats	44,516
16th Dec	2 Leg 2	(a)	Anderlecht	"	1-0	Hunt	60,000
10th Feb	3 Leg 1	(a)	FC Cologne	W.Ger	0-0		40,000
17th Mar	3 Leg 2	(h)	FC Cologne	"	0-0		48,432
24th Mar	Replay	Rotterdam	FC Cologne	"	2-2	St John, Hunt	45,000
			(Liverpool won on toss of a coin)				
4th May	SF Leg 1	(h)	Inter Milan	Ita	3-1	Hunt, Callaghan, St John	54,082
12th May	SF Leg 1	(a)	Inter Milan	"	0-3		90,000
1965/66	**CUP WINNERS' CUP**		**(WINNERS – BORUSSIA DORTMUND)**				
29th Sept	Pr Leg 1	(a)	Juventus	Ita	0-1		12,000
13th Oct	Pr Leg 2	(h)	Juventus	"	2-0	Lawler, Strong	51,055
1st Dec	1 Leg 1	(h)	Standard Liege	Bel	3-1	Lawler 2, Thompson	46,112
15th Dec	1 Leg 2	(a)	Standard Liege	"	2-1	Hunt, St John	35,000
1st Mar	2 Leg 1	(a)	Honved	Hun	0-0		20,000
8th Mar	2 Leg 2	(h)	Honved	"	2-0	Lawler, St John	54,631
14th Apr	SF Leg 1	(a)	Celtic	Sco	0-1		80,000
19th Apr	SF Leg 2	(h)	Celtic	"	2-0	Smith, Strong	54,208
5th May	Final	Glasgow	B. Dortmund	W.Ger	1-2 aet	Hunt	41,657
1966/67	**EUROPEAN CUP**		**(WINNERS – CELTIC)**				
28th Sept	Pr Leg 1	(h)	Petrolul Ploesti	Rom	2-0	St John, Callaghan	44,463
12th Oct	Pr Leg 2	(a)	Petrolul Ploesti	"	1-3	Hunt	20,000
19th Oct	Replay	Brussels	Petrolul Ploesti	"	2-0	St John, Thompson	15,000
7th Dec	1 Leg 1	(a)	Ajax Amsterdam	Hol	1-5	Lawler	65,000
14th Dec	1 Leg 2	(h)	Ajax Amsterdam	"	2-2	Hunt 2	53,846
1967/68	**I-C FAIRS CUP**		**(WINNERS – LEEDS UNITED)**				
19th Sept	1 Leg 1	(a)	Malmo	Swe	2-0	Hateley 2	14,314
4th Oct	1 Leg 2	(h)	Malmo	"	2-1	Yeats, Hunt	39,795
7th Nov	2 Leg 1	(h)	TSV Munich 1860	W.Ger	8-0	St John, Hateley, Smith (pen) Hunt 2, Thompson, Callaghan 2	44,812
14th Nov	2 Leg 2	(a)	TSV Munich 1860	"	1-2	Callaghan	10,000
28th Nov	3 Leg 1	(a)	Ferencvaros	Hun	0-1		30,000
9th Jan	3 Leg 2	(h)	Ferencvaros	"	0-1		46,892
1968/69	**I-C FAIRS CUP**		**(WINNERS – NEWCASTLE UNITED)**				
18th Sept	1 Leg 1	(a)	Athletic Bilbao	Spa	1-2	Hunt	35,000
2nd Oct	1 Leg 2	(h)	Athletic Bilbao	"	2-1 aet	Lawler, Hughes	49,567
			(Liverpool lost on toss of coin)				
1969/70	**I-C FAIRS CUP**		**(WINNERS – ARSENAL)**				
16th Sept	1 Leg 1	(h)	Dundalk	Rep. Ire	10-0	Evans 2, Lawler, Smith 2, Graham 2, Lindsay, Thompson, Callaghan	32,562
30th Sept	1 Leg 2	(a)	Dundalk	"	4-0	Thompson 2, Graham, Callaghan	6,000
12th Nov	2 Leg 1	(a)	Vitoria Setubal	Por	0-1		16,000
26th Nov	2 Leg 2	(h)	Vitoria Setubal	"	3-2	Smith (pen), Evans, Hunt	41,633

LIVERPOOL'S RESULTS IN EUROPEAN COMPETITION

Season	Round	Venue	Opponents	Opponent Country	Score	Scorers	Att
1970/71	**I-C FAIRS CUP**		**(WINNERS – LEEDS UNITED)**				
15th Sept	1 Leg 1	(h)	Ferencvaros	Hun	1-0	Graham	37,531
29th Sept	1 Leg 2	(a)	Ferencvaros	"	1-1	Hughes	25,000
21st Oct	2 Leg 1	(h)	D. Bucharest	Rom	3-0	Lindsay, Lawler, Hughes	36,525
4th Nov	2 Leg 2	(a)	D. Bucharest	"	1-1	Boersma	45,000
9th Dec	3 Leg 1	(a)	Hibernian	Sco	1-0	Toshack	30,296
22nd Dec	3 Leg 2	(h)	Hibernian	"	2-0	Heighway, Boersma	37,815
10th Mar	4 Leg 1	(h)	Bayern Munich	W.Ger	3-0	Evans 3	45,616
24th Mar	4 Leg 2	(a)	Bayern Munich	"	1-1	Ross	23,000
14th Apr	SF Leg 1	(h)	Leeds United	Eng	0-1		52,577
28th Apr	SF Leg 2	(a)	Leeds United	"	0-0		40,462
1971/72	**CUP WINNERS' CUP**		**(WINNERS – RANGERS)**				
15th Sept	1 Leg 1	(a)	Servette Geneva	Swi	1-2	Lawler	16,000
29th Sept	1 Leg 2	(h)	Servette Geneva	"	2-0	Hughes, Heighway	38,591
20th Oct	2 Leg 1	(h)	Bayern Munich	W.Ger	0-0		42,949
3rd Nov	2 Leg 2	(a)	Bayern Munich	"	1-3	Evans	40,000
1972/73	**UEFA CUP**		**(WINNERS – LIVERPOOL)**				
12th Sept	1 Leg 1	(h)	E. Frankfurt	W.Ger	2-0	Keegan, Hughes	33,380
26th Sept	1 Leg 2	(a)	E. Frankfurt	"	0-0		20,000
24th Oct	2 Leg 1	(h)	AEK Athens	Gre	3-0	Boersma, Cormack, Smith (pen)	31,906
7th Nov	2 Leg 2	(a)	AEK Athens	"	3-1	Hughes 2, Boersma	25,000
29th Nov	3 Leg 1	(a)	Dynamo Berlin	E.Ger	0-0		19,000
13th Dec	3 Leg 2	(h)	Dynamo Berlin	"	3-1	Boersma, Heighway, Toshack	34,140
7th Mar	4 Leg 1	(h)	Dynamo Dresden	E.Ger	2-0	Hall, Boersma	33,270
21st Mar	4 Leg 2	(a)	Dynamo Dresden	"	1-0	Keegan	35,000
10th Apr	SF Leg 1	(h)	Tottenham H.	Eng	1-0	Lindsay	42,174
25th Apr	SF Leg 2	(a)	Tottenham H.	"	1-2	Heighway	46,919
10th May	F Leg 1	(h)	B. Moench'bach	W.Ger	3-0	Keegan 2, Lloyd	41,169
23rd May	F Leg 2	(a)	B. Moench'bach	"	0-2		35,000
1973/74	**EUROPEAN CUP**		**(WINNERS – BAYERN MUNICH)**				
19th Sept	1 Leg 1	(a)	Jeunesse D'Esch	Lux	1-1	Hall	5,000
3rd Oct	1 Leg 2	(h)	Jeunesse D'Esch	"	2-0	Mond o.g., Toshack	28,714
24th Oct	2 Leg 1	(a)	R.S. Belgrade	Yug	1-2	Lawler	40,000
6th Nov	2 Leg 2	(h)	R.S. Belgrade"		1-2	Lawler	41,774
1974/75	**CUP WINNERS' CUP**		**(WINNERS – DYNAMO KIEV)**				
17th Sept	1 Leg 1	(h)	Stromsgodset	Nor	11-0	Lindsay (pen), Boersma 2, Thompson 2, Heighway, Cormack, Hughes, Smith Callaghan, Kennedy	24,743
1st Oct	1 Leg 2	(a)	Stromsgodset	"	1-0	Kennedy	17,000
23rd Oct	2 Leg 1	(h)	Ferencvaros	Hun	1-1	Keegan	35,027
5th Nov	2 Leg 2	(a)	Ferencvaros	"	0-0		30,000
1975/76	**UEFA CUP**		**(WINNERS – LIVERPOOL)**				
17th Sept	1 Leg 1	(a)	Hibernian	Sco	0-1		19,219
30th Sept	1 Leg 2	(h)	Hibernian	"	3-1	Toshack 3	29,963
22nd Oct	2 Leg 1	(a)	Real Sociedad	Spa	3-1	Heighway, Callaghan, Thompson	20,000
4th Nov	2 Leg 2	(h)	Real Sociedad	"	6-0	Toshack, Kennedy 2, Fairclough Heighway, Neal	23,796

LIVERPOOL'S RESULTS IN EUROPEAN COMPETITION

Season	Round	Venue	Opponents	Opponent Country	Score	Scorers	Att
1975/76	**UEFA CUP (cont)**		**(WINNERS – LIVERPOOL)**				
26th Nov	3 Leg 1	(a)	Slask Wroclaw	Pol	2-1	Kennedy, Toshack	46,000
10th Dec	3 Leg 2	(h)	Slask Wroclaw	"	3-0	Case 3	17,886
3rd Mar	4 Leg 1	(a)	Dynamo Dresden	E.Ger	0-0		33,000
17th Mar	4 Leg 2	(h)	Dynamo Dresden	"	2-1	Case, Keegan	39,300
30th Mar	SF Leg 1	(a)	Barcelona	Spa	1-0	Toshack	70,000
14th Apr	SF Leg 2	(h)	Barcelona	"	1-1	Thompson	55,104
28th Apr	F Leg 1	(h)	FC Bruges	Bel	3-2	Kennedy, Case, Keegan (pen)	49,981
19th May	F Leg 2	(a)	FC Bruges	"	1-1	Keegan	33,000
1976/77	**EUROPEAN CUP**		**(WINNERS – LIVERPOOL)**				
14th Sept	1 Leg 1	(h)	Crusaders	N.Ire	2-0	Neal (pen), Toshack	22,442
28th Sept	1 Leg 2	(a)	Crusaders	"	5-0	Keegan, Johnson 2, McDermott Heighway	10,500
20th Oct	2 Leg 1	(a)	Trabzonspor	Tur	0-1		25,000
3rd Nov	2 Leg 2	(h)	Trabzonspor	"	3-0	Heighway, Johnson, Keegan	42,275
2nd Mar	3 Leg 1	(a)	St Etienne	Fra	0-1		38,000
16th Mar	3 Leg 2	(h)	St Etienne	"	3-1	Keegan, Kennedy, Fairclough	55,043
6th Apr	SF Leg 1	(a)	FC Zurich	Swi	3-1	Neal 2 (1 pen), Heighway	30,500
20th Apr	SF Leg 2	(h)	FC Zurich	"	3-0	Case 2, Keegan	50,611
25th May	Final	Rome	B. Moench'bach	W.Ger	3-1	McDermott, Smith, Neal (pen)	52,078
1977/78	**EUROPEAN CUP**		**(WINNERS – LIVERPOOL)**				
19th Oct	2 Leg 1	(h)	Dynamo Dresden	E.Ger	5-1	Hansen, Case 2, Neal (pen) Kennedy	39,835
2nd Nov	2 Leg 2	(a)	Dynamo Dresden	"	1-2	Heighway	33,000
1st Mar	3 Leg 1	(a)	Benfica	Por	2-1	Case, Hughes	70,000
15th Mar	3 Leg 2	(h)	Benfica	"	4-1	Callaghan, Dalglish, McDermott, Neal	48,364
29th Mar	SF Leg 1	(a)	B. Moench'bach	W.Ger	1-2	Johnson	66,000
12th Apr	SF Leg 2	(h)	B. Moench'bach	"	3-0	Kennedy, Dalglish, Case	51,500
10th May	Final	Wembley	FC Bruges	Bel	1-0	Dalglish	92,000
1977/78	**EURO. SUPER CUP**		**(WINNERS – LIVERPOOL)**				
22nd Nov	Leg 1	(a)	SV Hamburg	W.Ger	1-1	Fairclough	16,000
6th Dec	Leg 2	(h)	SV Hamburg	"	6-0	Thompson, McDermott 3 Fairclough, Dalglish	34,931
1978/79	**EUROPEAN CUP**		**(WINNERS – NOTTINGHAM FOREST)**				
13th Sept	1 Leg 1	(a)	Nottingham Forest	Eng	0-2		38,316
27th Sept	1 Leg 2	(h)	Nottingham Forest	"	0-0		51,679
1978/79	**EURO. SUPER CUP**		**(WINNERS – ANDERLECHT)**				
4th Dec	1 Leg 1	(a)	Anderlecht	Bel	1-3	Case	35,000
19th Dec	1 Leg 2	(h)	Anderlecht	"	2-1	Hughes, Fairclough	23,598

LIVERPOOL'S RESULTS IN EUROPEAN COMPETITION

Season	Round	Venue	Opponents	Opponent Country	Score	Scorers	Att
1979/80	**EUROPEAN CUP**		**(WINNERS – NOTTINGHAM FOREST)**				
19th Sept	1 Leg 1	(h)	Dynamo Tblisi	Rus	2-1	Johnson, Case	35,270
3rd Oct	1 Leg 2	(a)	Dynamo Tblisi	"	0-3		80,000
1980/81	**EUROPEAN CUP**		**(WINNERS – LIVERPOOL)**				
17th Sept	1 Leg 1	(a)	Oulu Palloseura	Fin	1-1	McDermott	14,000
1st Oct	1 Leg 2	(h)	Oulu Palloseura	"	10-1	Souness 3 (1pen), McDermott 3, Lee, R.Kennedy, Fairclough 2	21,013
22nd Oct	2 Leg 1	(a)	Aberdeen	Sco	1-0	McDermott	24,000
5th Nov	2 Leg 2	(h)	Aberdeen	"	4-0	Miller o.g., Neal, Dalglish, Hansen	36,182
4th Mar	3 Leg 1	(h)	CSKA Sofia	Bul	5-1	Souness 3, Lee, McDermott	37,255
18th Mar	3 Leg 2	(a)	CSKA Sofia	"	1-0	Johnson	65,000
8th Apr	SF Leg 1	(h)	Bayern Munich	W.Ger	0-0		44,543
22nd Apr	SF Leg 2	(a)	Bayern Munich	"	1-1	R.Kennedy	77,600
27th May	Final	Paris	Real Madrid	Spa	1-0	A.Kennedy	48,360
1981/82	**EUROPEAN CUP**		**(WINNERS – ASTON VILLA)**				
16th Sept	1 Leg 1	(a)	Oulu Palloseura	Fin	1-0	Dalglish	8,400
30th Sept	1 Leg 2	(h)	Oulu Palloseura	"	7-0	Dalglish, McDermott 2, R.Kennedy, Johnson, Rush, Lawrenson	20,789
21st Oct	2 Leg 1	(a)	AZ '67 Alkmaar	Hol	2-2	Johnson, Lee	15,000
4th Nov	2 Leg 2	(h)	AZ '67 Alkmaar	"	3-2	McDermott (pen), Rush, Hansen	29,703
3rd Mar	3 Leg 1	(h)	CSKA Sofia	Bul	1-0	Whelan	27,388
17th Mar	3 Leg 2	(a)	CSKA Sofia	"	0-2 aet		60,000
1982/83	**EUROPEAN CUP**		**(WINNERS – HAMBURG)**				
14th Sept	1 Leg 1	(a)	Dundalk	Rep. Ire	4-1	Whelan 2, Rush, Hodgson	16,500
28th Sept	1 Leg 2	(h)	Dundalk	"	1-0	Whelan	12,021
19th Oct	2 Leg 1	(a)	HJK Helsinki	Fin	0-1		5,722
2nd Nov	2 Leg 2	(h)	HJK Helsinki	"	5-0	Dalglish, Johnson, Neal, A.Kennedy 2	16,434
2nd Mar	3 Leg 1	(a)	Widzew Lodz	Pol	0-2		45,531
16th Mar	3 Leg 2	(h)	Widzew Lodz	"	3-2	Neal (pen), Rush, Hodgson	44,494
1983/84	**EUROPEAN CUP**		**(WINNERS – LIVERPOOL)**				
14th Sept	1 Leg 1	(a)	BK Odense	Den	1-0	Dalglish	30,000
28th Sept	1 Leg 2	(h)	BK Odense	"	5-0	Robinson 2, Dalglish 2, Clausen o.g.	14,985
19th Oct	2 Leg 1	(h)	Athletic Bilbao	Spa	0-0		33,063
2nd Nov	2 Leg 2	(a)	Athletic Bilbao	"	1-0	Rush	47,500
7th Mar	3 Leg 1	(h)	Benfica	Por	1-0	Rush	39,096
21st Mar	3 Leg 2	(a)	Benfica	"	4-1	Whelan 2, Johnston, Rush	70,000
11th Apr	SF Leg 1	(h)	D. Bucharest	Rom	1-0	Lee	36,941
25th Apr	SF Leg 2	(a)	D. Bucharest	"	2-1	Rush 2	60,000
30th May	Final	Rome	AS Roma	Ita	1-1 aet	Neal	69,693
			(Liverpool won 4-2 on penalties)				

LIVERPOOL'S RESULTS IN EUROPEAN COMPETITION

Season	Round	Venue	Opponents	Opponent Country	Score	Scorers	Att
1984/85	**EUROPEAN CUP**		**(WINNERS – JUVENTUS)**				
19th Sept	1 Leg 1	(a)	Lech Poznan	Pol	1-0	Wark	35,000
3rd Oct	1 Leg 2	(h)	Lech Poznan	"	4-0	Wark 3, Walsh	22,143
24th Oct	2 Leg 1	(h)	Benfica	Por	3-1	Rush 3	27,733
7th Nov	2 Leg 2	(a)	Benfica	"	0-1		50,000
6th Mar	3 Leg 1	(a)	Austria Vienna	Aut	1-1	Nicol	21,000
20th Mar	3 Leg 2	(h)	Austria Vienna	"	4-1	Walsh 2, Nicol, Obermayer o.g.	32,761
10th Apr	SF Leg 1	(h)	Panathinaikos	Gre	4-0	Wark, Rush 2, Beglin	39,488
24th Apr	SF Leg 2	(a)	Panathinaikos	"	1-0	Lawrenson	60,000
29th May	Final	Brussels	Juventus	Ita	0-1		60,000
1984/85	**EURO. SUPER CUP**		**(WINNERS – JUVENTUS)**				
16th Jan		(a)	Juventus	Ita	0-2		60,000
1991/92	**UEFA CUP**		**(WINNERS – AJAX)**				
18th Sept	1 Leg 1	(h)	Kuusysi Lahti	Fin	6-1	Saunders 4, Houghton 2	17,131
2nd Oct	1 Leg 2	(a)	Kuusysi Lahti	"	0-1		8,435
23rd Oct	2 Leg 1	(a)	Auxerre	Fra	0-2		16,500
6th Nov	2 Leg 2	(h)	Auxerre	"	3-0	Molby (pen), Marsh, Walters	23,094
27th Nov	3 Leg 1	(a)	Swarovski Tirol	Aut	2-0	Saunders 2	12,500
11th Dec	3 Leg 2	(h)	Swarovski Tirol	"	4-0	Saunders 3, Venison	16,007
4th Mar	4 Leg 1	(a)	Genoa	Ita	0-2		40,000
18th Mar	4 Leg 2	(h)	Genoa	"	1-2	Rush	38,840
1992/93	**CUP WINNERS' CUP**		**(WINNERS – PARMA)**				
16th Sept	1 Leg 1	(h)	Apollon Limassol	Cyp	6-1	Stewart 2, Rush 4	12,769
29th Sept	1 Leg 2	(a)	Apollon Limassol	"	2-1	Rush, Hutchison	8,000
22nd Oct	2 Leg 1	(a)	Spartak Moscow	Rus	2-4	Wright, McManaman	60,000
4th Nov	2 Leg 2	(h)	Spartak Moscow	"	0-2		37,993
1995/96	**UEFA CUP**		**(WINNERS – BAYERN MUNICH)**				
12th Sept	1 Leg 1	(a)	S. Vladikavkaz	Rus	2-1	McManaman, Redknapp	43,000
26th Sept	1 Leg 2	(h)	S. Vladikavkaz	"	0-0		35,042
17th Oct	2 Leg 1	(a)	Brondby	Den	0-0		37,648
31st Oct	2 Leg 2	(h)	Brondby	"	0-1		35,878
1996/97	**CUP WINNERS' CUP**		**(WINNERS – FC BARCELONA)**				
12th Sept	1 Leg 1	(a)	MyPa 47	Fin	1-0	Bjornebye	5,500
26th Sept	1 Leg 2	(h)	MyPa 47	"	3-1	Berger, Collymore, Barnes	39,013
17th Oct	2 Leg 1	(a)	Sion	Swi	2-1	Fowler, Barnes	16,500
31st Oct	2 Leg 2	(h)	Sion	"	6-3	McManaman, Bjornebye Barnes, Fowler 2, Berger	38,514
6th Mar	3 Leg 1	(a)	Brann Bergen	Nor	1-1	Fowler	12,700
20th Mar	3 Leg 2	(h)	Brann Bergen	"	3-0	Fowler 2 (1 pen), Collymore	40,326
10th Apr	SF Leg 1	(a)	Paris St Germain	Fra	0-3		35,142
24th Apr	SF Leg 2	(h)	Paris St Germain	"	2-0	Fowler, Wright	38,984

LIVERPOOL'S RESULTS IN EUROPEAN COMPETITION

Season	Round	Venue	Opponents	Opponent Country	Score	Scorers	Att
1997/98	**UEFA CUP**		**(WINNERS – INTER MILAN)**				
16th Sept	1 Leg 1	(a)	Celtic	Sco	2-2	Owen, McManaman	48,526
30th Sept	1 Leg 2	(h)	Celtic	"	0-0		38,205
21st Oct	2 Leg 1	(a)	RC Strasbourg	Fra	0-3		18,813
4th Nov	2 Leg 2	(h)	RC Strasbourg	"	2-0	Fowler (pen), Riedle	32,426
1998/99	**UEFA CUP**		**(WINNERS – PARMA)**				
15th Sept	1 Leg 1	(a)	FC Kosice	Slovakia	3-0	Berger, Riedle, Owen	4,500
29th Sept	1 Leg 2	(h)	FC Kosice	"	5-0	Redknapp 2, Ince, Fowler 2	23,792
20th Oct	2 Leg 1	(h)	Valencia	Spa	0-0		36,004
3rd Nov	2 Leg 2	(a)	Valencia	"	2-2	McManaman, Berger	49,000
24th Nov	3 Leg 1	(a)	Celta Vigo	Spa	1-3	Owen	32,000
8th Dec	3 Leg 2	(h)	Celta Vigo	"	0-1		30,289
2000/01	**UEFA CUP**		**(WINNERS – LIVERPOOL)**				
14th Sept	1 Leg 1	(a)	Rapid Bucharest	Rom	1-0	Barmby	12,000
28th Sept	1 Leg 2	(h)	Rapid Bucharest	"	0-0		37,954
26th Oct	2 Leg 1	(h)	Slovan Liberec	Cz Rep	1-0	Heskey	29,662
9th Nov	2 Leg 2	(a)	Slovan Liberec	"	3-2	Barmby, Heskey, Owen	6,808
23rd Nov	3 Leg 1	(a)	Olympiakos	Gre	2-2	Barmby, Gerrard	43,855
7th Dec	3 Leg 2	(h)	Olympiakos	"	2-0	Heskey, Barmby	35,484
15th Feb	4 Leg 1	(a)	AS Roma	Ita	2-0	Owen 2	59,718
22nd Feb	4 Leg 2	(h)	AS Roma	"	0-1		43,688
8th Mar	5 Leg 1	(a)	FC Porto	Por	0-0		21,150
15th Mar	5 Leg 2	(h)	FC Porto	"	2-0	Murphy, Owen	40,502
5th Apr	SF Leg 1	(a)	Barcelona	Spa	0-0		90,000
19th Apr	SF Leg 2	(h)	Barcelona	"	1-0	McAllister	44,203
16th May	Final	Dortmund	Alaves	Spa	5-4 aet	Babbel, Gerrard, McAllister (pen), Fowler, Geli o.g.	65,000
			(Liverpool won on golden goal)				
2001/02	**EUROPEAN CUP**		**(WINNERS – REAL MADRID)**				
8th Aug	Q. Leg 1	(a)	FC Haka	Fin	5-0	Heskey, Owen 3, Hyypia	33,217
21st Aug	Q. Leg 2	(h)	FC Haka	"	4-1	Fowler, Redknapp, Heskey, Wilson o.g.	31,602
	First Group Stage						
11th Sept	Group B	(h)	Boavista	Por	1-1	Owen	30,015
19th Sept	Group B	(a)	B. Dortmund	Ger	0-0		50,000
26th Sept	Group B	(h)	Dynamo Kiev	Ukr	1-0	Litmanen	33,513
16th Oct	Group B	(a)	Dynamo Kiev	"	2-1	Murphy, Gerrard	55,000
24th Oct	Group B	(a)	Boavista	Por	1-1	Murphy	6,000
30th Oct	Group B	(h)	B. Dortmund	Ger	2-0	Smicer, Wright	41,507
	Second Group Stage						
20th Nov	Group B	(h)	Barcelona	Spa	1-3	Owen	41,521
5th Dec	Group B	(a)	AS Roma	Ita	0-0		57,819
20th Feb	Group B	(h)	Galatasaray	Tur	0-0		41,605
26th Feb	Group B	(a)	Galatasaray	"	1-1	Heskey	22,100
13th Mar	Group B	(a)	Barcelona	Spa	0-0		75,362
19th Mar	Group B	(h)	AS Roma	Ita	2-0	Litmanen (pen), Heskey	41,794
3rd Apr	QF Leg 1	(h)	B. Leverkusen	Ger	1-0	Hyypia	42,454
9th Apr	QF Leg 2	(a)	B. Leverkusen	"	2-4	Xavier, Litmanen	22,500

LIVERPOOL'S RESULTS IN EUROPEAN COMPETITION

Season	Round	Venue	Opponents	Opponent Country	Score	Scorers	Att
2001/02	**EURO. SUPER CUP**	**(WINNERS – LIVERPOOL)**					
24th Aug		Monaco	Bayern Munich	Ger	3-2	Riise, Heskey, Owen	15,000
2002/03	**EUROPEAN CUP**	**(WINNERS – AC MILAN)**					
			First Group Stage				
17th Sept	Group B (a)		Valencia	Spa	0-2		43,000
25th Sept	Group B (h)		FC Basel	Swi	1-1	Baros	37,634
2nd Oct	Group B (h)		Spartak Moscow	Rus	5-0	Heskey 2, Cheyrou, Hyypia, Diao	40,812
22nd Oct	Group B (a)		Spartak Moscow	"	3-1	Owen 3	15,000
30th Oct	Group B (h)		Valencia	Spa	0-1		41,831
12th Nov	Group B (a)		FC Basel	Swi	3-3	Murphy, Smicer, Owen	35,000
2002/03	**UEFA CUP**	**(WINNERS – FC PORTO)**					
28th Nov	3 Leg 1 (a)		Vitesse Arnhem	Hol	1-0	Owen	28,000
12th Dec	3 Leg 2 (h)		Vitesse Arnhem	"	1-0	Owen	23,576
20th Feb	4 Leg 1 (a)		Auxerre	Fra	1-0	Hyypia	20,452
27th Feb	4 Leg 2 (h)		Auxerre	"	2-0	Owen, Murphy	34,252
13th Mar	5 Leg 1 (a)		Celtic	Sco	1-1	Heskey	59,759
20th Mar	5 Leg 2 (h)		Celtic	"	0-2		44,238
2003/04	**UEFA CUP**	**(WINNERS – VALENCIA)**					
24th Sept	1 Leg 1 (a)		Olimpija Ljubljana	Slovenia	1-1	Owen	10,000
15th Oct	1 Leg 2 (h)		Olimpija Ljubljana	"	3-0	LeTallec, Heskey, Kewell	42,880
6th Nov	2 Leg 1 (a)		Steaua Bucharest	Rom	1-1	Traore	25,000
27th Nov	2 Leg 2 (h)		Steaua Bucharest	"	1-0	Kewell	42,837
26th Feb	3 Leg 1 (h)		Levski Sofia	Bul	2-0	Gerrard, Kewell	39,149
3rd Mar	3 Leg 2 (a)		Levski Sofia	"	4-2	Gerrard, Owen, Hamann, Hyypia	40,281
11th Mar	4 Leg 1 (h)		O. Marseille	Fra	1-1	Baros	41,270
25th Mar	4 Leg 2 (a)		O. Marseille	"	1-2	Heskey	50,000
2004/05	**EUROPEAN CUP**	**(WINNERS – LIVERPOOL)**					
10th Aug	Q. Leg 1 (a)		AK Graz	Aut	2-0	Gerrard 2	15,000
24th Aug	Q. Leg 2 (h)		AK Graz	"	0-1		42,950
			Group Stage				
15th Sept	Group A (h)		AS Monaco	Fra	2-0	Cisse, Baros	33,517
28th Sept	Group A (a)		Olympiakos	Gre	0-1		33,000
19th Oct	Group A (h)		D. La Coruna	Spa	0-0		40,236
3rd Nov	Group A (a)		D. La Coruna	"	1-0	Andrade o.g.	32,000
23rd Nov	Group A (a)		AS Monaco	Fra	0-1		15,000
8th Dec	Group A (h)		Olympiakos	Gre	3-1	Sinama-Pongolle, Mellor, Gerrard	42,045
22nd Feb	L. 16 L1 (h)		B. Leverkusen	Ger	3-1	Garcia, Riise, Hamann	40,942
9th Mar	L. 16 L2 (a)		B. Leverkusen	"	3-1	Garcia 2, Baros	23,000
5th Apr	QF Leg 1 (h)		Juventus	Ita	2-1	Hyypia, Garcia	41,216
13th Apr	QF Leg 2 (a)		Juventus	"	0-0		55,464
27th Apr	SF Leg 1 (a)		Chelsea	Eng	0-0		40,497
3rd May	SF Leg 2 (h)		Chelsea	"	1-0	Garcia	42,529
25th May	Final	Istanbul	AC Milan	Ita	3-3 aet	Gerrard, Smicer, Alonso	65,000
			(Liverpool won 3-2 on penalties)				

LIVERPOOL'S RESULTS IN EUROPEAN COMPETITION

Season	Round	Venue	Opponents	Opponent Country	Score	Scorers	Att
2005/06	**EUROPEAN CUP**	**(WINNERS – BARCELONA)**					
13th July	Q.1 Leg 1	(h)	TNS	Wal	3-0	Gerrard 3	44,760
19th July	Q.1 Leg 2	(a)	TNS	"	3-0	Cisse, Gerrard 2	8,009
26th July	Q.2 Leg 1	(a)	FBK Kaunas	Lith	3-1	Cisse, Carragher, Gerrard (pen)	8,300
2nd Aug	Q.2 Leg 2	(h)	FBK Kaunas	"	2-0	Gerrard, Cisse	43,717
10th Aug	Q.3 Leg 1	(a)	CSKA Sofia	Bul	3-1	Cisse, Morientes 2	16,512
23rd Aug	Q.3 Leg 2	(h)	CSKA Sofia	"	0-1		42,175
	Group Stage						
13th Sept	Group G	(a)	Real Betis	Spa	2-1	Sinama-Pongolle, Garcia	45,000
28th Sept	Group G	(h)	Chelsea	Eng	0-0		42,743
19th Oct	Group G	(a)	Anderlecht	Bel	1-0	Cisse	25,000
1st Nov	Group G	(h)	Anderlecht	Bel	3-0	Morientes, Garcia, Cisse	42,607
23rd Nov	Group G	(h)	Real Betis	Spa	0-0		42,077
6th Dec	Group G	(a)	Chelsea	Eng	0-0		41,598
21st Feb	L. 16 L1	(a)	Benfica	Por	0-1		65,000
8th Mar	L. 16 L2	(h)	Benfica	Por	0-2		42,745
2005/06	**EURO. SUPER CUP**	**(WINNERS – LIVERPOOL)**					
26th Aug		Monaco	CSKA Moscow	Rus	3-1 aet	Cisse 2, Garcia	18,000
2006/07	**EUROPEAN CUP**	**(WINNERS – AC MILAN)**					
9th Aug	Q.3 Leg 1	(h)	Maccabi Haifa	Isr	2-1	Bellamy, Gonzalez	40,058
22nd Aug	Q.3 Leg 2	(a)	Maccabi Haifa	"	1-1	Crouch	12,500
	Group Stage						
12th Sept	Group C	(a)	PSV Eindhoven	Hol	0-0		35,000
27th Sept	Group C	(h)	Galatasaray	Tur	3-2	Crouch 2, Garcia	41,976
18th Oct	Group C	(a)	Bordeaux	Fra	1-0	Crouch	33,000
31st Oct	Group C	(h)	Bordeaux	Fra	3-0	Garcia 2, Gerrard	41,978
22nd Nov	Group C	(a)	PSV Eindhoven	Hol	2-0	Gerrard, Crouch	41,948
5th Dec	Group C	(h)	Galatasaray	Tur	2-3	Fowler 2	23,000
21st Feb	L. 16 L1	(a)	Barcelona	Spa	2-1	Bellamy, Riise	88,000
6th Mar	L. 16 L2	(h)	Barcelona	Spa	0-1		42,579
3rd Apr	QF L1	(a)	PSV Eindhoven	Hol	3-0	Gerrard, Riise, Crouch	36,500
11th Apr	QF L2	(h)	PSV Eindhoven	Hol	1-0	Crouch	41,447
25th Apr	SF L1	(a)	Chelsea	Eng	0-1		39,483
1st May	SF L2	(h)	Chelsea	Eng aet	1-0	Agger	42,554
	(Liverpool won 4-1 on penalties)						
23rd May	Final	Athens	AC Milan	Ita	1-2	Kuyt	74,000
2007/08	**EUROPEAN CUP**	**(WINNERS – MANCHESTER UNITED)**					
15th Aug	Q. Leg 1 (a)		Toulouse	Fra	1-0	Voronin	30,380
28th Aug	Q. Leg 2 (h)		Toulouse	"	4-0	Crouch, Hyypia, Kuyt 2	43,118
	Group Stage						
18th Sept	Group A	(a)	FC Porto	Por	1-1	Kuyt	41,208
3rd Oct	Group A	(h)	Marseille	Fra	0-1		41,355
24th Oct	Group A	(a)	Besiktas	Tur	1-2	Gerrard	32,500
6th Nov	Group A	(h)	Besiktas	"	8-0	Crouch 2, Benayoun 3, Gerrard, Babel 2	41,143

LIVERPOOL'S RESULTS IN EUROPEAN COMPETITION

Season	Round	Venue	Opponents	Opponent Country	Score	Scorers	Att
2007/08	**EURO. CUP (cont)**		**(WINNERS – MANCHESTER UNITED)**				
28th Nov	Group A (h)		FC Porto	Por	4-1	Torres 2, Gerrard (pen), Crouch	41,095
11th Dec	Group A (a)		Marseille	Fra	4-0	Gerrard, Torres, Kuyt, Babel	53,000
19th Feb	L. 16 L1 (h)		Inter Milan	Ita	2-0	Kuyt, Gerrard	41,999
11th Mar	L. 16 L2 (a)		Inter Milan	"	1-0	Torres	80,000
2nd Apr	QF Leg 1 (a)		Arsenal	Eng	1-1	Kuyt	60,041
8th Apr	QF Leg 2 (h)		Arsenal	"	4-2	Hyypia, Torres, Gerrard (pen), Babel	41,985
22nd Apr	SF Leg 1 (h)		Chelsea	Eng	1-1	Kuyt	42,180
30th Apr	SF Leg 2 (a)		Chelsea	"	2-3 aet	Torres, Babel	38,900
2008/09	**EUROPEAN CUP**		**(WINNERS – BARCELONA)**				
13th Aug	Q.3 Leg 1 (a)		Standard Liege	Bel	0-0		25,000
27th Aug	Q.3 Leg 2 (h)		Standard Liege	"	1-0 aet	Kuyt	43,889
42,175			**Group Stage**				
16th Sept	Group D (a)		Marseille	Fra	2-1	Gerrard 2 (1 pen)	45,000
1st Oct	Group D (h)		PSV Eindhoven	Hol	3-1	Kuyt, Keane, Gerrard	41,097
22nd Oct	Group D (a)		Atletico Madrid	Spa	1-1	Keane	48,769
4th Nov	Group D (h)		Atletico Madrid	Spa	1-1	Gerrard (pen)	42,010
26th Nov	Group D (h)		Marseille	Fra	1-0	Gerrard	40,024
9th Dec	Group D (a)		PSV Eindhoven	Hol	3-1	Babel, Riera, Ngog	35,000
25th Feb	L. 16 L1 (a)		Real Madrid	Spa	1-0	Benayoun	85,000
10th Mar	L. 16 L2 (h)		Real Madrid	"	4-0	Torres, Gerrard 2 (1 pen), Dossena	42,550
8th Apr	QF Leg 1 (h)		Chelsea	Eng	1-3	Torres	42,543
14th Apr	QF Leg 2 (a)		Chelsea	"	4-4	Aurelio, Alonso (pen), Lucas, Kuyt	38,286

Liverpool line up ahead of their last 16, second leg clash against Real Madrid in March 2009

CLASSIC EUROPEAN SEASON – 1976/77

Liverpool's first European Cup triumph, only the third by a British club, proved lucky 13 – the number of seasons the Reds had competed in continental competition.
The campaign began with a first-round tie against Northern Irish part-timers Crusaders, Liverpool eventually cruising to a 7-0 aggregate triumph – they had struggled to a 2-0 win at Anfield.
Next up was a first – Turkish opposition, in the former of Trabzonspor. A disputed penalty meant a narrow defeat in the away leg, but at Anfield quickfire goals from Steve Heighway, David Johnson and Kevin Keegan silenced the vocal Turkish masses.

The 1976 European Cup runners-up St Etienne were the last eight opposition, and the French champions would travel to Liverpool one goal ahead after a late Dominique Bathenay strike.
The return match did much to create the sense of occasion only a European night at Anfield can. Around 55,000 were packed in, including another sizeable visiting following. Keegan's early cross deceived visiting keeper Ivan Curkovic to level the tie, only for Bathenay's stunning long-ranger to put the French side ahead again – crucially an away goal. Ray Kennedy made the scores level again, but with the Reds behind on away goals, sub David Fairclough was brought on for John Toshack. With six minutes left, the youngster latched onto Kennedy's lob forward to finish like a seasoned pro. The goal sparked off wild celebrations, scenes that have gone down in club folklore. Swiss champions Zurich proved easier opposition in the semi-finals. Despite taking the lead, two from Phil Neal and one from Heighway secured a 3-1 away win, before the Reds eased to a 3-0 victory at Anfield, Case netting the first early on to all but end the tie.

Paired against West German champions Borussia Moenchengladbach in the final in Rome's Olympic Stadium, the only change from the side beaten by Manchester United in the FA Cup final the previous Saturday was Ian Callaghan, who was brought into a five-man midfield in place of Johnson. Veteran Cally produced a controlled display in his 83rd European game – a then English record. He had a hand in setting up the opener for the onrushing Terry McDermott, this after Borussia had hit the post through Rainer Bonhof's long-range effort.
Allan Simonsen, who would be named European Footballer of the Year at the end of 1977, levelled early in the second half, before Tommy Smith headed Liverpool back into the lead, the ideal time to net his first goal of the season in his 600th game for the club. Borussia were always dangerous, but the 20,000+ Liverpool supporters could rejoice when Neal coolly converted from the spot after Keegan, in his last game in a red shirt, was brought down by his tired man-marker Berti Vogts.
It completed a memorable double for manager Bob Paisley, Liverpool having already won the league. The season before they had been league and UEFA Cup winners.

EUROPEAN CUP STATISTICS 1976/77

PLAYER	AGE (START OF 76/77)	GAMES	GOALS
Ian Callaghan	34	7	0
Jimmy Case	22	6	2
Ray Clemence	28	9	0
David Fairclough	19	1 + 2	1
Steve Heighway	28	9	3
Emlyn Hughes	28	9	0
David Johnson	24	4 + 2	3
Joey Jones	21	9	0
Kevin Keegan	25	8	4
Ray Kennedy	25	9	1
Terry McDermott	24	6 + 1	2
Phil Neal	25	8	4
Tommy Smith	31	7	1
John Toshack	27	4	1
Phil Thompson	22	3	0
Alan Waddle	22	0 + 1	0

Team line-ups

🏴 Liverpool (4-5-1):

Keegan

McDermott
Kennedy   Case   Callaghan   Heighway

Jones   Hughes   Smith   Neal

Clemence

Subs not used: McDonnell, Lindsay, Waddle, Fairclough, Johnson

B. Moenchengladbach (3-5-2):

Stielike   Heynckes

Simonsen   Schaffer   Wimmer   Wohlers
Bonhof

Wittkamp   Klinkhammer   Vogts

Kneib

Subs: Kulik (Wimmer) 24, Hannes (Wohlers) 79
Subs not used: Koppell, Kleff, Herdenreich

LIVERPOOL 3
B. MOENCHENGLADBACH 1

European Cup
Final
Stadio Olimpico, Rome, Italy
Wednesday May 25, 1977.
Attendance: 52,078

Goals: McDermott (27), Simonsen (51), Smith (64), Neal (82 pen)
Booking: Stielike (Borussia Moenchengladbach)
Referee: Robert Wurtz (France)

EUROPEAN PLAYER RECORDS

CORRECT AT END OF 2008/2009 SEASON – Games played includes substitute appearances

EUROPEAN APPEARANCES – ALL COMPETITIONS (46+ GAMES)

		FIRST-TEAM CAREER	GAMES
1	Jamie Carragher	1997-	116
2	Steven Gerrard	1998-	101
3	Sami Hyypia	1999-2009	94
4	Ian Callaghan	1960-1978	89
5	Tommy Smith	1963-1978	85
6	Ray Clemence	1968-1981	80
7	Emlyn Hughes	1967-1979	79
=	John Arne Riise	2001-2008	79
9	Phil Neal	1974-1985	74
10	Steve Heighway	1970-1981	67
11	Chris Lawler	1963-1975	66
12	Dietmar Hamann	1999-2006	61
13	Pepe Reina	2005-	52
14	Kenny Dalglish	1977-1990	51
=	Steve Finnan	2003-2008	51
16	Ray Kennedy	1974-1981	50
=	Michael Owen	1997-2004	50
=	Phil Thompson	1972-1983	50
19	Xabi Alonso	2004-	48
20	Alan Hansen	1977-1990	46
=	Danny Murphy	1997-2004	46

EUROPEAN CUP/UEFA CHAMPIONS LEAGUE APPEARANCES (30+ GAMES)

		FIRST-TEAM CAREER	GAMES
1	Jamie Carragher	1997-	86
2	Steven Gerrard	1998-	76
2	John Arne Riise	2001-2008	68
3	Sami Hyypia	1999-2009	67
5	Phil Neal	1974-1985	57
6	Pepe Reina	2005-	51
7	Xabi Alonso	2004-2009	47
=	Kenny Dalglish	1977-1990	47
9	Steve Finnan	2003-2008	44
10	Alan Hansen	1977-1990	43
11	Dietmar Hamann	1999-2006	37
12	Graeme Souness	1978-1984	36
13	Alan Kennedy	1978-1985	34
=	Dirk Kuyt	2006-	34
15	Ray Clemence	1968-1981	33
=	Sammy Lee	1978-1986	33
17	Ray Kennedy	1974-1981	32
=	Phil Thompson	1972-1983	32
19	Luis Garcia	2004-2007	31
=	Terry McDermott	1974-1982	31
21	Ian Callaghan	1960-1978	30
=	Peter Crouch	2005-2008	30
=	Bruce Grobbelaar	1981-1994	30

First-team career noted as the year a player made his first appearance for the first team, and the year they made their last appearance

EUROPEAN PLAYER RECORDS

CORRECT AT END OF 2008/2009 SEASON – Games played includes substitute appearances

INTER-CITIES FAIRS CUP/UEFA CUP APPEARANCES (19+ GAMES)

		FIRST-TEAM CAREER	GAMES
1	Emlyn Hughes	1967-1979	45
2	Ian Callaghan	1960-1978	41
=	Tommy Smith	1963-1978	41
4	Ray Clemence	1968-1981	36
5	Chris Lawler	1963-1975	35
6	Michael Owen	1997-2004	33
7	Steve Heighway	1970-1981	30
8	Jamie Carragher	1997-	28
9	Brian Hall	1969-1976	25
=	Sami Hyypia	1999-2009	25
11	Robbie Fowler	1993-2001 & 2006-2007	24
=	Steven Gerrard	1998-	24
=	Danny Murphy	1997-2004	24
=	John Toshack	1970-1977	24
15	Larry Lloyd	1969-1974	23
16	Dietmar Hamann	1999-2006	22
=	Emile Heskey	2000-2004	22
=	Kevin Keegan	1971-1977	22
=	Alec Lindsay	1969-1977	22
20	Peter Thompson	1963-1972	20
21	Steve McManaman	1990-1999	19

EUROPEAN CUP WINNERS' CUP APPEARANCES (8+ GAMES)

		FIRST-TEAM CAREER	GAMES
1	Ian Callaghan	1960-1978	17
2	Tommy Smith	1963-1978	16
3	Chris Lawler	1963-1975	15
4	Steve McManaman	1990-1999	11
=	Jamie Redknapp	1991-2001	11
=	Peter Thompson	1963-1972	11
7	Gerry Byrne	1957-1969	9
=	David James	1992-1999	9
=	Tommy Lawrence	1962-1971	9
=	Willie Stevenson	1962-1967	9
=	Ian St John	1961-1971	9
=	Ron Yeats	1961-1971	9
13	Stig Inge Bjornebye	1992-1999	8
=	Ray Clemence	1968-1981	8
=	Steve Heighway	1970-1981	8
=	Emlyn Hughes	1967-1979	8
=	Jason McAteer	1995-1999	8
=	Michael Thomas	1991-1998	8
=	Mark Wright	1991-1998	8

First-team career noted as the year a player made his first appearance for the first team, and the year they made their last appearance

EUROPEAN PLAYER RECORDS

CORRECT AT END OF 2008/09 SEASON- Games played includes substitute appearances

EUROPEAN GOALS

		FIRST-TEAM CAREER	GAMES	GOALS
1	Steven Gerrard	1998-	101	32
2	Michael Owen	1997-2004	50	22
3	Ian Rush	1980-87 & 1988-96	38	20
4	Roger Hunt	1959-1969	31	17
5	Terry McDermott	1974-1982	34	15
6	Robbie Fowler	1993-2001 & 2006-07	44	14
7	Jimmy Case	1975-1981	35	13
=	Emile Heskey	2000-2004	45	13
9	Kevin Keegan	1971-1977	40	12
=	Ray Kennedy	1974-1981	50	12
11	Peter Crouch	2005-2008	30	11
=	Luis Garcia	2004-2007	32	11
=	Dirk Kuyt	2006-	34	11
=	Kenny Dalglish	1977-1990	51	11
=	Chris Lawler	1963-1975	66	11
=	Steve Heighway	1970-1981	67	11
=	Phil Neal	1974-1985	74	11

(There are 107 different Liverpool goalscorers in European competition)

EUROPEAN CUP/UEFA CHAMPIONS LEAGUE GOALS

		FIRST-TEAM CAREER	GAMES	GOALS
1	Steven Gerrard	1998-	76	28
2	Ian Rush	1980-87 & 1988-96	25	14
3	Terry McDermott	1974-1982	31	12
4	Peter Crouch	2005-2008	30	11
=	Dirk Kuyt	2006-	34	11
6	Roger Hunt	1959-1969	14	10
=	Luis Garcia	2004-2007	31	10
=	Kenny Dalglish	1977-1990	47	10
=	Phil Neal	1974-1985	57	10
10	Michael Owen	1997-2004	16	9
11	David Johnson	1976-1982	20	8
=	Fernando Torres	2007-	20	8
13	Ian St John	1961-1971	13	7
=	Jimmy Case	1975-1981	22	7
=	Djibril Cisse	2004-2006	22	7
16	Ryan Babel	2007-	23	6
=	Emile Heskey	2000-2004	22	6
=	Ronnie Whelan	1981-1994	23	6
=	Ray Kennedy	1974-1981	32	6
=	Graeme Souness	1978-1984	36	6
=	Sami Hyypia	1999-2009	67	6
22	John Wark	1984-1987	9	5

First-team career noted as the year a player made his first appearance for the first team,
and the year they made their last appearance

EUROPEAN PLAYER RECORDS

CORRECT AT END OF 2008/09 SEASON - Games played includes substitute appearances

INTER-CITIES FAIRS CUP/UEFA CUP GOALS

		FIRST-TEAM CAREER	GAMES	GOALS
1	Michael Owen	1997-2004	33	12
2	Dean Saunders	1991-1992	5	9
3	John Toshack	1970-1977	24	8
4	Kevin Keegan	1971-1977	22	7
5	Phil Boersma	1969-1975	13	6
=	Ian Callaghan	1960-1978	41	6
=	Alun Evans	1968-1972	10	6
=	Emile Heskey	2000-2004	22	6
=	Emlyn Hughes	1967-1979	45	6
10	Jimmy Case	1975-1981	9	5
=	Steve Heighway	1970-1981	30	5
=	Roger Hunt	1959-1969	10	5
=	Tommy Smith	1963-1978	41	5

EUROPEAN CUP WINNERS' CUP GOALS

		FIRST-TEAM CAREER	GAMES	GOALS
1	Robbie Fowler	1993-2001 & 2006-2007	7	7
2	Chris Lawler	1963-1975	15	5
=	Ian Rush	1980-1987 & 1988-1996	4	5
4	John Barnes	1987-1997	7	3

EUROPEAN RANKINGS 2009/10

Based on UEFA co-efficient points taken from a club's performances in European competition over the last five seasons, the following table is the ranking of the continent's top sides, as noted at 31 August 2009.

	CLUB	RANKING POINTS
1	FC Barcelona	110.708
2	Manchester United	101.157
3	Chelsea	100.157
4	**Liverpool**	**95.157**
5	Arsenal	92.157
6	Sevilla	90.708
7	AC Milan	85.153
8	Bayern Munich	84.524
9	Werder Bremen	78.024
10	AS Roma	73.153
11	Inter Milan	71.153
12	Lyon	71.048
13	Real Madrid	66.708
14	Hamburg	66.524
15	Shakhtar Donetsk	64.590
16	Villarreal	62.208
17	Zenit St. Petersburg	60.325
18	FC Porto	59.875
19	Rangers	53.858
20	PSV Eindhoven	53.726

BIGGEST EUROPEAN VICTORIES

DATE	OPPONENTS	VENUE	COMPETITION	SCORE
17th Sept 1974	Stromsgodset	Home	European Cup Winners' Cup	11-0
16th Sept 1969	Dundalk	Home	Inter Cities' Fairs Cup	10-0
1st Oct 1980	Oulu Palloseura	Home	European Cup	10-1
7th Nov 1967	TSV Munich 1860	Home	Inter Cities' Fairs Cup	8-0
6th Nov 2008	Besiktas	Home	Champions League	8-0
30th Sept 1981	Oulu Palloseura	Home	European Cup	7-0
4th Nov 1975	Real Sociedad	Home	UEFA Cup	6-0
6th Dec 1977	SV Hamburg	Home	European Super Cup	6-0
14th Sept 1964	Reykjavik	Home	European Cup	6-1
18th Sept 1991	Kuusysi Lahti	Home	UEFA Cup	6-1
16th Sept 1992	Apollon Limassol	Home	European Cup Winners' Cup	6-1

BIGGEST EUROPEAN DEFEATS

DATE	OPPONENTS	VENUE	COMPETITION	SCORE
7th Dec 1966	Ajax	Away	European Cup	1-5
12th May 1965	Inter Milan	Away	European Cup	0-3
3rd Oct 1979	Dynamo Tblisi	Away	European Cup	0-3
10th Apr 1997	Paris St Germain	Away	European Cup Winners' Cup	0-3
21st Oct 1997	RC Strasbourg	Away	UEFA Cup	0-3
22nd Oct 1992	Spartak Moscow	Away	European Cup Winners' Cup	2-4
9th Apr 2002	Bayer Leverkusen	Away	Champions League	2-4
12th Oct 1966	Petrolul Ploesti	Away	European Cup	1-3
3rd Nov 1971	Bayern Munich	Away	European Cup Winners' Cup	1-3
4th Dec 1978	Anderlecht	Away	European Super Cup	1-3
24th Nov 1998	Celta Vigo	Away	UEFA Cup	1-3
20th Nov 2001	Barcelona	Home	Champions League	1-3
8th Apr 2009	Chelsea	Home	Champions League	1-3

LIVERPOOL MANAGERS – EUROPE

BIGGEST WIN RATIO ENJOYED BY LIVERPOOL MANAGERS IN EUROPEAN COMPETITION

MANAGER	P	W	D	L	F	A	% WINS
Joe Fagan	19	14	2	3	34	10	73.7
Bob Paisley	61	39	11	11	140	49	63.9
Rafael Benitez	71	42	15	14	121	54	59.2
Bill Shankly	65	34	13	18	114	54	52.3
Gerard Houllier	52	26	17	9	78	45	50.0
Roy Evans	16	8	5	3	24	16	50.0
Graeme Souness	12	6	0	6	26	16	50.0
Roy Evans/Gerard Houllier	4	2	2	0	10	2	50.0

PENALTIES SAVED BY LIVERPOOL GOALKEEPERS

EUROPEAN COMPETITION ONLY

DATE	COMPETITION	ROUND	OPPOSITION	GOALKEEPER
10/05/1973	UEFA Cup	Final, 1st leg	B. Moenchengladbach	Ray Clemence
17/09/1975	UEFA Cup	1st round, 1st leg	Hibernian	Ray Clemence
03/03/1976	UEFA Cup	QF, 1st leg	Dynamo Dresden	Ray Clemence
18/03/1981	European Cup	QF, 2nd leg	CSKA Sofia	Ray Clemence
13/08/2008	European Cup	3rd QR, 1st leg	Standard Liege	Pepe Reina

Ray Clemence – Four-time European penalty saver

LIVERPOOL'S EUROPEAN OPPONENTS

Liverpool will add three new teams to their list of European opponents in the 2009/10 campaign. The draw for the Champions League groups paired the Reds against Lyon (France), Fiorentina (Italy) and Debrecen (Hungary) in Group E.

Atletico Madrid became the 10th Spanish club the Reds had faced during 2008/09, while the last 16 tie against Real Madrid was the first competitive meeting between the sides since the 1981 European Cup final – Liverpool winning out on both occasions.

The 19 remaining countries that the club have yet to visit in European competition are listed below. Qualifiers for the 2009/10 UEFA Champions League competition are noted in brackets – note that there are no Liechtenstein champions as they are the only UEFA member without their own organised national league.

Albania (KF Tirana), **Andorra** (Sant Julia), **Armenia** (Pyunik FC), **Azerbaijan** (FK Baku), **Belarus** (FC BATE Borisov), **Bosnia-Herzegovina** (HSK Zrinjski Mostar), **Croatia** (Dinamo Zagreb), **Estonia** (FC Levadia Tallinn), **FYR Macedonia** (Makedonija Gjorce Petrov), **Faroe Islands** (EB/Streymur), **Georgia** (FC WIT Georgia), **Kazakhstan** (FC Aktobe), **Latvia** (FK Ventspils), **Liechtenstein**, **Malta** (Hibernians), **Moldova** (FC Sheriff Tiraspol), **Montenegro** (Mogren), **San Marino** (Tre Fiori), **Serbia** (FK Partizan Belgrade).

The countries, and the clubs, that Liverpool have faced (up to and including the 2008/2009 season) are listed below and opposite:

AUSTRIA (3)
AK Graz, Austria Vienna, Swarovski Tirol.
BELGIUM (3)
FC Bruges, Anderlecht, Standard Liege.
BULGARIA (2)
CSKA Sofia, Levski Sofia.
CYPRUS (1)
Apollon Limassol.
CZECH REPUBLIC (1)
Slovan Liberec.
DENMARK (2)
Brondby, Odense.
ENGLAND (5)
Arsenal, Chelsea, Leeds United, Nottingham Forest, Tottenham Hotspur.
EAST GERMANY (2)
Dynamo Berlin, Dynamo Dresden.
FINLAND (5)
FC Haka, HJK Helsinki, Kuusysi Lahti, MyPa 47, Oulu Palloseura.
FRANCE (8)
Auxerre, Bordeaux, Olimpique Marseille, Monaco, Paris St Germain, RC Strasbourg, St Etienne, Toulouse.
GERMANY (2)
Bayer Leverkusen, Borussia Dortmund.
GREECE (3)
AEK Athens, Olympiakos, Panathinaikos.
HOLLAND (4)
Ajax Amsterdam, AZ '67 Alkmaar, PSV Eindhoven, Vitesse Arnhem.
HUNGARY (2)
Ferencvaros, Honved.
ICELAND (1)
Reykjavik.

LIVERPOOL'S EUROPEAN OPPONENTS

ISRAEL (1)
Maccabi Haifa.

ITALY (5)
AC Milan, AS Roma, Genoa, Inter Milan,
Juventus.

LITHUANIA (1)
FBK Kaunas.

LUXEMBOURG (1)
Jeunesse D'Esch.

NORTHERN IRELAND (1)
Crusaders.

NORWAY (2)
Brann Bergen, Stromsgodset.

POLAND (3)
Lech Poznan, Slask Wroclaw, Widzew Lodz.

PORTUGAL (4)
Benfica, Boavista, FC Porto, Vitoria Setubal.

REPUBLIC OF IRELAND (1)
Dundalk.

ROMANIA (4)
Dinamo Bucharest, Petrolul Ploesti,
Rapid Bucharest, Steaua Bucharest.

RUSSIA (4)
Dynamo Tblisi, Spartak Moscow,
Spartak Vladikavkaz, CSKA Moscow.

SCOTLAND (3)
Aberdeen, Celtic, Hibernian.

SLOVAKIA (1)
FC Kosice.

SLOVENIA (1)
Olimpija Ljubljana.

SPAIN (10)
Alaves, Athletic Bilbao, Atletico Madrid,
Celta Vigo, Deportivo La Coruna, FC Barcelona,
Real Betis, Real Madrid, Real Sociedad,
Valencia.

SWEDEN (1)
Malmo.

SWITZERLAND (4)
FC Basel, FC Sion, FC Zurich, Servette Geneva.

TURKEY (3)
Besiktas, Galatasaray, Trabzonspor.

WALES (1)
Total Network Solutions.

WEST GERMANY (7)
Bayern Munich, Borussia Moenchengladbach,
Borussia Dortmund, FC Cologne,
Eintracht Frankfurt, Hamburg, 1860 Munich.

UKRAINE (1)
Dynamo Kiev.

YUGOSLAVIA (1)
Red Star Belgrade.

**Spanish capital – Liverpool faced Madrid's
two biggest sides, Real and Atletico, during
the 2008/09 Champions League campaign**

LIVERPOOL IN EUROPE: CLUB-BY-CLUB RECORD

OPPOSITION	PLAYED	WON	DRAWN	LOST	FOR	AGAINST
Aberdeen	2	2	0	0	5	0
AC Milan	2	1	0	1	4	5
AEK Athens	2	2	0	0	6	1
Ajax Amsterdam	2	0	1	1	3	7
Alaves	1	1	0	0	5	4
Anderlecht	6	5	0	1	11	4
Apollon Limassol	2	2	0	0	8	2
Arsenal	2	1	1	0	5	3
AS Monaco	2	1	0	1	2	1
AS Roma	5	3	1	1	5	2
Athletic Bilbao	4	2	1	1	4	3
Atletico Madrid	2	0	2	0	2	2
Austria Vienna	2	1	1	0	5	2
Auxerre	4	3	0	1	6	2
AZ '67 Alkmaar	2	1	1	0	5	4
Basel FC	2	0	2	0	4	4
Bayer Leverkusen	4	3	0	1	9	6
Bayern Munich	7	2	4	1	9	7
Benfica	8	5	0	3	14	8
Besiktas	2	1	0	1	9	2
Boavista	2	0	2	0	2	2
Bordeaux	2	2	0	0	4	0
Borussia Dortmund	3	1	1	1	3	2
Bor. Moenchengladbach	5	3	0	2	10	5
Brann Bergen	2	1	1	0	4	1
Brondby	2	0	1	1	0	1
Celta Vigo	2	0	0	2	1	4
Celtic	6	1	3	2	5	6
Chelsea	10	2	5	3	10	12
Club Brugge KV	3	2	1	0	5	3
Crusaders	2	2	0	0	7	0
CSKA Moscow	1	1	0	0	3	1
CSKA Sofia	6	4	0	2	10	5
Deportivo La Coruna	2	1	1	0	1	0
Dinamo Bucharest	4	3	1	0	7	2
Dundalk	4	4	0	0	19	1
Dynamo Berlin	2	1	1	0	3	1
Dynamo Dresden	6	4	1	1	11	4
Dynamo Kiev	2	2	0	0	3	1
Dynamo Tblisi	2	1	0	1	2	4
Eintracht Frankfurt	2	1	1	0	2	0
FC Barcelona	8	3	3	2	6	6
FC Cologne	3	0	3	0	2	2
FC Porto	4	2	2	0	7	2
Ferencvaros	6	1	3	2	3	4
Galatasaray	4	1	2	1	6	6
Genoa	2	0	0	2	1	4
Graz AK	2	1	0	1	2	1
Haka FC	2	2	0	0	9	1
Hamburg	2	1	1	0	7	1
Hibernian	4	3	0	1	6	2
HJK Helsinki	2	1	0	1	5	1
Honved	2	1	1	0	2	0

LIVERPOOL IN EUROPE: CLUB-BY-CLUB RECORD

OPPOSITION	PLAYED	WON	DRAWN	LOST	FOR	AGAINST
Inter Milan	4	3	0	1	6	4
Jeunesse D'Esch	2	1	1	0	3	1
Juventus	6	2	1	3	4	5
Kaunas FBK	2	2	0	0	5	1
Kosice FC	2	2	0	0	8	0
Kuusysi Lahti	2	1	0	1	6	2
Lech Poznan	2	2	0	0	5	0
Leeds United	2	0	1	1	0	1
Levski Sofia	2	2	0	0	6	2
Maccabi Haifa	2	1	1	0	3	2
Malmo	2	2	0	0	4	1
Munich 1860	2	1	0	1	9	2
MyPa 47	2	2	0	0	4	1
Nottingham Forest	2	0	1	1	0	2
Odense	2	2	0	0	6	0
Olimpija Ljubljana	2	1	1	0	4	1
Olympiakos	4	2	1	1	7	4
Olympique Marseille	6	3	1	2	9	5
Oulu Palloseura	4	3	1	0	19	2
Panathinaikos	2	2	0	0	5	0
Paris St Germain	2	1	0	1	2	3
Petrolul Ploesti	3	2	0	1	5	3
PSV Eindhoven	6	5	1	0	12	2
Rapid Bucharest	2	1	1	0	1	0
RC Strasbourg	2	1	0	1	2	3
Real Betis	2	1	1	0	2	1
Real Madrid	3	3	0	0	6	0
Real Sociedad	2	2	0	0	9	1
Red Star Belgrade	2	0	0	2	2	4
Reykjavik	2	2	0	0	11	1
St Etienne	2	1	0	1	3	2
Servette Geneva	2	1	0	1	3	2
Sion FC	2	2	0	0	8	4
Slask Wroclaw	2	2	0	0	5	1
Slovan Liberec	2	2	0	0	4	2
Spartak Moscow	4	2	0	2	10	7
Spartak Vladikavkaz	2	1	1	0	2	1
Standard Liege	4	3	1	0	6	2
Steaua Bucharest	2	1	1	0	2	1
Stromsgodset	2	2	0	0	12	0
Swarowski Tirol	2	2	0	0	6	0
Total Network Solutions	2	2	0	0	6	0
Tottenham Hotspur	2	1	0	1	2	2
Toulouse	2	2	0	0	5	0
Trabzonspor	2	1	0	1	3	1
Valencia	4	0	2	2	2	5
Vitesse Arnhem	2	2	0	0	2	0
Vitoria Setubal	2	1	0	1	3	3
Widzew Lodz	2	1	0	1	3	4
Zurich FC	2	2	0	0	6	1
OVERALL	**300**	**171**	**65**	**64**	**547**	**246**

Games decided on toss of coin (Petrolul) in a third game counted as a draw. One-game ties decided on penalties count as wins or losses.

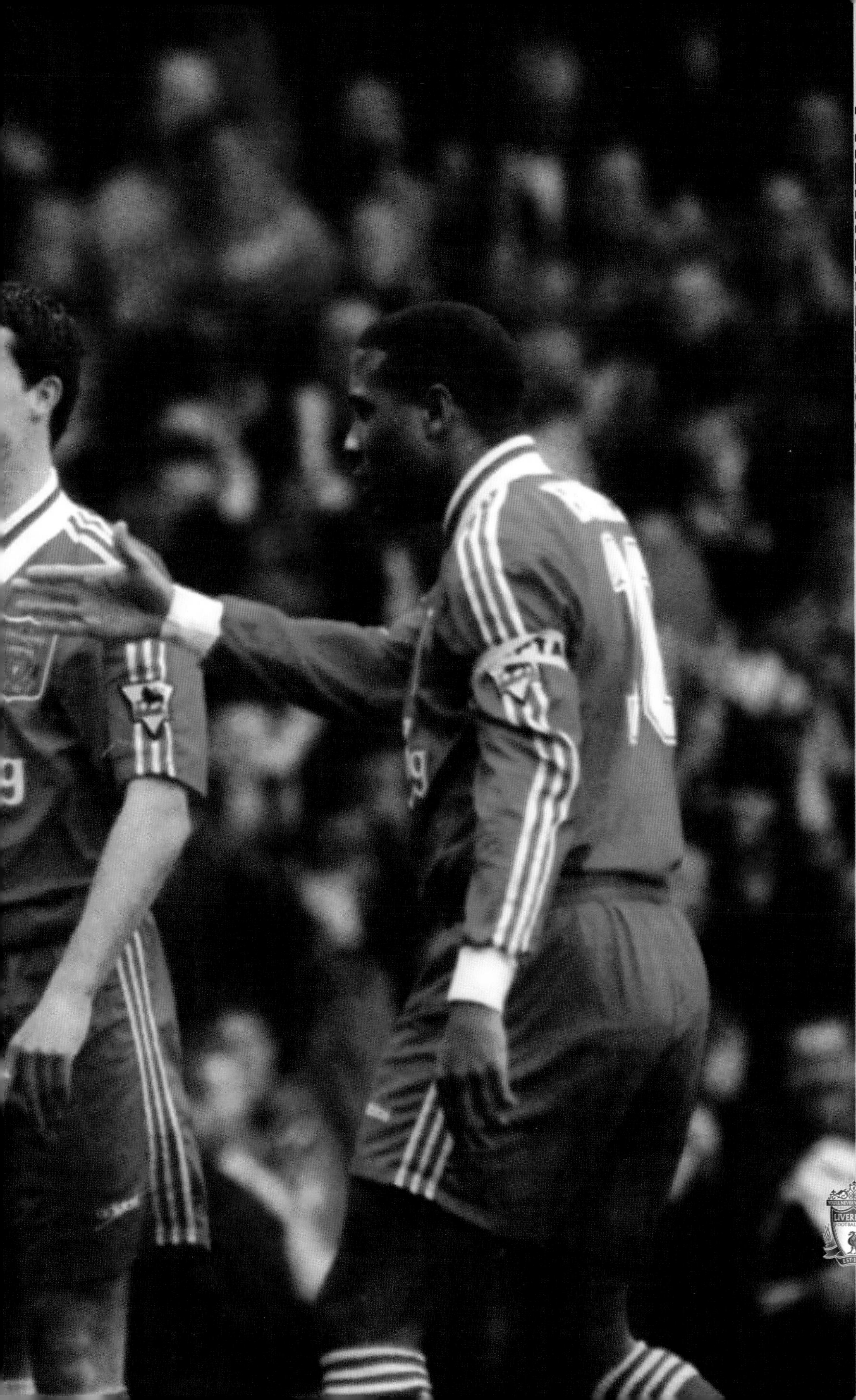

MOST POINTS WON BY TEAMS
IN PREMIER LEAGUE HISTORY

08/09 POS.	POS.	CLUB	POINTS	HIGHEST POS	SEASONS IN PREMIERSHIP
1	1	Manchester United	1409	1st (11 times)	17
2	2	Arsenal	1236	1st (3 times)	17
3	3	Chelsea	1181	1st (2 times)	17
4	4	Liverpool	1161	2nd (2 times)	17
5	5	Aston Villa	939	2nd (1992/1993)	17
6	6	Newcastle United	906	2nd (2 times)	16
7	7	Tottenham Hotspur	885	5th (2 times)	17
9	8	Everton	863	4th (2004/2005)	17
8	9	Blackburn Rovers	846	1st (1994/1995)	15
11	10	West Ham United	696	5th (1998/1999)	14
10	11	Leeds United	692	3rd (1999/2000)	12
12	12	Middlesbrough	633	7th (2004/2005)	14
13	13	Southampton	587	8th (2002/2003)	13
14	14	Manchester City	557	8th (2004/2005)	12
15	15	Bolton Wanderers	454	6th (2004/2005)	10
16	16	Coventry City	409	11th (2 times)	9
17	17	Sheffield Wednesday	392	7th (3 times)	8
18	18	Wimbledon (MK Dons)	391	6th (1993/1994)	8
21	19	Fulham	364	7th (2008/2009)	8
19	20	Charlton Athletic	361	7th (2003/2004)	8
20	21	Leicester City	342	8th (1999/2000)	8
23	22	Sunderland	304	7th (2 times)	8
25	23	Portsmouth	274	8th (2007/2008)	6
22	24	Derby County	274	8th (1998/1999)	7
24	25	Nottingham Forest	239	3rd (1994/1995)	5
26	26	Ipswich Town	224	5th (2000/2001)	5
27	27	Queens Park Rangers	216	5th (1992/1993)	4
28	28	Birmingham City	212	10th (2003/2004)	5
29	29	Norwich City	201	3rd (1992/1993)	4
32	30	Wigan Athletic	174	10th (2005/2006)	4
30	31	Crystal Palace	160	18th (2004/2005)	4
31	32	Sheffield United	132	14th (1992/1993)	3
34	33	West Bromwich Albion	132	17th (2004/2005)	4
33	34	Reading	91	8th (2006/2007)	2
35	35	Oldham Athletic	89	19th (1992/1993)	2
36	36	Bradford City	62	17th (1999/2000)	2
37	37	Watford	52	20th (1999/2000)	2
–	38	Stoke City	45	12th (2008/09)	1
38	39	Barnsley	35	19th (1997/1998)	1
–	=	Hull City	35	17th (2008/09)	1
39	41	Wolverhampton Wanderers	33	20th (2003/2004)	1
40	42	Swindon Town	30	22nd (1994/1995)	1

THE PREMIER LEAGUE FINISHES

17 SEASONS		
POSITION	NUMBER OF TIMES	MOST RECENT FINAL POSITION
1st	0	-
2nd	2	2008/09
3rd	5	2006/07
4th	5	2007/08
5th	2	2004/05
6th	1	1992/93
7th	1	1998/99
8th	1	1993/94

PREMIER LEAGUE FACTS & FIGURES

LEAGUE RECORD								
SEASON	P	W	D	L	F	A	PTS	POS
1992/1993	42	16	11	15	62	55	59	6
1993/1994	42	17	9	16	59	55	60	8
1994/1995	42	21	11	10	65	37	74	4
1995/1996	38	20	11	7	70	34	71	3
1996/1997	38	19	11	8	62	37	68	4
1997/1998	38	18	11	9	68	42	65	3
1998/1999	38	15	9	14	68	49	54	7
1999/2000	38	19	10	9	51	30	67	4
2000/2001	38	20	9	9	71	39	69	3
2001/2002	38	24	8	6	67	30	80	2
2002/2003	38	18	10	10	61	41	64	5
2003/2004	38	16	12	10	55	37	60	4
2004/2005	38	17	7	14	52	41	58	5
2005/2006	38	25	7	6	57	25	82	3
2006/2007	38	20	8	10	57	27	68	3
2007/2008	38	21	13	4	67	28	76	4
2008/2009	38	25	11	2	77	27	86	2

Robbie Fowler – Major Premier League player for the Reds

FULL PREMIER LEAGUE RECORD - CLUB-BY-CLUB

	PLAYED	WON	DRAWN	LOST	FOR	AGAINST
Arsenal	34	14	11	9	48	36
Aston Villa	34	18	8	8	57	32
Barnsley	2	1	0	1	3	3
Birmingham City	10	2	5	3	14	13
Blackburn Rovers	30	14	10	6	49	33
Bolton Wanderers	20	13	4	3	40	18
Bradford City	4	3	0	1	6	2
Charlton Athletic	16	8	3	5	27	16
Chelsea	34	13	7	14	38	42
Coventry City	18	9	3	6	27	17
Crystal Palace	8	5	2	1	20	6
Derby County	14	10	1	3	30	9
Everton	34	14	12	8	41	33
Fulham	16	10	3	3	29	11
Hull City	2	1	1	0	5	3
Ipswich Town	10	5	3	2	20	7
Leeds United	24	14	4	6	48	23
Leicester City	16	7	4	5	19	14
Manchester City	24	12	9	3	38	21
Manchester United	34	9	7	18	37	50
Middlesbrough	28	13	9	6	40	24
Newcastle United	32	19	6	7	66	35
Norwich City	8	5	1	2	17	7
Nottingham Forest	10	4	4	2	18	11
Oldham Athletic	4	3	0	1	8	4
Portsmouth	12	7	3	2	21	9
Queens Park Rangers	8	6	1	1	13	7
Reading	4	3	0	1	7	5
Sheffield United	6	2	2	2	8	5
Sheffield Wednesday	16	9	4	3	27	16
Southampton	26	12	7	7	45	33
Stoke City	2	0	2	0	0	0
Sunderland	16	10	5	1	21	6
Swindon Town	2	1	1	0	7	2
Tottenham Hotspur	34	16	10	8	58	37
Watford	4	3	0	1	8	3
West Bromwich Albion	8	8	0	0	24	0
West Ham United	28	16	7	5	45	19
Wigan Athletic	8	6	2	0	16	4
Wimbledon	16	5	6	5	22	17
Wolverhampton Wanderers	2	1	1	0	2	1

PREMIER LEAGUE FACTS & FIGURES

BIGGEST WINS (ALL HOME UNLESS STATED)

DATE	OPPONENTS	SCORE	LIVERPOOL SCORERS	ATT.
16th Jan 1999	Southampton	7-1	Fowler 3, Matteo, Carragher, Owen, Thompson	44,011
1st Sept 2007	Derby County	6-0	Alonso 2, Babel, Torres 2, Voronin	44,076
26th Apr 2003	West Brom	6-0	Owen 4, Baros 2	27,128*
9th Feb 2002	Ipswich Town	6-0	Abel Xavier, Heskey 2, Hyypia, Owen 2	25,608**
28th Oct 1995	Manchester City	6-0	Rush 2, Redknapp, Fowler 2, Ruddock	39,267

(*At The Hawthorns)
(**At Portman Road)

BIGGEST DEFEATS (ALL AWAY UNLESS STATED)

DATE	OPPONENTS	SCORE	LIVERPOOL SCORER	ATT.
19th Dec 1992	Coventry City	1-5	Redknapp	19,779
5th Apr 2003	Manchester Utd	0-4		67,639
2nd Oct 2005	Chelsea	1-4	Gerrard	44,235*
16th Dec 2001	Chelsea	0-4		41,174
25th Apr 1998	Chelsea	1-4	Riedle	34,639
3rd Apr 1992	Blackburn Rovers	1-4	Rush	15,032

(*At Anfield)

AVERAGE HOME ATTENDANCES

SEASON	HIGH	LOW	AVERAGE	HIGH/LOW
1992/1993	44,619	29,574	37,009	
1993/1994	44,601	24,561	38,503	LOWEST ATTENDANCE, v QPR
1994/1995	40,014	27,183	34,175	LOWEST SEASON AVERAGE
1995/1996	40,820	34,063	39,552	
1996/1997	40,892	36,126	39,776	
1997/1998	44,532	34,705	40,628	
1998/1999	44,852	36,019	43,321	
1999/2000	44,929	40,483	44,074	
2000/2001	44,806	38,474	43,698	
2001/2002	44,371	37,153	43,389	
2002/2003	44,250	41,462	43,243	
2003/2004	44,374	34,663	42,677	
2004/2005	44,224	35,064	42,587	
2005/2006	44,983	42,293	44,236	HIGHEST SEASON AVERAGE HIGHEST ATTENDANCE, v SPURS
2006/2007	44,403	41,370	43,561	
2007/2008	44,459	42,308	43,532	
2008/2009	44,424	41,169	43,608	

PREMIER LEAGUE NUMBERS GAME

SHIRT NUMBER	PLAYERS (PREMIER LEAGUE APPEARANCES IN BRACKETS)				
1	Grobbelaar (29),	James (171),	Westerveld (75),	Dudek (92)	
2	R.Jones (125),	Henchoz (135),	Kromkamp (14),	Arbeloa (9),	Dossena (16)
3	Burrows (4),	Dicks (24),	Scales (3),	Kvarme (45),	Ziege (16),
	Xavier (14),	Finnan (145)			
4	Nicol (35),	McAteer (100),	Song (34),	Hyypia (245)	
5	M.Wright (104),	Staunton (44),	Baros (68),	Agger (54)	
6	Hutchison (11),	Babb (128),	Babbel (42),	Riise (131)	
7	Clough (39),	McManaman (101),	Smicer (91),	Kewell (93),	Keane (19)
8	Stewart (8),	Collymore (61),	Leonhardsen (37),	Heskey (150),	Gerrard (163)
9	Rush (98),	Fowler (144),	Anelka (20),	Diouf (55),	Cisse (49),
	Torres (57)				
10	Barnes (135),	Owen (178),	Garcia (77),	Voronin (19)	
11	Walters (35),	Redknapp (103),	Smicer (30),	Fowler (14),	Gonzalez (25),
	Benayoun (30),	Riera (28)			
12	Whelan (23),	Scales (62),	Harkness (38),	Hyypia (73),	Dudek (35),
	P.Jones (2),	Pellegrino (12),	Aurelio (57)		
13	James (14),	Riedle (60),	Murphy (130),	Le Tallec (4)	
14	Molby (25),	Ruddock (19),	Heggem (54),	Alonso (143)	
15	Redknapp (99),	Berger (148),	Diao (11),	Crouch (85),	Benayoun (32)
16	Thomas (99),	Dundee (3),	Hamann (191),	Pennant (55)	
17	McManaman (108),	Ince (65),	Gerrard (129),	Josemi (21)	Bellamy (27),
	Arbeloa (57)				
18	Rosenthal (3),	Owen (38),	Ferri (2),	Meijer (24),	Riise (103),
	Nunez (18),	Kuyt (104)			
19	Piechnik (1),	Kennedy (16),	Friedel (14),	Arphexad (2),	Morientes (41),
	Babel (57)				
20	Bjornebye (128),	Barmby (32),	Le Tallec (13),	Carson (4),	Mascherano (59)
21	Marsh (2),	Matteo (127),	McAllister (55),	Diao (26),	Traore (48),
	Lucas (43)				
22	Harkness (43),	Camara (33),	Kirkland (25),	Sissoko (51),	Insua (10)
23	Fowler (108),	Carragher (398)			
24	L.Jones (3),	Murphy (40),	Diomede (2),	S-Pongolle (38),	Ngog (14)
25	Ruddock (96),	Thompson (48),	Biscan (72),	Reina (144)	
27	Vignal (11)				
28	Gerrard (41),	Cheyrou (31),	Warnock (40),	Plessis (1)	
29	Friedel (11),	S.Wright (14),	Luzi (1),	Paletta (3)	
30	Traore (40),	Zenden (7),	Padelli (1)		
31	Raven (1),	El Zhar (15)			
32	Newby (1),	Welsh (4),	Zenden (16)		
33	Mellor (12)				
34	Potter (2)				
35	Guthrie (3)				
36	Otsemobor (4)				
37	Litmanen (26),	Skrtel (35)			
42	El Zhar (3)				
46	Hobbs (2)				
47	Plessis (2)				
48	Insua (5)				

MOST APPEARANCES IN PREMIER LEAGUE

POS.	PLAYER	GAMES	POS.	PLAYER	GAMES
1	Jamie Carragher	398	24	Jerzy Dudek	127
2	Steven Gerrard	333	=	Dominic Matteo	127
3	Sami Hyypia	318	26	Vladimir Smicer	121
4	Robbie Fowler	266	27	Neil Ruddock	115
5	Steve McManaman	240	28	Michael Thomas	107
6	John Arne Riise	234	29	Dirk Kuyt	104
7	Jamie Redknapp	231	30	Jason McAteer	100
8	Michael Owen	216			
9	David James	214			
10	Dietmar Hamann	191			
11	Danny Murphy	170			
12	John Barnes	162			
13	Rob Jones	155			
14	Emile Heskey	150			
15	Patrik Berger	148			
16	Steve Finnan	145			
17	Pepe Reina	144			
18	Xabi Alonso	143			
19	Stig Inge Bjornebye	139			
20	Mark Wright	137			
21	Stephane Henchoz	135			
22	Ian Rush	130			
23	Phil Babb	128			

No 5: Steve McManaman

MOST GOALS IN PREMIER LEAGUE

POS.	PLAYER	GOALS
1	Robbie Fowler	128
2	Michael Owen	118
3	Steven Gerrard	71
4	Ian Rush	45
5	Steve McManaman	41
6	Emile Heskey	39
7	Fernando Torres	38
8	Jamie Redknapp	29
9	Patrik Berger	28
=	Own Goals	28
11	Dirk Kuyt	27
12	Stan Collymore	26
13	Danny Murphy	25
14	John Barnes	22
=	Peter Crouch	22
=	Sami Hyypia	22
17	John Arne Riise	21
18	Milan Baros	19
19	Luis Garcia	18
20	Xabi Alonso	15
21	Paul Ince	14
22	Djibril Cisse	13
23	Yossi Benayoun	12
=	Harry Kewell	12

No 1: Robbie Fowler

LANDMARK LIVERPOOL PREMIER LEAGUE GOALS

GOAL	SCORER	OPPONENT	VENUE	DATE	RESULT
1st	Mark Walters	Sheffield United	Home	19/08/92	2-1
100th	Nigel Clough	Manchester United	Home	04/01/94	3-3
200th	Robbie Fowler	Manchester United	Away	01/10/95	2-2
300th	Stan Collymore	Leeds United	Home	19/02/97	4-0
400th	Michael Owen	Nottingham Forest	Home	24/10/98	5-1
500th	Michael Owen	Coventry City	Away	01/04/00	3-0
600th	Michael Owen	Middlesbrough	Home	08/12/01	2-0
700th	Michael Owen	West Bromwich Albion	Away	26/04/03	6-0
800th	Milan Baros	Fulham	Home	05/02/05	3-1
900th	Dirk Kuyt	Bolton Wanderers	Home	01/01/07	3-0
1000th	Fernando Torres	Manchester City	Away	05/10/08	3-2

LANDMARK PREMIER LEAGUE AWAY GOALS

GOAL	PLAYER	DATE	SCORE	OPPOSITION
1	Mark Walters	25th August 1992	2-2	Ipswich Town
50	Robbie Fowler	20th August 1994	6-1	Crystal Palace
100	John Barnes	17th August 1996	3-3	Middlesbrough
150	Michael Owen	16th August 1998	2-1	Southampton
200	Emile Heskey	15th October 2000	4-0	Derby County
250	Abel Xavier	9th February 2002	6-0	Ipswich Town
300	Emile Heskey	2nd November 2003	2-1	Fulham
350	Luis Garcia	2nd January 2006	2-2	Bolton Wanderers
400	Jermaine Pennant	19th April 2008	2-0	Fulham

Emile Heskey – Landmark goalscorer away from Anfield

AWAY GOALSCORERS IN THE PREMIER LEAGUE

Fourteen different players have reached double figures away from Anfield since 1992, a total of 66 past and present Liverpool players. Incidentally it was Fernando Torres who helped the Reds reach 1000 Premier League goals, scored at Manchester City, in October 2008.

GOALS	PLAYER	GOALS	PLAYER
55	Michael Owen	3	Jan Molby
43	Robbie Fowler	2	Bruno Cheyrou
27	Steven Gerrard	2	Julian Dicks
23	Steve McManaman	2	Dietmar Hamann
22	Emile Heskey	2	Paul Ince
21	Ian Rush	2	Oyvind Leonhardsen
13	Dirk Kuyt	2	Fernando Morientes
12	Danny Murphy	2	Ronny Rosenthal
12	John Arne Riise	2	Andriy Voronin
11	John Barnes	2	Mark Walters
11	Sami Hyypia	2	Ronnie Whelan
11	Jamie Redknapp	2	Mark Wright
10	Milan Baros	1	Nicolas Anelka
10	Fernando Torres	1	Alvaro Arbeloa
10	Own Goals	1	Phil Babb
9	Peter Crouch	1	Markus Babbel
8	Patrik Berger	1	Igor Biscan
8	Djibril Cisse	1	Stig Inge Bjornebye
8	Luis Garcia	1	Nigel Clough
7	Xabi Alonso	1	Salif Diao
7	Stan Collymore	1	Andrea Dossena
7	Karlheinz Riedle	1	Steve Harkness
5	Yossi Benayoun	1	Vegard Heggem
5	Titi Camara	1	Robbie Keane
5	Craig Bellamy	1	Jason McAteer
5	Harry Kewell	1	Mike Marsh
5	Vladimir Smicer	1	Steve Nicol
4	Ryan Babel	1	Jermaine Pennant
4	Don Hutchison	1	Florent Sinama-Pongolle
4	Neil Ruddock	1	Momo Sissoko
4	Michael Thomas	1	David Thompson
3	Fabio Aurelio	1	Abel Xavier
3	Jari Litmanen	1	Christian Ziege
3	Gary McAllister		

LIVERPOOL PREMIER LEAGUE AWAY GOALS

SEASON	GAMES	GOALS	SEASON	GAMES	GOALS
1992/93	21	21	2001/02	19	34
1993/94	21	26	2002/03	19	31
1994/95	21	27	2003/04	19	26
1995/96	19	24	2004/05	19	21
1996/97	19	24	2005/06	19	25
1997/98	19	26	2006/07	19	18
1998/99	19	24	2007/08	19	24
1999/00	19	23	2008/09	19	36
2000/01	19	31			

PREMIER LEAGUE PLAYERS' RECORD (A-G)

The following statistics are the full records of players who have played for Liverpool since the inception of the Premier League in 1992. However, the figures are their full record for the club, which includes the period prior to 1992 (all figures correct at end of 2008/09 season).

PLAYER	FIRST GAME-LAST GAME	LEAGUE		FA CUP		LEAGUE CUP		EUROPE		OTHER GAMES		LFC CAREER	
		A	G	A	G	A	G	A	G	A	G	A	G
Daniel Agger	2006-2009	54	3	2	0	4	2	18	1	1	0	79	6
Xabi Alonso	2004-2009	143	15	12	2	4	0	48	2	3	0	210	19
Nicolas Anelka	2001-2002	20	4	2	1	0	0	0	0	0	0	22	5
Alvaro Arbeloa	2007-2009	66	2	3	0	3	0	26	0	0	0	98	2
Pegguy Arphexad	2000-2002	2	0	0	0	2	0	2	0	0	0	6	0
Fabio Aurelio	2006-2009	57	3	3	0	4	0	22	1	1	0	87	4
Phil Babb	1994-1999	128	1	12	0	16	0	14	0	0	0	170	1
Markus Babbel	2000-2002	42	3	5	1	7	1	17	1	2	0	73	6
Ryan Babel	2007-2009	57	7	7	1	4	0	23	6	0	0	91	14
Nick Barmby	2000-2002	32	2	5	1	7	1	13	4	1	0	58	8
John Barnes	1987-1997	314	84	51	16	26	3	12	3	4	2	407	108
Milan Baros	2002-2005	68	19	3	0	8	4	28	4	1	0	108	27
Antonio Barragan	2005-2005	0	0	0	0	0	0	1	0	0	0	1	0
Craig Bellamy	2006-2007	27	7	0	0	2	0	12	2	1	0	42	9
Yossi Benayoun	2007-2009	62	12	4	3	3	1	20	4	0	0	89	20
Patrik Berger	1996-2003	148	28	8	0	11	3	28	4	1	0	196	35
Igor Biscan	2000-2005	72	2	7	0	15	1	23	0	1	0	118	3
Stig I. Bjornebye	1992-1999	139	2	13	0	16	0	16	2	0	0	184	4
David Burrows	1988-1993	146	3	17	0	16	0	11	0	3	0	193	3
Titi Camara	1999-2000	33	9	2	1	2	0	0	0	0	0	37	10
Jamie Carragher	1997-2009	398	4	32	0	27	0	116	1	4	0	577	5
Scott Carson	2005-2006	4	0	1	0	1	0	3	0	0	0	9	0
Diego Cavalieri	2008-2009	0	0	1	0	2	0	1	0	0	0	4	0
Phil Charnock	1992-1992	0	0	0	0	1	0	1	0	0	0	2	0
Bruno Cheyrou	2002-2004	31	2	6	2	2	0	8	1	1	0	48	5
Djibril Cisse	2004-2006	49	13	6	2	0	0	23	9	1	0	79	24
Nigel Clough	1993-1995	39	7	2	0	3	2	0	0	0	0	44	9
Stan Collymore	1995-1997	61	26	9	7	4	0	7	2	0	0	81	35
Peter Crouch	2005-2008	85	22	11	5	5	1	30	11	3	3	134	42
Stephen Darby	2008-2008	0	0	0	0	1	0	1	0	0	0	2	0
Philipp Degen	2008-2008	0	0	0	0	2	0	0	0	0	0	2	0
Salif Diao	2002-2005	37	1	2	0	8	1	14	1	0	0	61	3
Julian Dicks	1993-1994	24	3	1	0	3	0	0	0	0	0	28	3
Bernard Diomede	2000-2001	2	0	0	0	0	0	3	0	0	0	5	0
El-Hadji Diouf	2002-2004	55	3	4	0	7	3	13	0	1	0	80	6
Andrea Dossena	2008-2009	16	1	2	0	1	0	7	1	0	0	26	2
Jerzy Dudek	2001-2007	127	0	9	0	11	0	38	0	1	0	186	0
Sean Dundee	1998-1999	3	0	0	0	1	0	1	0	0	0	5	0
Nabil El Zhar	2006-2009	18	0	1	0	4	1	2	0	0	0	25	1
Jean Michel Ferri	1999-1999	2	0	0	0	0	0	0	0	0	0	2	0
Steve Finnan	2003-2008	145	1	13	0	6	0	51	0	2	0	217	1
Robbie Fowler	1993-2007	266	128	24	12	35	29	44	14	0	0	369	183
Brad Friedel	1998-1999	25	0	0	0	4	0	2	0	0	0	31	0
Luis Garcia	2004-2007	77	18	4	1	5	0	32	11	3	0	121	30
Steven Gerrard	1998-2009	333	71	26	9	19	7	101	32	4	1	483	120
Mark Gonzalez	2006-2007	25	2	0	0	2	0	8	1	1	0	36	3
Bruce Grobbelaar	1981-1994	440	0	62	0	70	0	38	0	18	0	628	0
Danny Guthrie	2006-2007	3	0	0	0	3	0	1	0	0	0	7	0

PREMIER LEAGUE PLAYERS' RECORD (H-N)

PLAYER	FIRST GAME-LAST GAME	LEAGUE		FA CUP		LEAGUE CUP		EUROPE		OTHER GAMES		LFC CAREER	
		A	G	A	G	A	G	A	G	A	G	A	G
Dietmar Hamann	1999-2006	191	8	16	1	12	0	61	2	3	0	283	11
Steve Harkness	1991-1999	102	2	6	0	15	1	16	0	0	0	139	3
Vegard Heggem	1998-2000	54	3	1	0	4	0	6	0	0	0	65	3
Stephane Henchoz	1999-2004	135	0	15	0	16	0	37	0	2	0	205	0
Emile Heskey	2000-2004	150	39	14	6	12	2	45	13	2	0	223	60
Jack Hobbs	2007-2007	2	0	0	0	3	0	0	0	0	0	5	0
Mike Hooper	1986-1993	51	0	5	0	10	0	4	0	3	0	73	0
Don Hutchison	1992-1994	45	7	3	0	8	2	3	1	1	0	60	10
Sami Hyypia	1999-2009	318	22	29	2	19	3	94	8	4	0	464	35
Paul Ince	1997-1999	65	14	3	1	6	1	7	1	0	0	81	17
Emiliano Insua	2007-2009	15	0	1	0	2	0	0	0	0	0	18	0
Charles Itandje	2007-2008	0	0	4	0	3	0	0	0	0	0	7	0
David James	1992-1999	214	0	19	0	22	0	22	0	0	0	277	0
Lee Jones	1994-1996	3	0	0	0	1	0	0	0	0	0	4	0
Paul Jones	2004-2004	2	0	0	0	0	0	0	0	0	0	2	0
Rob Jones	1991-1998	183	0	27	0	22	0	11	0	0	0	243	0
Josemi	2004-2005	21	0	0	0	1	0	12	0	1	0	35	0
Robbie Keane	2008-2009	19	5	1	0	1	0	7	2	0	0	28	7
Martin Kelly	2008-2008	0	0	0	0	0	0	1	0	0	0	1	0
Mark Kennedy	1995-1998	16	0	1	0	2	0	2	0	0	0	21	0
Harry Kewell	2003-2008	93	12	10	0	5	1	30	3	1	0	139	16
Frode Kippe	1999-2001	0	0	0	0	2	0	0	0	0	0	2	0
Chris Kirkland	2001-2004	25	0	3	0	6	0	11	0	0	0	45	0
Istvan Kozma	1992-1992	6	0	2	0	1	0	0	0	1	0	10	0
Jan Kromkamp	2006-2006	14	0	4	0	0	0	0	0	0	0	18	0
Dirk Kuyt	2006-2009	104	27	7	2	2	0	34	11	0	0	147	40
Bjorn Tore Kvarme	1997-1999	45	0	2	0	2	0	5	0	0	0	54	0
Lucas Leiva	2007-2009	43	1	6	1	5	1	17	1	0	0	71	4
O. Leonhardsen	1997-1999	37	7	1	0	6	0	5	0	0	0	49	7
Anthony Le Tallec	2003-2005	17	0	4	0	2	0	9	1	0	0	32	1
Sebastian Leto	2007-2007	0	0	0	0	2	0	2	0	0	0	4	0
Jari Litmanen	2001-2002	26	5	3	1	3	0	11	3	0	0	43	9
Patrice Luzi	2004-2004	1	0	0	0	0	0	0	0	0	0	1	0
Gary McAllister	2000-2002	55	5	5	0	6	1	20	2	1	1	87	9
Jason McAteer	1995-1999	100	3	12	3	13	0	14	0	0	0	139	6
Steve McManaman	1990-1999	272	46	29	5	33	10	30	5	0	0	364	66
Mike Marsh	1989-1993	69	2	8	0	11	3	12	1	1	0	101	6
Javier Mascherano	2007-2009	59	1	5	0	1	0	25	0	0	0	90	1
Dominic Matteo	1993-2000	127	1	8	0	9	0	11	0	0	0	155	2
Layton Maxwell	1999-1999	0	0	0	0	1	1	0	0	0	0	1	1
Erik Meijer	1999-2000	24	0	0	0	3	2	0	0	0	0	27	2
Neil Mellor	2002-2005	12	2	2	0	6	3	2	1	0	0	22	6
Jan Molby	1984-1995	218	44	28	4	28	9	7	1	11	3	292	61
F. Morientes	2005-2006	41	8	5	1	3	0	11	3	1	0	61	12
Danny Murphy	1997-2004	170	25	15	3	16	11	46	5	2	0	249	44
Jon Newby	1999-2000	1	0	2	0	1	0	0	0	0	0	4	0
David Ngog	2008-2009	14	2	0	0	2	0	3	1	0	0	19	3
Steve Nicol	1982-1994	343	36	50	3	42	4	20	2	13	1	468	46
Antonio Nunez	2004-2005	18	0	1	0	3	1	5	0	0	0	27	1

PREMIER LEAGUE PLAYERS' RECORD (O-Z)

PLAYER	FIRST GAME-LAST GAME	LEAGUE		FA CUP		LEAGUE CUP		EUROPE		OTHER GAMES		LFC CAREER	
		A	G	A	G	A	G	A	G	A	G	A	G
Jon Otsemobor	2002-2003	4	0	0	0	2	0	0	0	0	0	6	0
Michael Owen	1997-2004	216	118	15	8	14	9	50	22	2	1	297	158
Daniele Padelli	2007-2007	1	0	0	0	0	0	0	0	0	0	1	0
Gabriel Paletta	2006-2007	3	0	0	0	3	1	2	0	0	0	8	1
Richie Partridge	2000-2004	0	0	0	0	3	0	0	0	0	0	3	0
M. Pellegrino	2005-2005	12	0	0	0	1	0	0	0	0	0	13	0
Lee Peltier	2006-2007	0	0	0	0	3	0	1	0	0	0	4	0
Jermaine Pennant	2006-2008	55	3	3	0	3	0	19	0	1	0	81	3
Torben Piechnik	1992-1993	17	0	2	0	5	0	0	0	0	0	24	0
Damien Plessis	2008-2009	3	0	0	0	2	1	2	0	0	0	7	1
Darren Potter	2004-2005	2	0	1	0	5	0	9	0	0	0	17	0
David Raven	2004-2005	1	0	1	0	2	0	0	0	0	0	4	0
Jamie Redknapp	1991-2001	237	30	18	2	27	5	26	4	0	0	308	41
Pepe Reina	2005-2009	144	0	7	0	1	0	52	0	3	0	207	0
Karlheinz Riedle	1997-1999	60	11	2	0	7	2	7	2	0	0	76	15
Albert Riera	2008-2009	28	3	3	1	0	0	9	1	0	0	40	5
John Arne Riise	2001-2008	234	21	17	3	13	2	79	4	5	1	348	31
Miki Roque	2006-2006	0	0	0	0	0	0	1	0	0	0	1	0
Ronny Rosenthal	1990-1993	74	21	8	0	9	1	4	0	2	0	97	22
Neil Ruddock	1993-1997	115	11	11	0	20	1	6	0	0	0	152	12
Ian Rush	1980-1996	469	229	61	39	78	48	38	20	14	10	660	346
Dean Saunders	1991-1992	42	11	8	2	5	2	5	9	1	1	61	25
John Scales	1994-1996	65	2	14	0	10	2	5	0	0	0	94	4
F. S-Pongolle	2003-2006	38	4	5	2	8	1	12	2	3	0	66	9
Mohamed Sissoko	2005-2007	51	1	6	0	4	0	23	0	3	0	87	1
Martin Skrtel	2008-2009	35	0	3	0	0	0	12	0	0	0	50	0
Vladimir Smicer	1999-2005	121	10	10	1	15	5	37	3	1	0	184	19
Jamie Smith	2006-2006	0	0	0	0	1	0	0	0	0	0	1	0
Mark Smyth	2004-2004	0	0	0	0	1	0	0	0	0	0	1	0
Rigobert Song	1999-2000	34	0	1	0	2	0	1	0	0	0	38	0
Jay Spearing	2008-2008	0	0	0	0	0	0	2	0	0	0	2	0
Steve Staunton	1988-2000	109	0	18	1	13	5	7	0	1	1	148	7
Paul Stewart	1992-1993	32	1	1	0	6	0	2	2	1	0	42	3
Nick Tanner	1989-1992	40	1	2	0	8	0	8	0	1	0	59	1
Michael Thomas	1991-1998	124	9	17	2	10	1	12	0	0	0	163	12
David Thompson	1996-2000	48	5	1	0	5	0	2	0	0	0	56	5
Fernando Torres	2007-2009	57	38	4	1	3	3	20	8	0	0	84	50
Djimi Traore	1999-2006	88	0	5	0	14	0	32	1	2	0	141	1
Gregory Vignal	2001-2003	11	0	1	0	3	0	5	0	0	0	20	0
Andriy Voronin	2007-2008	19	5	1	0	1	0	7	1	0	0	28	6
Mark Walters	1991-1995	94	14	9	0	12	4	8	1	1	0	124	19
Stephen Warnock	2004-2007	40	1	3	0	8	0	15	0	1	0	67	1
John Welsh	2002-2005	4	0	1	0	3	0	2	0	0	0	10	0
Sander Westerveld	1999-2001	75	0	8	0	5	0	14	0	1	0	103	0
Ronnie Whelan	1981-1994	362	46	41	7	50	14	24	6	16	0	493	73
Zak Whitbread	2004-2005	0	0	1	0	4	0	2	0	0	0	7	0
Mark Wright	1991-1997	158	5	18	0	16	2	17	2	1	0	210	9
Stephen Wright	2000-2002	14	0	2	0	2	0	3	1	0	0	21	1
Abel Xavier	2002-2002	14	1	0	0	1	0	5	1	1	0	21	2
Boudewijn Zenden	2005-2007	23	2	0	0	2	0	21	0	1	0	47	2
Christian Ziege	2000-2001	16	1	3	0	4	1	9	0	0	0	32	2

GOALS SCORED BY OVERSEAS PLAYERS

PREMIER LEAGUE ONLY

PLAYER	GOALS	PLAYER	GOALS
Fernando Torres	38	Nicolas Anelka	4
Patrik Berger	28	Florent Sinama-Pongolle	4
Dirk Kuyt	27	Daniel Agger	3
Sami Hyypia	22	Fabio Aurelio	3
John Arne Riise	21	Markus Babbel	3
Milan Baros	19	El-Hadji Diouf	3
Luis Garcia	18	Vegard Heggem	3
Xabi Alonso	15	Albert Riera	3
Djibril Cisse	13	Alvaro Arbeloa	2
Yossi Benayoun	12	Igor Biscan	2
Harry Kewell	12	Stig Inge Bjornebye	2
Karlheinz Riedle	11	Bruno Cheyrou	2
Vladimir Smicer	10	Mark Gonzalez	2
Titi Camara	9	David Ngog	2
Dietmar Hamann	8	Bolo Zenden	2
Fernando Morientes	8	Salif Diao	1
Ryan Babel	7	Andrea Dossena	1
Oyvind Leonhardsen	7	Lucas Leiva	1
Jan Molby	7	Javier Mascherano	1
Ronny Rosenthal	6	Momo Sissoko	1
Jari Litmanen	5	Abel Xavier	1
Andriy Voronin	5	Christian Ziege	1

BEST PREMIER LEAGUE GOAL DIFFERENCE

LIVERPOOL RECORD SINCE 1992

SEASON	GOAL DIFFERENCE	GOALS FOR	GOALS AGAINST	FINAL POSITION
2008/09	50	77	27	2nd
2007/08	39	67	28	4th
2001/02	37	67	30	2nd
1995/96	36	70	34	3rd
2000/01	32	71	39	3rd
2005/06	32	57	25	3rd
2006/07	30	57	27	3rd
1994/95	28	65	37	4th
1997/98	26	68	42	3rd
1996/97	25	62	37	4th
1999/00	21	51	30	4th
2002/03	20	61	41	5th
1998/99	19	68	49	7th
2003/04	18	55	37	4th
2004/05	11	52	41	5th
1992/93	7	62	55	6th
1993/94	4	59	55	8th

PREMIER LEAGUE EVER-PRESENTS

David James remains the record-holder for Liverpool ever-presents in the Premier League era, playing every league game for three consecutive seasons between 1994-96. Twelve different players have appeared in every game for at least one season.

Pepe Reina has been an ever present in the last two campaigns, while Jamie Carragher has played every league game in two out of the last three Premier League seasons.

PLAYERS WHO HAVE PLAYED EVERY LEAGUE GAME FOR LIVERPOOL DURING ONE SEASON

SEASON	GAMES	PLAYER
1993/94	42	Ian Rush
1994/95	42	Robbie Fowler, David James
1995/96	38	Steve McManaman, Robbie Fowler, David James
1996/97	38	Stig Inge Bjornebye, David James
1999/00	38	Sami Hyypia
2000/01	38	Markus Babbel, Sander Westerveld
2001/02	38	John Arne Riise
2003/04	38	Sami Hyypia
2004/05	38	Jamie Carragher
2007/08	38	Pepe Reina
2008/09	38	Jamie Carragher, Dirk Kuyt, Pepe Reina

Sami Hyypia – League regular in two different seasons

PREMIER LEAGUE CAPTAINS

A total of 13 players have started as captain during Liverpool's 17 Premier League campaigns, ahead of the 2009/10 season. Statistically in terms of points won per match, Steve Nicol has enjoyed most success, skippering the team to six wins from nine games while vice-captain Jamie Carragher has seen the team lose only twice in his 22 games as captain.

LIVERPOOL CAPTAINS IN PREMIER LEAGUE GAMES (MOST SUCCESSFUL FIRST)							
CAPTAIN	PLD	W	D	L	PTS	WIN %	AVE PTS. PER GAME
Steve Nicol	9	6	2	1	20	66.67	2.22
Steve McManaman	8	5	1	2	16	62.50	2.00
Jamie Carragher	22	12	8	2	44	55.55	2.00
Steven Gerrard	185	102	47	36	353	55.14	1.91
Robbie Fowler	22	12	4	6	40	54.55	1.82
Sami Hyypia	131	69	32	30	239	52.67	1.82
John Barnes	87	43	25	19	154	49.43	1.77
Ian Rush	87	40	20	27	140	45.98	1.61
Jamie Redknapp	22	10	5	7	35	45.45	1.59
Paul Ince	65	28	18	19	102	43.08	1.57
Neil Ruddock	2	0	2	0	2	0.00	1.00
Mark Wright	17	4	4	9	16	23.53	0.94
Phil Babb	1	0	0	1	0	0.00	0.00
TOTAL	**658**	**331**	**168**	**159**	**1161**	**50.30**	**1.76**

Jamie Carragher – In the top three

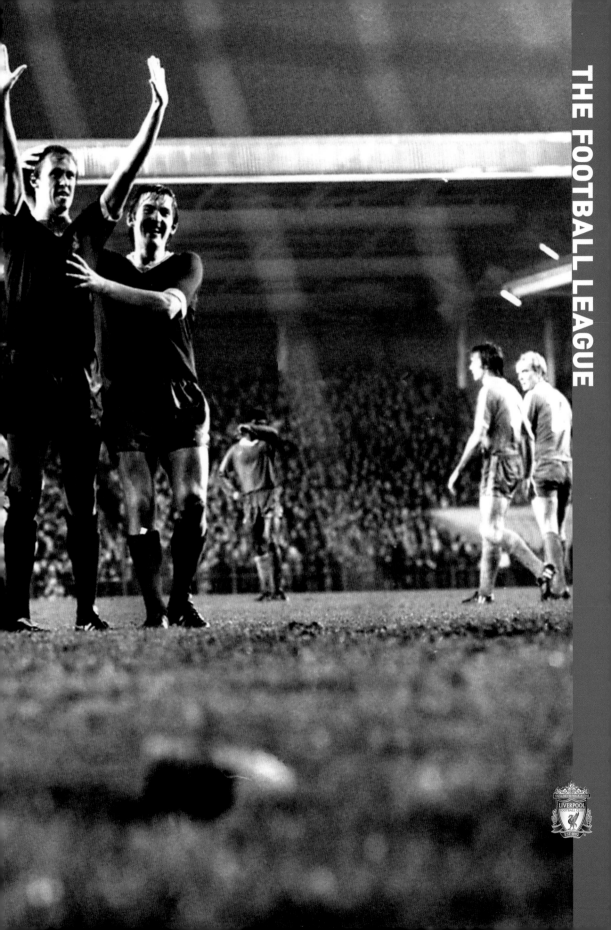

FULL FOOTBALL LEAGUE RECORD - CLUB-BY-CLUB

TEAM	PLAYED	WON	DRAWN	LOST	FOR	AGAINST
Arsenal	170	68	44	58	243	217
Aston Villa	168	79	38	51	298	244
Barnsley	12	7	2	3	23	15
Birmingham City	96	46	22	28	159	134
Blackburn Rovers	122	51	37	34	218	165
Blackpool	40	18	9	13	72	62
Bolton Wanderers	112	48	29	35	179	135
Bradford City	26	18	2	6	45	22
Bradford Park Avenue	6	3	1	2	10	8
Brentford	10	4	3	3	16	16
Brighton & Hove Albion	16	8	6	2	36	20
Bristol City	30	16	3	11	52	39
Bristol Rovers	16	10	1	5	32	21
Burnley	74	29	19	26	117	95
Burton Swifts	4	3	1	0	17	3
Burton United	2	1	0	1	3	2
Burton Wanderers	2	1	0	1	5	3
Bury	48	26	14	8	92	53
Cardiff City	26	8	2	16	35	51
Carlisle United	2	2	0	0	3	0
Charlton Athletic	56	29	8	19	93	70
Chelsea	132	60	28	44	206	183
Chesterfield	2	1	1	0	7	2
Coventry City	68	39	16	13	113	45
Crewe Alexandra	4	4	0	0	20	1
Crystal Palace	26	15	6	5	57	17
Darwen	2	1	1	0	4	0
Derby County	126	66	28	32	248	156
Doncaster Rovers	10	5	2	3	19	13
Everton	180	68	56	56	244	214
Fulham	44	25	12	7	83	41
Gainsborough Trinity	2	2	0	0	8	2
Glossop	4	3	1	0	11	5
Grimsby Town	36	18	10	8	87	47
Huddersfield Town	68	25	17	26	113	113
Hull City	8	6	2	0	20	10
Ipswich Town	60	28	19	13	110	59
Leeds United	100	51	25	24	164	101
Leicester City	88	36	19	33	143	121
Leyton Orient	14	9	2	3	37	15
Lincoln City	20	11	4	5	42	28
Loughborough Town	2	2	0	0	5	2
Luton Town	28	13	9	6	52	33
Manchester City	146	74	35	37	263	191
Manchester United	152	51	43	58	198	211
Middlesbrough	134	57	39	38	229	172
Middlesbrough Ironopolis	2	2	0	0	8	0
Millwall	4	3	1	0	6	3
Newcastle United	148	71	37	40	259	184
Northampton Town	2	1	1	0	5	0

FULL LEAGUE RECORD - CLUB-BY-CLUB

TEAM	PLAYED	WON	DRAWN	LOST	FOR	AGAINST
Northwich Victoria	2	2	0	0	7	2
Norwich City	46	24	11	11	84	47
Nottingham Forest	100	50	24	26	167	99
Notts County	60	34	12	14	110	63
Oldham Athletic	24	14	4	6	39	30
Oxford United	6	5	1	0	20	3
Plymouth Argyle	10	5	3	2	22	15
Portsmouth	58	24	15	19	102	87
Port Vale	12	7	3	2	38	20
Preston North End	64	26	17	21	114	99
Queens Park Rangers	40	28	6	6	68	34
Reading	4	3	0	1	7	5
Rotherham United	20	14	3	3	57	21
Scunthorpe United	8	6	2	0	17	8
Sheffield United	118	55	27	36	192	153
Sheffield Wednesday	116	54	26	36	197	165
Southampton	74	35	18	21	112	86
Stoke City	108	53	29	26	176	113
Sunderland	144	64	31	49	242	210
Swansea City	20	10	4	6	51	27
Swindon Town	2	1	1	0	7	2
Tottenham Hotspur	132	62	34	36	211	148
Walsall	4	2	2	0	11	3
Watford	16	12	1	3	37	16
West Bromwich Albion	116	55	33	28	181	127
West Ham United	104	54	29	21	169	93
Wigan Athletic	8	6	2	0	16	4
Wimbledon	28	11	10	7	41	31
Wolverhampton Wanderers	88	43	16	29	136	106

First Division action from 1978 – Liverpool v Manchester City

THE FOOTBALL LEAGUE POSITIONS

DIVISION ONE - 77 SEASONS

POSITION	NUMBER OF FINISHES	MOST RECENT FINAL POSITION
1st	18	1989/90
2nd	10	1990/91
3rd	2	1971/72
4th	3	1924/25
5th	7	1980/81
6th	1	1991/92
7th	3	1964/65
8th	3	1962/63
9th	4	1950/51
10th	2	1931/32
11th	5	1951/52
12th	4	1948/49
13th	2	1914/15
14th	1	1932/33
15th	1	1906/07
16th	4	1927/28
17th	3	1952/53
18th	2	1936/37
19th	1	1935/36
20th	0	–
21st	0	–
22nd	1	1953/54

DIVISION TWO - 11 SEASONS

POSITION	NUMBER OF FINISHES	MOST RECENT FINAL POSITION
1st	4	1961/62
3rd	4	1960/61
4th	2	1958/59
11th	1	1954/55

1989/90 – First place

BIGGEST-EVER VICTORIES

DATE	OPPONENTS	VENUE	DIVISION	SCORE
18th Feb 1896	Rotherham United	Home	Two	10-1
12th Sept 1989	Crystal Palace	Home	One	9-0
26th Dec 1928	Burnley	Home	One	8-0
6th Dec 1902	Grimsby Town	Home	One	9-2
8th Apr 1905	Burslem Port Vale	Home	Two	8-1
29th Feb 1896	Burton Swifts	Away	Two	7-0
28th Mar 1896	Crewe Alexandra	Away	Two	7-0
4th Jan 1902	Stoke City	Home	One	7-0
26th Nov 1955	Fulham	Home	Two	7-0
2nd Sept 1978	Tottenham Hotspur	Home	One	7-0

BIGGEST-EVER DEFEATS

DATE	OPPONENTS	VENUE	DIVISION	SCORE
11th Dec 1954	Birmingham City	Away	Two	1-9
10th Nov 1934	Huddersfield Town	Away	One	0-8
1st Jan 1934	Newcastle United	Away	One	2-9
7th May 1932	Bolton Wanderers	Away	One	1-8
1st Sept 1934	Arsenal	Away	One	1-8
7th Dec 1912	Sunderland	Away	One	0-7
1st Sept 1930	West Ham United	Away	One	0-7
19th Apr 1930	Sunderland	Home	One	0-6
28th Nov 1931	Arsenal	Away	One	0-6
11th Sept 1935	Manchester City	Away	One	0-6
26th Sept 1953	Charlton Athletic	Away	One	0-6

John Aldridge, in action during the 9-0 victory over Crystal Palace in 1989

FOOTBALL LEAGUE EVER-PRESENTS

PLAYERS WHO HAVE PLAYED EVERY LEAGUE GAME FOR LIVERPOOL DURING ONE SEASON

SEASON	GAMES	PLAYER
1894/95	30	Tom Bradshaw
1896/97	30	John McCartney
1897/98	30	Thomas Cleghorn, Harry Storer
1899/00	34	Billy Dunlop, Tom Robertson
1900/01	34	Bill Goldie, Bill Perkins, Tom Robertson
1901/02	34	Bill Goldie
1902/03	34	Bill Goldie
1904/05	34	Ned Doig
1905/06	38	Arthur Goddard
1909/10	38	Tom Chorlton
1910/11	38	Robbie Robinson
1912/13	38	Robert Ferguson
1913/14	38	Thomas Fairfoul
1914/15	38	Jimmy Nicholl
1920/21	42	Walter Wadsworth
1921/22	42	Dick Forshaw, Fred Hopkin
1922/23	42	Dick Forshaw, Donald McKinlay, Elisha Scott
1923/24	42	Elisha Scott
1924/25	42	Danny Shone
1925/26	42	Harry Chambers
1926/27	42	Harry Chambers
1927/28	42	Tom Bromilow, Dick Edmed
1928/29	42	James Jackson, Tom Morrison
1930/31	42	Tommy Lucas, Archie McPherson
1931/32	42	Tom Bradshaw, Gordon Gunson
1932/33	42	Willie Steel
1936/37	42	Alf Hanson
1938/39	42	Jack Balmer, Matt Busby
1948/49	42	Jack Balmer
1950/51	42	Eddie Spicer
1955/56	42	Geoff Twentyman
1956/57	42	Ronnie Moran
1958/59	42	Dick White
1959/60	42	Alan A'Court, Ronnie Moran
1960/61	42	Bert Slater, Dick White
1961/62	42	Alan A'Court, Gerry Byrne, Jimmy Melia, Gordon Milne
1962/63	42	Roger Hunt
1963/64	42	Ian Callaghan, Gordon Milne, Peter Thompson
1965/66	42	Gerry Byrne, Ian Callaghan, Tommy Lawrence, Tommy Smith, Ron Yeats
1966/67	42	Chris Lawler, Tommy Smith, Peter Thompson
1967/68	42	Chris Lawler, Tommy Lawrence
1968/69	42	Ian Callaghan, Chris Lawler, Tommy Lawrence, Tommy Smith, Peter Thompson
1969/70	42	Bobby Graham, Chris Lawler
1971/72	42	Ray Clemence, Emlyn Hughes, Chris Lawler
1972/73	42	Ian Callaghan, Chris Lawler, Larry Lloyd
1973/74	42	Ian Callaghan, Ray Clemence, Peter Cormack,

EVER-PRESENTS

PLAYERS WHO HAVE PLAYED EVERY LEAGUE GAME FOR LIVERPOOL DURING ONE SEASON

SEASON	GAMES	PLAYER
1973/74	42	Emlyn Hughes, Kevin Keegan
1974/75	42	Ray Clemence, Emlyn Hughes
1975/76	42	Ray Clemence, Phil Neal
1976/77	42	Ray Clemence, Emlyn Hughes, Phil Neal
1977/78	42	Kenny Dalglish, Phil Neal
1978/79	42	Ray Clemence, Kenny Dalglish, Ray Kennedy, Phil Neal
1979/80	42	Kenny Dalglish, Phil Neal, Phil Thompson
1980/81	42	Phil Neal
1981/82	42	Kenny Dalglish, Bruce Grobbelaar, Phil Neal
1982/83	42	Kenny Dalglish, Bruce Grobbelaar, Alan Kennedy, Phil Neal
1983/84	42	Bruce Grobbelaar, Alan Hansen, Alan Kennedy, Mark Lawrenson, Sammy Lee
1984/85	42	Bruce Grobbelaar, Phil Neal
1985/86	42	Bruce Grobbelaar
1986/87	42	Ian Rush
1987/88	40	Steve McMahon, Steve Nicol
1988/89	38	Ray Houghton, Steve Nicol
1989/90	38	Bruce Grobbelaar, Steve McMahon

Steve Nicol – Ever present in two successive seasons

PLAYER RECORDS – APPEARANCES

FOOTBALL LEAGUE 1893-1992 – Games played includes substitute appearances

TOTAL APPEARANCES (300+ GAMES)

	PLAYER	FIRST-TEAM CAREER	GAMES
1	Ian Callaghan	1960-1978	640
2	Billy Liddell	1946-1960	492
3	Emlyn Hughes	1967-1979	474
4	Ray Clemence	1968-1981	470
5	Tommy Smith	1963-1978	467
6	Phil Neal	1974-1985	455
7	Alan Hansen	1977-1990	434
8	Elisha Scott	1913-1934	430
9	Bruce Grobbelaar	1981-1994	406
=	Chris Lawler	1963-1975	406
11	Roger Hunt	1959-1969	404
12	Donald MacKinlay	1910-1928	393
13	Arthur Goddard	1902-1914	386
14	Gordon Hodgson	1926-1935	358
=	Ron Yeats	1961-1971	358
16	Kenny Dalglish	1977-1990	355
17	Alan A'Court	1953-1964	354
18	Ephraim Longworth	1910-1928	342
=	Ronnie Moran	1952-1965	342
20	Tom Bromilow	1919-1930	341
=	Tommy Lucas	1919-1932	341
22	Phil Thompson	1972-1983	340
23	Ian Rush	1980-1987 & 1988-1996	339
24	Jimmy McDougall	1928-1938	338
25	Ian St John	1961-1971	336
26	Fred Hopkin	1921-1931	335
27	Steve Heighway	1970-1981	331
28	Jack Cox	1898-1909	328
29	Billy Dunlop	1895-1909	325
30	Arthur Riley	1925-1939	322
=	Peter Thompson	1963-1972	322
=	Ronnie Whelan	1981-1994	322
33	Alex Raisbeck	1898-1909	312
=	Phil Taylor	1936-1954	312
35	Harry Chambers	1919-1928	310
36	Ray Lambert	1946-1955	308
37	Tommy Lawrence	1962-1971	306
38	Laurie Hughes	1946-1957	303

*NOTE FIGURES INCLUDE FOOTBALL LEAGUE GAMES ONLY.
FIRST-TEAM CAREER NOTED AS THE YEAR A PLAYER MADE HIS FIRST APPEARANCE FOR THE
FIRST TEAM, AND THE YEAR THEY MADE THEIR LAST APPEARANCE.
PREMIER LEAGUE APPEARANCES WOULD GIVE THE FOLLOWING APPEARANCE FIGURES, AT
END OF 2008/09 SEASON (300+ APPEARANCES ONLY):

Ian Rush 469, Bruce Grobbelaar 440, Jamie Carragher 398, Ronnie Whelan 362, Steve Nicol 343,
Steven Gerrard 333, Sami Hyypia 318, John Barnes 314.

PLAYER RECORDS – GOALS

	PLAYER	FIRST-TEAM CAREER	GOALS
FOOTBALL LEAGUE 1893-1992			
TOTAL GOALS (60+ GOALS)			
1	Roger Hunt	1959-1969	245
2	Gordon Hodgson	1926-1935	233
3	Billy Liddell	1946-1960	215
4	Ian Rush	1980-1987 & 1988-1996	184
5	Harry Chambers	1919-1928	135
6	Jack Parkinson	1903-1914	124
7	Sam Raybould	1900-1907	119
8	Kenny Dalglish	1977-1990	118
9	Dick Forshaw	1919-1927	117
10	Jack Balmer	1935-1952	98
11	Ian St John	1961-1971	95
12	Jimmy Melia	1955-1964	77
13	Albert Stubbins	1946-1953	75
14	Berry Nieuwenhuys	1933-1947	74
=	John Toshack	1970-1977	74
16	Jack Cox	1898-1909	73
17	Arthur Goddard	1902-1914	72
18	Joe Hewitt	1904-1909	68
=	Kevin Keegan	1971-1977	68
20	Robert Robinson	1904-1912	63
21	John Barnes	1987-1997	62
22	Alan A'Court	1953-1964	61

*NOTE FIGURES INCLUDE FOOTBALL LEAGUE GAMES ONLY.
FIRST-TEAM CAREER NOTED AS THE YEAR A PLAYER MADE HIS FIRST APPEARANCE FOR THE FIRST TEAM, AND THE YEAR THEY MADE THEIR LAST APPEARANCE.
PREMIER LEAGUE GOALS WOULD GIVE THE FOLLOWING FIGURES, AT END OF 2008/09 SEASON (50+ GOALS ONLY):

Ian Rush 229, Robbie Fowler 128, Michael Owen 118, John Barnes 84, Steven Gerrard 71.

Football League scorers – Keegan and Barnes

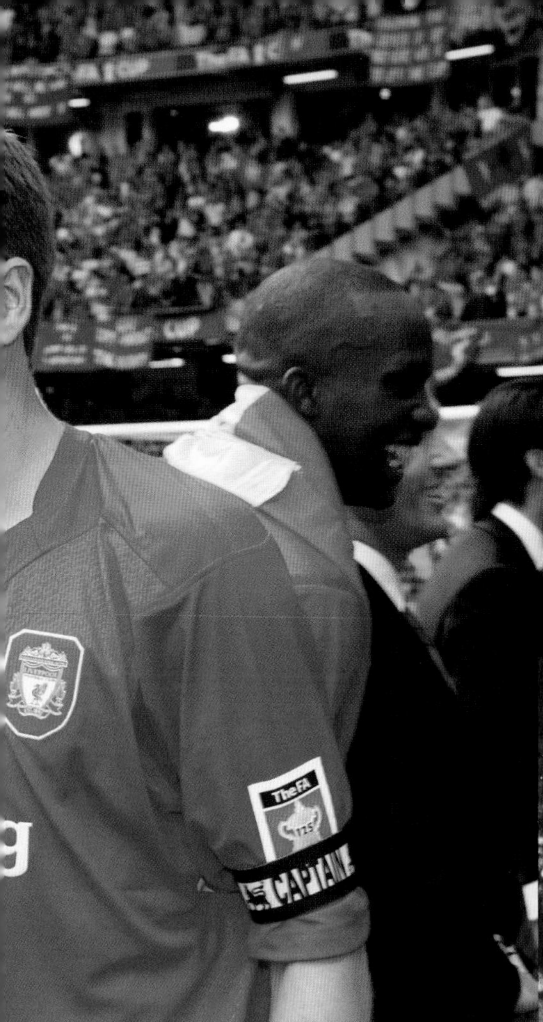

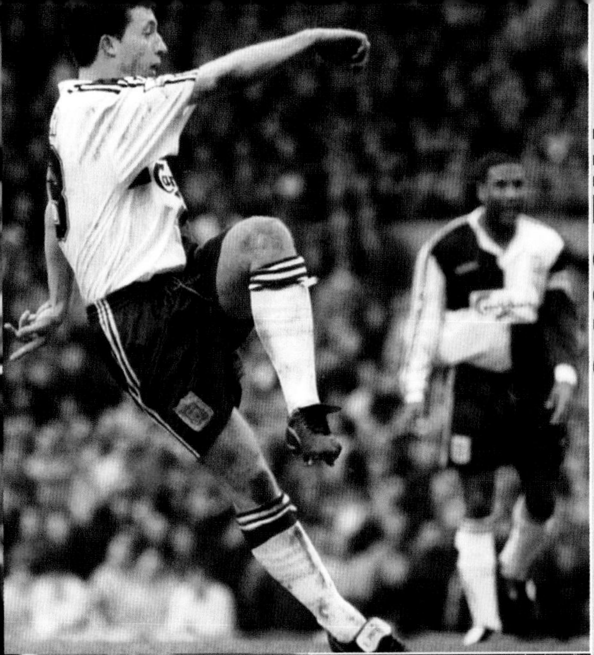

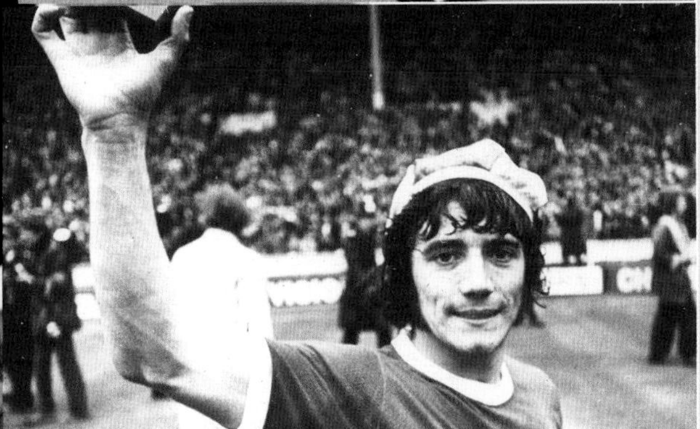

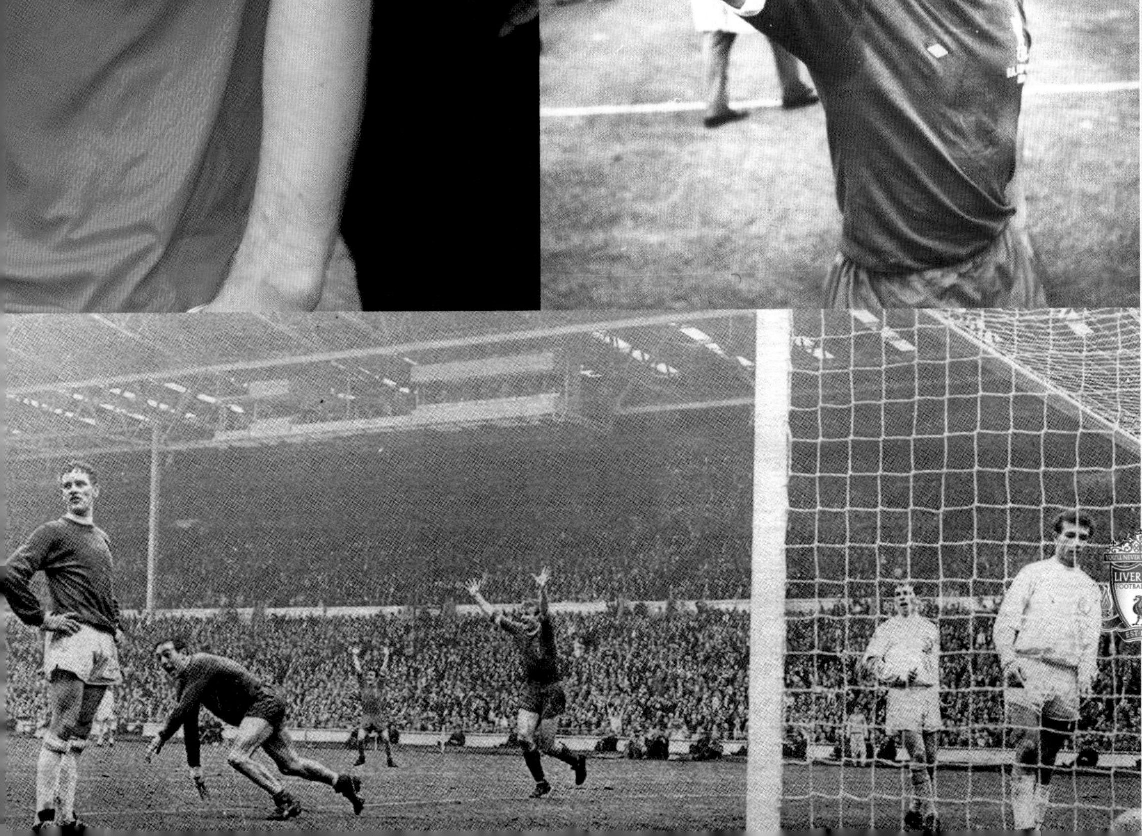

THE FA CUP RESULTS

(*1970-2009 - Full record available in The Official Guides 2006-2008*)

Date	Round	Venue	Opponents	Opponent Division	Score	Scorers	Att
1969/70	**(WINNERS - CHELSEA)**						
7th Jan	3	(a)	Coventry City	1	1-1	Graham	33,688
12th Jan	3 Rep	(h)	Coventry City	1	3-0	Ross, Thompson, Graham	51,261
24th Jan	4	(h)	Wrexham	4	3-1	Graham 2, St John	54,096
7th Feb	5	(h)	Leicester City	2	0-0		53,785
11th Feb	5 Rep	(a)	Leicester City	2	2-0	Evans 2	42,100
21st Feb	6	(a)	Watford	2	0-1		34,047
1970/71	**(WINNERS - ARSENAL)**						
2nd Jan	3	(h)	Aldershot	4	1-0	McLaughlin	45,500
23rd Jan	4	(h)	Swansea Town	3	3-0	Toshack, St John, Lawler	47,229
13th Feb	5	(h)	Southampton	1	1-0	Lawler	50,226
6th Mar	6	(h)	Tottenham Hotspur	1	0-0		54,731
16th Mar	6 Rep	(a)	Tottenham Hotspur	1	1-0	Heighway	56,283
27th Mar	S.F.	Old Trafford	Everton	1	2-1	Evans, Hall	62,144
8th May	Final	Wembley	Arsenal	1	1-2 aet	Heighway	100,000
1971/72	**(WINNERS - LEEDS UNITED)**						
15th Jan	3	(a)	Oxford United	2	3-0	Keegan 2, Lindsay	18,000
5th Feb	4	(h)	Leeds United	1	0-0		56,300
9th Feb	4 Rep	(a)	Leeds United	1	0-2		45,821
1972/73	**(WINNERS - SUNDERLAND)**						
13th Jan	3	(a)	Burnley	2	0-0		35,730
16th Jan	3 Rep	(h)	Burnley	2	3-0	Toshack 2, Cormack	56,124
3rd Feb	4	(h)	Manchester City	1	0-0		56,296
7th Feb	4 Rep	(a)	Manchester City	1	0-2		49,572
1973/74	**(WINNERS - LIVERPOOL)**						
5th Jan	3	(h)	Doncaster Rovers	4	2-2	Keegan 2	31,483
8th Jan	3 Rep	(a)	Doncaster Rovers	4	2-0	Heighway, Cormack	22,499
26th Jan	4	(h)	Carlisle United	2	0-0		47,211
29th Jan	4 Rep	(a)	Carlisle United	2	2-0	Boersma, Toshack	21,262
16th Feb	5	(h)	Ipswich Town	1	2-0	Hall, Keegan	45,340
9th Mar	6	(a)	Bristol City	2	1-0	Toshack	37,671
30th Mar	S.F.	Old Trafford	Leicester City	1	0-0		60,000
3rd Apr	S.F. Rep	Villa Park	Leicester City	1	3-1	Hall, Keegan, Toshack	55,619
4th May	Final	Wembley	Newcastle United	1	3-0	Keegan 2, Heighway	100,000
1974/75	**(WINNERS - WEST HAM UNITED)**						
4th Jan	3	(h)	Stoke City	1	2-0	Heighway, Keegan	48,723
25th Jan	4	(a)	Ipswich Town	1	0-1		34,708
1975/76	**(WINNERS - SOUTHAMPTON)**						
3rd Jan	3	(a)	West Ham United	1	2-0	Keegan, Toshack	32,363
24th Jan	4	(a)	Derby County	1	0-1		38,200

THE FA CUP RESULTS

Date	Round	Venue	Opponents	Opponent Division	Score	Scorers	Att
1976/77	**(WINNERS - MANCHESTER UNITED)**						
8th Jan	3	(h)	Crystal Palace	3	0-0		44,730
11th Jan	3 Rep	(a)	Crystal Palace	3	3-2	Keegan, Heighway 2	42,644
29th Jan	4	(h)	Carlisle United	2	3-0	Keegan, Toshack, Heighway	45,358
26th Feb	5	(h)	Oldham Athletic	2	3-1	Keegan, Case, Neal (pen)	52,455
19th Mar	6	(h)	Middlesbrough	1	2-0	Fairclough, Keegan	55,881
23rd Apr	S.F.	Maine Rd	Everton	1	2-2	McDermott, Case	52,637
27th Apr	S.F. Rep	Maine Rd	Everton	1	3-0	Neal (pen), Case, Kennedy	52,579
21st May	Final	Wembley	Manchester United	1	1-2	Case	100,000
1977/78	**(WINNERS - IPSWICH TOWN)**						
7th Jan	3	(a)	Chelsea	1	2-4	Johnson, Dalglish	45,449
1978/79	**(WINNERS - ARSENAL)**						
10th Jan	3	(a)	Southend United	3	0-0		31,033
17th Jan	3 Rep	(h)	Southend United	3	3-0	Case, Dalglish, R.Kennedy	37,797
30th Jan	4	(h)	Blackburn Rovers	2	1-0	Dalglish	43,432
28th Feb	5	(h)	Burnley	2	3-0	Johnson 2, Souness	47,161
10th Mar	6	(a)	Ipswich Town	1	1-0	Dalglish	31,322
31st Mar	S.F.	Maine Rd	Manchester United	1	2-2	Dalglish, Hansen	52,584
4th Apr	S.F. Rep	Goodison	Manchester United	1	0-1		53,069
1979/80	**(WINNERS - WEST HAM UNITED)**						
5th Jan	3	(h)	Grimsby Town	3	5-0	Souness, Johnson 3, Case	49,706
26th Jan	4	(a)	Nottingham Forest	1	2-0	Dalglish, McDermott (pen)	33,277
16th Feb	5	(h)	Bury	3	2-0	Fairclough 2	43,769
8th Mar	6	(a)	Tottenham Hotspur	1	1-0	Mc Dermott	48,033
12th Apr	S.F.	Hillsborough	Arsenal	1	0-0		50,174
16th Apr	S.F. Rep	Villa Park	Arsenal	1	1-1 aet	Fairclough	40,679
28th Apr	S.F.Rep (2)	Villa Park	Arsenal	1	1-1 aet	Dalglish	42,975
1st May	S.F.Rep (3)	Highfield Rd	Arsenal	1	0-1		35,335
1980/81	**(WINNERS - TOTTENHAM HOTSPUR)**						
3rd Jan	3	(h)	Altrincham	Non Lge	4-1	McDermott, Dalglish 2, R.Kennedy	37,170
24th Jan	4	(a)	Everton	1	1-2	Case	53,804
1981/82	**(WINNERS - TOTTENHAM HOTSPUR)**						
2nd Jan	3	(a)	Swansea City	1	4-0	Hansen, Rush 2, Lawrenson	24,179
23rd Jan	4	(a)	Sunderland	1	3-0	Dalglish 2, Rush	28,582
13th Feb	5	(a)	Chelsea	2	0-2		41,422
1982/83	**(WINNERS - MANCHESTER UNITED)**						
8th Jan	3	(a)	Blackburn Rovers	2	2-1	Hodgson, Rush	21,967
29th Jan	4	(h)	Stoke City	1	2-0	Dalglish, Rush	36,666
20th Feb	5	(h)	Brighton	1	1-2	Johnston	44,868
1983/84	**(WINNERS - EVERTON)**						
6th Jan	3	(h)	Newcastle United	2	4-0	Robinson, Rush 2, Johnston	33,566
29th Jan	4	(a)	Brighton	2	0-2		19,057

THE FA CUP RESULTS

Date	Round	Venue	Opponents	Opponent Division	Score	Scorers	Att
1984/85	**(WINNERS - MANCHESTER UNITED)**						
5th Jan	3	(h)	Aston Villa	1	3-0	Rush 2, Wark	36,877
27th Jan	4	(h)	Tottenham Hotspur	1	1-0	Rush	27,905
16th Feb	5	(a)	York City	3	1-1	Rush	13,485
20th Feb	5 Rep	(h)	York City	3	7-0	Whelan 2, Wark 3, Neal, Walsh	43,010
10th Mar	6	(a)	Barnsley	2	4-0	Rush 3, Whelan	19,838
13th Apr	S.F.	Goodison	Manchester United	1	2-2 aet	Whelan, Walsh	51,690
17th Apr	S.F. Rep	Maine Rd	Manchester United	1	1-2	McGrath o.g.	45,775
1985/86	**(WINNERS - LIVERPOOL)**						
4th Jan	3	(h)	Norwich City	2	5-0	MacDonald, Walsh, McMahon Whelan, Wark	29,082
26th Jan	4	(a)	Chelsea	1	2-1	Rush, Lawrenson	33,625
15th Feb	5	(a)	York City	3	1-1	Molby (pen)	12,443
18th Feb	5 Rep	(h)	York City	3	3-1 aet	Wark, Molby, Dalglish	29,362
11th Mar	6	(h)	Watford	1	0-0		36,775
17th Mar	6 Rep	(a)	Watford	1	2-1 aet	Molby (pen), Rush	28,097
5th Apr	S.F.	Tottenham	Southampton	1	2-0 aet	Rush 2	44,605
10th May	Final	Wembley	Everton	1	3-1	Rush 2, Johnston	98,000
1986/87	**(WINNERS - COVENTRY CITY)**						
11th Jan	3	(a)	Luton Town	1	0-0		11,085
26th Jan	3 Rep	(h)	Luton Town	1	0-0 aet		34,822
28th Jan	3 Rep (2)	(a)	Luton Town	1	0-3		14,687
1987/88	**(WINNERS - WIMBLEDON)**						
9th Jan	3	(a)	Stoke City	2	0-0		31,979
12th Jan	3 Rep	(h)	Stoke City	2	1-0	Beardsley	39,147
31st Jan	4	(a)	Aston Villa	2	2-0	Barnes, Beardsley	46,324
21st Feb	5	(a)	Everton	1	1-0	Houghton	48,270
13th Mar	6	(a)	Manchester City	2	4-0	Houghton, Beardsley (pen) Johnston, Barnes	44,077
9th Apr	S.F.	Hillsborough	Nottingham Forest	1	2-1	Aldridge 2 (1 pen)	51,627
14th May	Final	Wembley	Wimbledon	1	0-1		98,203
1988/89	**(WINNERS - LIVERPOOL)**						
7th Jan	3	(a)	Carlisle United	4	3-0	Barnes, McMahon 2	18,556
29th Jan	4	(a)	Millwall	1	2-0	Aldridge, Rush	23,615
18th Feb	5	(a)	Hull City	2	3-2	Barnes, Aldridge 2	20,058
18th Mar	6	(h)	Brentford	3	4-0	McMahon, Barnes, Beardsley 2	42,376
7th May	S.F.	Old Trafford	Nottingham Forest	1	3-1	Aldridge, Laws o.g.	38,000
20th May	Final	Wembley	Everton	1	3-2aet	Aldridge, Rush 2	82,800
1989/90	**(WINNERS - MANCHESTER UNITED)**						
6th Jan	3	(a)	Swansea City	3	0-0		16,098
9th Jan	3 Rep	(h)	Swansea City	3	8-0	Barnes 2, Whelan, Rush 3, Beardsley, Nicol	29,194
28th Jan	4	(a)	Norwich City	1	0-0		23,152
31st Jan	4 Rep	(h)	Norwich City	1	3-1	Nicol, Barnes, Beardsley (pen)	29,339
17th Feb	5	(h)	Southampton	1	3-0	Rush, Beardsley, Nicol	35,961
11th Mar	6	(a)	QPR	1	2-2	Barnes, Rush	21,057
14th Mar	6 Rep	(h)	QPR	1	1-0	Beardsley	38,090
8th Apr	S.F.	Villa Park	Crystal Palace	1	3-4 aet	Rush, McMahon, Barnes (pen)	38,389

THE FA CUP RESULTS

Date	Round	Venue	Opponents	Opponent Division	Score	Scorers	Att
1990/91	**(WINNERS - TOTTENHAM HOTSPUR)**						
5th Jan	3	(a)	Blackburn Rovers	2	1-1	Atkins o.g.	18,524
8th Jan	3 Rep	(h)	Blackburn Rovers	2	3-0	Houghton, Rush, Staunton	34,175
26th Jan	4	(h)	Brighton	2	2-2	Rush 2	32,670
30th Jan	4 Rep	(a)	Brighton	2	3-2 aet	McMahon 2, Rush	14,392
17th Feb	5	(h)	Everton	1	0-0		38,323
20th Feb	5 Rep	(a)	Everton	1	4-4 aet	Beardsley 2, Rush, Barnes	37,766
27th Feb	5 Rep (2)	(a)	Everton	1	0-1		40,201
1991/92	**(WINNERS - LIVERPOOL)**						
6th Jan	3	(a)	Crewe Alexandra	4	4-0	McManaman, Barnes 3 (1 pen)	7,400
5th Feb	4	(a)	Bristol Rovers	2	1-1	Saunders	9,464
11th Feb	4 Rep	(h)	Bristol Rovers	2	2-1	McManaman, Saunders	30,142
16th Feb	5	(a)	Ipswich Town	2	0-0		26,140
26th Feb	5 Rep	(h)	Ipswich Town	2	3-2 aet	Houghton, Molby, McManaman	27,335
8th Mar	6	(h)	Aston Villa	1	1-0	Thomas	29,109
5th Apr	S.F.	Highbury	Portsmouth	2	1-1 aet	Whelan	41,869
13th Apr	S.F. Rep	Villa Park	Portsmouth	2	0-0 aet		40,077
			(Liverpool won 3-1 on penalties)				
9th May	Final	Wembley	Sunderland	2	2-0	Thomas, Rush	79,544
1992/93	**(WINNERS - ARSENAL)**						
3rd Jan	3	(a)	Bolton Wanderers	2	2-2	Winstanley o.g., Rush	21,502
13th Jan	3 Rep	(h)	Bolton Wanderers	2	0-2		34,790
1993/94	**(WINNERS - MANCHESTER UNITED)**						
19th Jan	3	(a)	Bristol City	1	1-1	Rush	21,718
25th Jan	3 Rep	(h)	Bristol City	1	0-1		36,720
1994/95	**(WINNERS - EVERTON)**						
7th Jan	3	(a)	Birmingham City	2	0-0		25,326
18th Jan	3 Rep	(h)	Birmingham City	2	1-1 aet	Redknapp	36,275
			(Liverpool won 2-0 on penalties)				
28th Jan	4	(a)	Burnley	1	0-0		20,551
7th Feb	4 Rep	(h)	Burnley	1	1-0	Barnes	32,109
19th Feb	5	(h)	Wimbledon	Prem	1-1	Fowler	25,124
28th Feb	5 Rep	(a)	Wimbledon	Prem	2-0	Barnes, Rush	12,553
11th Mar	6	(h)	Tottenham Hotspur	Prem	1-2	Fowler	39,592
1995/96	**(WINNERS - MANCHESTER UNITED)**						
6th Jan	3	(h)	Rochdale	3	7-0	Fowler, Collymore 3, Valentine o.g., Rush, McAteer	28,126
18th Feb	4	(a)	Shrewsbury Town	2	4-0	Collymore, Walton o.g., Fowler, McAteer	7,752
28th Feb	5	(h)	Charlton Athletic	1	2-1	Fowler, Collymore	36,818
10th Mar	6	(a)	Leeds United	Prem	0-0		34,632
20th Mar	6 Rep	(h)	Leeds United	Prem	3-0	McManaman 2, Fowler	30,812
31st Mar	S.F	Old Trafford	Aston Villa	Prem	3-0	Fowler 2, McAteer	39,072
11th May	Final	Wembley	Manchester United	Prem	0-1		79,007
1996/97	**(WINNERS - CHELSEA)**						
4th Jan	3	(h)	Burnley	2	1-0	Collymore	33,252
26th Jan	4	(a)	Chelsea	Prem	2-4	Fowler, Collymore	27,950

THE FA CUP RESULTS

Date	Round	Venue	Opponents	Opponent Division	Score	Scorers	Att
1997/98	**(WINNERS - ARSENAL)**						
3rd Jan	3	(h)	Coventry City	Prem	1-3	Redknapp	33,888
1998/99	**(WINNERS - MANCHESTER UNITED)**						
3rd Jan	3	(a)	Port Vale	1	3-0	Owen (pen), Ince, Fowler	16,557
24th Jan	4	(a)	Manchester United	Prem	1-2	Owen	54,591
1999/2000	**(WINNERS - CHELSEA)**						
12th Dec	3	(a)	Huddersfield Town.	1	2-0	Camara, Matteo	23,678
10th Jan	4	(h)	Blackburn Rovers	1	0-1		32,839
2000/01	**(WINNERS - LIVERPOOL)**						
6th Jan	3	(h)	Rotherham United	2	3-0	Heskey 2, Hamann	30,689
27th Jan	4	(a)	Leeds United	Prem	2-0	Barmby, Heskey	37,108
18th Feb	5	(h)	Manchester City	Prem	4-2	Litmanen (pen), Heskey, Smicer (pen), Babbel	36,231
11th Mar	6	(a)	Tranmere Rovers	1	4-2	Murphy, Owen, Gerrard, Fowler (pen)	16,334
8th Apr	S.F.	Villa Park	Wycombe W.	2	2-1	Heskey, Fowler	40,037
12th May	Final	Cardiff	Arsenal	Prem	2-1	Owen 2	74,200
2001/02	**(WINNERS - ARSENAL)**						
5th Jan	3	(h)	Birmingham City	1	3-0	Owen 2, Anelka	40,875
27th Jan	4	(a)	Arsenal	Prem	0-1		38,092
2002/03	**(WINNERS - ARSENAL)**						
5th Jan	3	(a)	Manchester City	Prem	1-0	Murphy (pen)	28,586
26th Jan	4	(a)	Crystal Palace	1	0-0		26,054
5th Feb	4 Rep	(h)	Crystal Palace	1	0-2		35,109
2003/04	**(WINNERS - MANCHESTER UNITED)**						
4th Jan	3	(a)	Yeovil Town	3	2-0	Heskey, Murphy (pen)	9,348
24th Jan	4	(h)	Newcastle United	Prem	2-1	Cheyrou 2	41,365
15th Feb	5	(h)	Portsmouth	Prem	1-1	Owen	34,669
22nd Feb	5 Rep	(a)	Portsmouth	Prem	0-1		19,529
2004/05	**(WINNERS - ARSENAL)**						
18th Jan	3	(a)	Burnley	Champ	0-1		19,033
2005/06	**(WINNERS - LIVERPOOL)**						
7th Jan	3	(a)	Luton Town	Champ	5-3	Gerrard, Sinama-Pongolle 2, Alonso 2	10,170
29th Jan	4	(a)	Portsmouth	Prem	2-1	Gerrard (pen), Riise	17,247
18th Feb	5	(h)	Manchester United	Prem	1-0	Crouch	44,039
21st Mar	6	(a)	Birmingham City	Prem	7-0	Hyypia, Crouch 2, Morientes, Riise, Tebily o.g., Cisse	27,378
22nd Apr	S.F.	Old Trafford	Chelsea	Prem	2-1	Riise, Garcia	64,575
13th May	Final	Cardiff	West Ham United (Liverpool won 3-1 on penalties)	Prem	3-3 aet	Cisse, Gerrard 2	74,000
2006/07	**(WINNERS - CHELSEA)**						
6th Jan	3	(h)	Arsenal	Prem	1-3	Kuyt	43,619
2007/08	**(WINNERS - PORTSMOUTH)**						
6th Jan	3	(a)	Luton Town	1	1-1	Crouch	10,226
15th Jan	3 Rep	(h)	Luton Town	1	5-0	Babel, Gerrard 3, Hyypia	41,446
26th Jan	4	(h)	Havant & Water.	Non Lge	5-2	Lucas, Benayoun 3, Crouch	42,566
16th Feb	5	(h)	Barnsley	Champ	1-2	Kuyt	42,449

THE FA CUP RESULTS

Date	Round	Venue	Opponents	Opponent Division	Score	Scorers	Att
2008/09	**(WINNERS - CHELSEA)**						
3rd Jan	3	(a)	Preston North End	Champ	2-0	Riera, Torres	23,046
25th Jan	4	(h)	Everton	Prem	1-1	Gerrard	43,524
4th Feb	4 Rep	(a)	Everton	Prem	0-1 aet		37,918

Steven Gerrard – FA Cup hero in 2006

PLAYER RECORDS – APPEARANCES

FA CUP 1892-2009 – Games played includes substitute appearances

TOTAL APPEARANCES

		FIRST-TEAM CAREER	GAMES
1	Ian Callaghan	1960-1978	79
2	Bruce Grobbelaar	1981-1994	62
=	Emlyn Hughes	1967-1979	62
4	Ian Rush	1980-1987 & 1988-1996	61
5	Alan Hansen	1977-1990	58
6	Ray Clemence	1968-1981	54
7	Tommy Smith	1963-1978	52
8	John Barnes	1987-1997	51
9	Steve Nicol	1982-1994	50
=	Ron Yeats	1961-1971	50
11	Ian St John	1961-1971	49
12	Chris Lawler	1963-1975	47
13	Phil Neal	1974-1985	45
14	Roger Hunt	1959-1969	44
15	Tommy Lawrence	1962-1971	42
=	Billy Liddell	1946-1960	42

PLAYER RECORDS – GOALS

FA CUP 1892-2009

TOTAL GOALS

		FIRST-TEAM CAREER	GOALS
1	Ian Rush	1980-1987 & 1988-1996	39
2	Roger Hunt	1959-1969	18
3	Harry Chambers	1919-1928	16
=	John Barnes	1987-1997	16
5	Kevin Keegan	1971-1977	14
6	Kenny Dalglish	1977-1990	13
=	Billy Liddell	1946-1960	13
8	Jack Balmer	1935-1952	12
=	Robbie Fowler	1993-2001 & 2006-2007	12
=	Ian St John	1961-1971	12
11	Peter Beardsley	1987-1991	11
=	Billy Lacey	1912-1924	11
13	Willie Fagan	1937-1951	10
14	Sam Raybould	1900-1907	9
=	Steven Gerrard	1998-	9
16	John Aldridge	1987-1989	8
=	Jack Cox	1898-1909	8
=	Tony Hateley	1967-1968	8
=	Steve Heighway	1970-1981	8
=	Gordon Hodgson	1926-1935	8
=	Michael Owen	1997-2004	8
=	Albert Stubbins	1946-1953	8
=	John Toshack	1970-1977	8

BIGGEST-EVER FA CUP VICTORIES

DATE	OPPONENTS	VENUE	OPPONENT DIVISION	SCORE
29th Oct 1892	Newtown	Home	Non-League	9-0
9th Jan 1990	Swansea City	Home	Three	8-0
20th Feb 1985	York City	Home	Three	7-0
6th Jan 1996	Rochdale	Home	Three	7-0
21st Mar 2006	Birmingham City	Away	Prem	7-0
11th Jan 1922	Sunderland	Home	One	5-0
4th Jan 1964	Derby County	Home	Two	5-0
5th Jan 1980	Grimsby Town	Home	Three	5-0
4th Jan 1986	Norwich City	Home	Two	5-0
12th Jan 1935	Yeovil & Petters	Away	Non-League	6-2

BIGGEST-EVER FA CUP DEFEATS

DATE	OPPONENTS	VENUE	OPPONENT DIVISION	SCORE
26th Jan 1946	Bolton Wanderers	Away	One	0-5
2nd Mar 1898	Derby County	Home	One	1-5
30th Jan 1929	Bolton Wanderers	Away	One	2-5 aet
8th Feb 1902	Southampton	Away	Non-League	1-4
11th Feb 1939	Wolverhampton W.	Away	One	1-4
24th Feb 1894	Bolton Wanderers	Away	One	0-3
20th Mar 1897	Aston Villa	Neutral	One	0-3
3rd Feb 1912	Fulham	Away	Two	0-3
17th Feb 1934	Bolton Wanderers	Home	Two	0-3
16th Jan 1937	Norwich City	Away	Two	0-3
24th Jan 1948	Manchester United	Away	One	0-3
28th Jan 1987	Luton Town	Away	One	0-3

Ian Callaghan – Record FA Cup appearance holder

THE LEAGUE CUP

(*1969-2009 - Full record available in The Official Guides 2006-2008*)

Date	Round	Venue	Opponents	Opponent Division	Score	Scorers	Att
1969/70	**(WINNERS - MANCHESTER CITY)**						
3rd Sept	2	(a)	Watford	2	2-1	Slater o.g., St John	21,149
24th Sept	3	(a)	Manchester City	1	2-3	A.Evans, Graham	28,019
1970/71	**(WINNERS - TOTTENHAM HOTSPUR)**						
8th Sept	2	(a)	Mansfield Town	3	0-0		12,532
22nd Sept	2 Rep	(h)	Mansfield Town	3	3-2 aet	Hughes, Smith (pen), A.Evans	31,087
6th Oct	3	(a)	Swindon Town	2	0-2		23,992
1971/72	**(WINNERS - STOKE CITY)**						
7th Sept	2	(h)	Hull City	2	3-0	Lawler, Heighway, Hall (pen)	31,612
5th Oct	3	(h)	Southampton	1	1-0	Heighway	28,964
27th Oct	4	(a)	West Ham United	1	1-2	Graham	40,878
1972/73	**(WINNERS - TOTTENHAM HOTSPUR)**						
5th Sept	2	(a)	Carlisle United	2	1-1	Keegan	16,257
19th Sept	2 Rep	(h)	Carlisle United	2	5-1	Keegan, Boersma 2, Lawler, Heighway	22,128
3rd Oct	3	(a)	West Bromwich Alb.1		1-1	Heighway	17,756
10th Oct	3 Rep	(h)	West Bromwich Alb.1		2-1 aet	Hughes, Keegan	26,461
31st Oct	4	(h)	Leeds United	1	2-2	Keegan, Toshack	44,609
22nd Nov	4 Rep	(a)	Leeds United	1	1-0	Keegan	34,856
4th Dec	5	(h)	Tottenham Hotspur	1	1-1	Hughes	48,677
6th Dec	5 Rep	(a)	Tottenham Hotspur	1	1-3	Callaghan	34,565
1973/74	**(WINNERS - WOLVERHAMPTON WANDERERS)**						
8th Oct	2	(a)	West Ham United	1	2-2	Cormack, Heighway	25,823
29th Oct	2 Rep	(h)	West Ham United	1	1-0	Toshack	26,002
21st Nov	3	(a)	Sunderland	2	2-0	Keegan, Toshack	36,208
27th Nov	4	(a)	Hull City	2	0-0		19,748
4th Dec	4 Rep	(h)	Hull City	2	3-1	Callaghan 3	17,120
19th Dec	5	(a)	Wolverhampton W.	1	0-1		15,242
1974/75	**(WINNERS - ASTON VILLA)**						
10th Sept	2	(h)	Brentford	4	2-1	Kennedy, Boersma	21,413
8th Oct	3	(a)	Bristol City	2	0-0		25,573
16th Oct	3 Rep	(h)	Bristol City	2	4-0	Heighway 2, Kennedy 2	23,694
12th Nov	4	(h)	Middlesbrough	1	0-1		24,906
1975/76	**(WINNERS - MANCHESTER CITY)**						
10th Sept	2	(a)	York City	2	1-0	Lindsay (pen)	9,421
7th Oct	3	(h)	Burnley	1	1-1	Case	24,607
14th Oct	3 Rep	(a)	Burnley	1	0-1		20,022
1976/77	**(WINNERS - ASTON VILLA)**						
31st Aug	2	(h)	West Bromwich Alb.1		1-1	Callaghan	23,378
6th Sept	2 Rep	(a)	West Bromwich Alb.1		0-1		22,662
1977/78	**(WINNERS - NOTTINGHAM FOREST)**						
30th Aug	2	(h)	Chelsea	1	2-0	Dalglish, Case	33,170
26th Oct	3	(h)	Derby County	1	2-0	Fairclough 2	30,400
29th Nov	4	(h)	Coventry City	1	2-2	Fairclough, Neal (pen)	33,817
20th Dec	4 Rep	(a)	Coventry City	1	2-0	Case, Dalglish	36,105

THE LEAGUE CUP

Date	Round	Venue	Opponents	Opponent Division	Score	Scorers	Att
1977/78	**(WINNERS - NOTTINGHAM FOREST)**						
17th Jan	5	(a)	Wrexham	3	3-1	Dalglish 3	25,641
7th Feb	S.F.Leg 1	(h)	Arsenal	1	2-1	Dalglish, Kennedy	44,764
14th Feb	S.F.Leg 2	(a)	Arsenal	1	0-0		49,561
18th Mar	Final	Wembley	Nottingham Forest	1	0-0 aet		100,000
22nd Mar	Final Rep.	Old Trafford	Nottingham Forest	1	0-1		54,375
1978/79	**(WINNERS - NOTTINGHAM FOREST)**						
28th Aug	2	(a)	Sheffield United	2	0-1		35,753
1979/80	**(WINNERS - WOLVERHAMPTON WANDERERS)**						
29th Aug	2 Leg 1	(a)	Tranmere Rovers	4	0-0		16,759
4th Sept	2 Leg 2	(h)	Tranmere Rovers	4	4-0	Thompson, Dalglish 2, Fairclough	24,785
25th Sept	3	(h)	Chesterfield	3	3-1	Fairclough, Dalglish, McDermott	20,960
30th Oct	4	(h)	Exeter City	3	2-0	Fairclough 2	21,019
5th Dec	5	(a)	Norwich City	1	3-1	Johnson 2, Dalglish	23,000
22nd Jan	S.F.Leg 1	(a)	Nottingham Forest	1	0-1		32,234
12th Feb	S.F.Leg 2	(h)	Nottingham Forest	1	1-1	Fairclough	50,880
1980/81	**(WINNERS - LIVERPOOL)**						
27th Aug	2 Leg 1	(a)	Bradford City	4	0-1		16,232
2nd Sept	2 Leg 2	(h)	Bradford City	4	4-0	Dalglish 2, R.Kennedy, Johnson	21,017
23rd Sept	3	(h)	Swindon Town	3	5-0	Lee 2, Dalglish, Cockerill o.g., Fairclough	16,566
28th Oct	4	(h)	Portsmouth	3	4-1	Dalglish, Johnson 2, Souness	32,021
5th Dec	5	(a)	Birmingham City	1	3-1	Dalglish, McDermott, Johnson	30,236
14th Jan	S.F.Leg 1	(a)	Manchester City	1	1-0	R.Kennedy	48,045
10th Feb	S.F.Leg 2	(h)	Manchester City	1	1-1	Dalglish	46,711
14th Mar	Final	Wembley	West Ham United	2	1-1 aet	A.Kennedy	100,000
1st Apr	Final Rep	Villa Park	West Ham United	2	2-1	Dalglish, Hansen	36,693
1981/82	**(WINNERS - LIVERPOOL)**						
7th Oct	2 Leg 1	(h)	Exeter City	3	5-0	Rush 2, McDermott, Dalglish, Whelan	11,478
28th Oct	2 Leg 2	(a)	Exeter City	3	6-0	Rush 2, Dalglish, Neal, Sheedy, Marker o.g.	11,740
10th Nov	3	(h)	Middlesbrough	1	4-1	Sheedy, Rush, Johnson 2	16,145
1st Dec	4	(a)	Arsenal	1	0-0		37,917
8th Dec	4 Rep	(h)	Arsenal	1	3-0 aet	Johnston, McDermott (pen), Dalglish	21,375
12th Jan	5	(h)	Barnsley	2	0-0		33,707
19th Jan	5 Rep	(a)	Barnsley	2	3-1	Souness, Johnson, Dalglish	29,639
2nd Feb	S.F.Leg 1	(a)	Ipswich Town	1	2-0	McDermott, Rush	26,690
9th Feb	S.F.Leg 2	(h)	Ipswich Town	1	2-2	Rush, Dalglish	34,933
13th Mar	Final	Wembley	Tottenham Hotspur	1	3-1 aet	Whelan 2, Rush	100,000
1982/83	**(WINNERS - LIVERPOOL)**						
5th Oct	2 Leg 1	(a)	Ipswich Town	1	2-1	Rush 2	19,328
26th Oct	2 Leg 2	(h)	Ipswich Town	1	2-0	Whelan, Lawrenson	17,698
11th Nov	3	(h)	Rotherham United	2	1-0	Johnston	20,412
30th Nov	4	(h)	Norwich City	1	2-0	Lawrenson, Fairclough	13,235
18th Jan	5	(h)	West Ham United	1	2-1	Hodgson, Souness	23,953
8th Feb	S.F.Leg 1	(h)	Burnley	2	3-0	Souness, Neal (pen), Hodgson	33,520
15th Feb	S.F.Leg 2	(a)	Burnley	2	0-1		20,000
26th Mar	Final	Wembley	Manchester United	1	2-1 aet	Kennedy, Whelan	100,000

THE LEAGUE CUP

Date	Round	Venue	Opponents	Opponent Division	Score	Scorers	Att
1983/84	**(WINNERS - LIVERPOOL)**						
5th Oct	2 Leg 1	(a)	Brentford	3	4-1	Rush 2, Robinson, Souness	17,859
25th Oct	2 Leg 2	(h)	Brentford	3	4-0	Souness (pen), Hodgson, Dalglish, Robinson	9,902
8th Nov	3	(a)	Fulham	2	1-1	Rush	20,142
22nd Nov	3 Rep	(h)	Fulham	2	1-1 aet	Dalglish	15,783
29th Nov	3 Rep (2)	(a)	Fulham	2	1-0 aet	Souness	20,905
20th Dec	4	(a)	Birmingham City	1	1-1	Souness	17,405
22nd Dec	4 Rep	(h)	Birmingham City	1	3-0	Nicol, Rush 2 (1 pen)	11,638
17th Jan	5	(a)	Sheffield Wed.	2	2-2	Nicol, Neal (pen)	49,357
25th Jan	5 Rep	(h)	Sheffield Wed.	2	3-0	Rush 2, Robinson	40,485
7th Feb	S.F.Leg 1	(h)	Walsall	3	2-2	Whelan 2	31,073
14th Feb	S.F.Leg 2	(a)	Walsall	3	2-0	Rush, Whelan	19,591
25th Mar	Final	Wembley	Everton	1	0-0 aet		100,000
28th Mar	Final Rep	Maine Rd	Everton	1	1-0	Souness	52,089
1984/85	**(WINNERS - NORWICH CITY)**						
24th Sept	2 Leg 1	(a)	Stockport County	4	0-0		11,169
9th Oct	2 Leg 2	(h)	Stockport County	4	2-0 aet	Robinson, Whelan	13,422
31st Oct	3	(a)	Tottenham Hotspur	1	0-1		38,690
1985/86	**(WINNERS - OXFORD UNITED)**						
24th Sept	2 Leg 1	(h)	Oldham Athletic	2	3-0	McMahon 2, Rush	16,150
9th Oct	2 Leg 2	(a)	Oldham Athletic	2	5-2	Whelan 2, Wark, Rush, MacDonald	7,719
29th Oct	3	(h)	Brighton	2	4-0	Walsh 3, Dalglish	15,291
26th Nov	4	(h)	Manchester United	1	2-1	Molby 2 (1 pen)	41,291
21st Jan	5	(h)	Ipswich Town	1	3-0	Walsh, Whelan, Rush	19,762
12th Feb	S.F.Leg 1	(a)	QPR	1	0-1		15,051
5th Mar	S.F.Leg 2	(h)	QPR	1	2-2	McMahon, Johnston	23,863
1986/87	**(WINNERS - ARSENAL)**						
23rd Sept	2 Leg 1	(h)	Fulham	3	10-0	Rush 2, Wark 2, Whelan, McMahon 4, Nicol	13,498
7th Oct	2 Leg 2	(a)	Fulham	3	3-2	McMahon, Parker o.g., Molby (pen)	7,864
29th Oct	3	(h)	Leicester City	1	4-1	McMahon 3, Dalglish	20,248
19th Nov	4	(a)	Coventry City	1	0-0		26,385
26th Nov	4 Rep	(h)	Coventry City	1	3-1	Molby 3 (3 pens)	19,179
21st Jan	5	(a)	Everton	1	1-0	Rush	53,325
11th Feb	S.F.Leg 1	(a)	Southampton	1	0-0		22,818
25th Feb	S.F.Leg 2	(h)	Southampton	1	3-0	Whelan, Dalglish, Molby	38,481
5th Apr	Final	Wembley	Arsenal	1	1-2	Rush	96,000
1987/88	**(WINNERS - LUTON TOWN)**						
23rd Sept	2 Leg 1	(a)	Blackburn Rovers	2	1-1	Nicol	13,924
6th Oct	2 Leg 2	(h)	Blackburn Rovers	2	1-0	Aldridge	28,994
28th Oct	3	(h)	Everton	1	0-1		44,071
1988/89	**(WINNERS - NOTTINGHAM FOREST)**						
28th Sept	2 Leg 1	(h)	Walsall	2	1-0	Gillespie	18,084
12th Oct	2 Leg 2	(a)	Walsall	2	3-1	Barnes, Rush, Molby (pen)	12,015
2nd Nov	3	(h)	Arsenal	1	1-1	Barnes	31,951
9th Nov	3 Rep	(a)	Arsenal	1	0-0		54,029
23rd Nov	3 Rep (2)	Villa Park	Arsenal	1	2-1	McMahon, Aldridge	21,708
30th Nov	4	(a)	West Ham United	1	1-4	Aldridge (pen)	26,971

THE LEAGUE CUP

Date	Round	Venue	Opponents	Opponent Division	Score	Scorers	Att
1989/90	**(WINNERS - NOTTINGHAM FOREST)**						
19th Sept	2 Leg 1	(h)	Wigan Athletic	3	5-2	Hysen, Rush 2, Beardsley, Barnes	19,231
4th Oct	2 Leg 2	(a)	Wigan Athletic (match played at Anfield)	3	3-0	Staunton 3	17,954
25th Oct	3	(a)	Arsenal	1	0-1		40,814
1990/91	**(WINNERS - SHEFFIELD WEDNESDAY)**						
25th Sept	2 Leg 1	(h)	Crewe Alexandra	3	5-1	McMahon, Gillespie, Houghton, Rush 2	17,228
9th Oct	2 Leg 2	(a)	Crewe Alexandra	3	4-1	Rush 3, Staunton	7,200
31st Oct	3	(a)	Manchester United	1	1-3	Houghton	42,033
1991/92	**(WINNERS - MANCHESTER UNITED)**						
25th Sept	2 Leg 1	(h)	Stoke City	3	2-2	Rush 2	18,389
9th Oct	2 Leg 2	(a)	Stoke City	3	3-2	McManaman, Saunders, Walters	22,335
29th Oct	3	(h)	Port Vale	2	2-2	McManaman, Rush	21,553
20th Nov	3 Rep	(a)	Port Vale	2	4-1	McManaman, Walters, Houghton, Saunders	18,725
3rd Dec	4	(a)	Peterborough Utd	3	0-1		14,114
1992/93	**(WINNERS - ARSENAL)**						
22nd Sept	2 Leg 1	(h)	Chesterfield	3	4-4	Rosenthal, Hutchison, Walters Wright	12,533
6th Oct	2 Leg 2	(a)	Chesterfield	3	4-1	Hutchison, Redknapp, Walters Rush	10,632
28th Oct	3	(a)	Sheffield United	Prem	0-0		17,856
11th Nov	3 Rep	(h)	Sheffield United	Prem	3-0	McManaman 2, Marsh (pen)	17,654
1st Dec	4	(h)	Crystal Palace	Prem	1-1	Marsh (pen)	18,525
16th Dec	4 Rep	(a)	Crystal Palace	Prem	1-2 aet	Marsh (pen)	19,622
1993/94	**(WINNERS - ASTON VILLA)**						
22nd Sept	2 Leg 1	(a)	Fulham	2	3-1	Rush, Clough, Fowler	13,599
5th Oct	2 Leg 2	(h)	Fulham	2	5-0	Fowler 5	12,541
27th Oct	3	(h)	Ipswich Town	Prem	3-2	Rush 3	19,058
1st Dec	4	(h)	Wimbledon	Prem	1-1	Molby (pen)	19,290
14th Dec	4 Rep	(a)	Wimbledon (Liverpool lost 3-4 on penalties)	Prem	2-2 aet	Ruddock, Segers o.g.	11,343
1994/95	**(WINNERS - LIVERPOOL)**						
21st Sept	2 Leg 1	(h)	Burnley	1	2-0	Scales, Fowler	23,359
5th Oct	2 Leg 2	(a)	Burnley	1	4-1	Redknapp 2, Fowler, Clough	19,032
25th Oct	3	(h)	Stoke City	1	2-1	Rush 2	32,060
30th Nov	4	(a)	Blackburn Rovers	Prem	3-1	Rush 3	30,115
11th Jan	5	(h)	Arsenal	Prem	1-0	Rush	36,004
15th Feb	S.F.Leg 1	(h)	Crystal Palace	Prem	1-0	Fowler	25,480
8th Mar	S.F.Leg 2	(a)	Crystal Palace	Prem	1-0	Fowler	18,224
2nd Apr	Final	Wembley	Bolton Wanderers	1	2-1	McManaman 2	75,595

THE LEAGUE CUP

Date	Round	Venue	Opponents	Opponent Division	Score	Scorers	Att
1995/96	**(WINNERS - ASTON VILLA)**						
20th Sept	2 Leg 1	(h)	Sunderland	1	2-0	McManaman, Thomas	25,579
4th Oct	2 Leg 2	(a)	Sunderland	1	1-0	Fowler	20,560
25th Oct	3	(h)	Manchester City	Prem	4-0	Scales, Fowler, Rush, Harkness	29,394
29th Nov	4	(h)	Newcastle United	Prem	0-1		40,077
1996/97	**(WINNERS - LEICESTER CITY)**						
23rd Oct	3	(a)	Charlton Athletic	1	1-1	Fowler	15,000
13th Nov	3 Rep	(h)	Charlton Athletic	1	4-1	Wright, Redknapp, Fowler 2	20,714
27th Nov	4	(h)	Arsenal	Prem	4-2	McManaman, Fowler 2 (1 pen) Berger	32,814
8th Jan	5	(a)	Middlesbrough	Prem	1-2	McManaman	28,670
1997/98	**(WINNERS - CHELSEA)**						
15th Oct	3	(a)	West Bromwich Alb.	1	2-0	Berger, Fowler	21,986
18th Nov	4	(h)	Grimsby Town	2	3-0	Owen 3	28,515
7th Jan	5	(a)	Newcastle United	Prem	2-0 aet	Owen, Fowler	33,207
27th Jan	S.F.Leg 1	(h)	Middlesbrough	1	2-1	Redknapp, Fowler	33,438
18th Feb	S.F.Leg 2	(a)	Middlesbrough	1	0-2		29,828
1998/99	**(WINNERS - TOTTENHAM HOTSPUR)**						
27th Oct	3	(h)	Fulham	2	3-1	Morgan o.g., Fowler (pen), Ince	22,296
10th Nov	4	(h)	Tottenham Hotspur	Prem	1-3	Owen	20,772
1999/2000	**(WINNERS - LEICESTER CITY)**						
14th Sept	2 Leg 1	(a)	Hull City	3	5-1	Murphy 2, Meijer 2, Staunton	10,034
21st Sept	2 Leg 2	(h)	Hull City	3	4-2	Murphy, Maxwell, Riedle 2	24,318
13th Oct	3	(a)	Southampton	Prem	1-2	Owen	13,822
2000/01	**(WINNERS - LIVERPOOL)**						
1st Nov	3	(h)	Chelsea	Prem	2-1 aet	Murphy, Fowler	29,370
29th Nov	4	(a)	Stoke City	2	8-0	Ziege, Smicer, Babbel, Fowler 3 (1 pen), Hyypia, Murphy	27,109
13th Dec	5	(h)	Fulham	1	3-0 aet	Owen, Smicer, Barmby	20,144
10th Jan	S.F.Leg 1	(a)	Crystal Palace	1	1-2	Smicer	25,933
24th Jan	S.F.Leg 2	(h)	Crystal Palace	1	5-0	Smicer, Murphy 2, Biscan Fowler	41,854
25th Feb	Final	Cardiff	Birmingham City	1	1-1 aet	Fowler	73,500
			(Liverpool won 5-4 on penalties)				
2001/02	**(WINNERS - BLACKBURN ROVERS)**						
9th Oct	3	(h)	Grimsby Town	1	1-2 aet	McAllister (pen)	32,672
2002/03	**(WINNERS - LIVERPOOL)**						
6th Nov	3	(h)	Southampton	Prem	3-1	Berger, Diouf, Baros	35,870
4th Dec	4	(h)	Ipswich Town	1	1-1	Diouf (pen)	26,305
			(Liverpool won 5-4 on penalties)				
18th Dec	5	(a)	Aston Villa	Prem	4-3	Murphy 2, Baros, Gerrard	38,530
8th Jan	S.F.Leg 1	(a)	Sheffield United	1	1-2	Mellor	30,095
21st Jan	S.F.Leg 2	(h)	Sheffield United	1	2-0 aet	Diouf, Owen	43,837
2nd Mar	Final	Cardiff	Manchester United	Prem	2-0	Gerrard, Owen	74,500
2003/04	**(WINNERS - MIDDLESBROUGH)**						
29th Oct	3	(a)	Blackburn Rovers	Prem	4-3	Murphy (pen), Heskey 2, Kewell	16,918
3rd Dec	4	(h)	Bolton Wanderers	Prem	2-3	Murphy, Smicer	33,185

THE LEAGUE CUP

Date	Round	Venue	Opponents	Opponent Division	Score	Scorers	Att
2004/05	**(WINNERS - CHELSEA)**						
26th Oct	3	(a)	Millwall	Champ	3-0	Diao, Baros 2	17,655
10th Nov	4	(h)	Middlesbrough	Prem	2-0	Mellor 2	28,176
1st Dec	5	(a)	Tottenham Hotspur	Prem	1-1 aet	Sinama-Pongolle (pen)	36,100
			(Liverpool won 4-3 on penalties)				
11th Jan	S.F.Leg 1	(h)	Watford	Champ	1-0	Gerrard	35,739
25th Jan	S.F.Leg 2	(a)	Watford	Champ	1-0	Gerrard	19,797
27th Feb	Final	Cardiff	Chelsea	Prem	2-3 aet	Riise, Nunez	71,622
2005/06	**(WINNERS - MANCHESTER UNITED)**						
25th Oct	3	(a)	Crystal Palace	Champ	1-2	Gerrard	19,673
2006/07	**(WINNERS - CHELSEA)**						
25th Oct	3	(h)	Reading	Prem	4-3	Fowler, Riise, Paletta, Crouch	42,445
8th Nov	4	(a)	Birmingham City	Champ	1-0	Agger	23,061
9th Jan	5	(h)	Arsenal	Prem	3-6	Fowler, Gerrard, Hyypia	42,614
2007/08	**(WINNERS - TOTTENHAM HOTSPUR)**						
25th Sept	3	(a)	Reading	Prem	4-2	Benayoun, Torres 3	23,563
31st Oct	4	(h)	Cardiff City	Champ	2-1	El Zhar, Gerrard	41,780
19th Dec	5	(a)	Chelsea	Prem	0-2		41,366
2008/09	**(WINNERS - MANCHESTER UNITED)**						
23rd Sept	3	(h)	Crewe Alexandra	1	2-1	Agger, Lucas	28,591
12th Nov	4	(a)	Tottenham Hotspur	Prem	2-4	Plessis, Hyypia	33,242

Last time – Liverpool line up ahead of the 2005 League Cup final

PLAYER RECORDS – APPEARANCES

LEAGUE CUP 1960-2008 – Games played includes substitute appearances

TOTAL APPEARANCES

		FIRST-TEAM CAREER	GAMES
1	Ian Rush	1980-1987 & 1988-1996	78
2	Bruce Grobbelaar	1981-1994	70
3	Alan Hansen	1977-1990	68
4	Phil Neal	1974-1985	66
5	Kenny Dalglish	1977-1990	59
6	Ray Clemence	1968-1981	55
7	Mark Lawrenson	1981-1988	50
=	Ronnie Whelan	1981-1994	50
9	Emlyn Hughes	1967-1979	46
10	Alan Kennedy	1978-1985	45
=	Graeme Souness	1978-1984	45
12	Phil Thompson	1972-1983	43
13	Ian Callaghan	1960-1978	42
=	Steve Nicol	1982-1994	42
15	Sammy Lee	1978-1986	39
16	Steve Heighway	1970-1981	38
17	Terry McDermott	1974-1982	36
18	Robbie Fowler	1993-2001 & 2006-2007	35
=	Craig Johnston	1981-1988	35
=	Ray Kennedy	1974-1981	35
21	Steve McManaman	1990-1999	33
22	Tommy Smith	1963-1978	30

PLAYER RECORDS – GOALS

LEAGUE CUP 1960-2008

TOTAL GOALS

		FIRST-TEAM CAREER	GOALS
1	Ian Rush	1980-1987 & 1988-1996	48
2	Robbie Fowler	1993-2001 & 2006-2007	29
3	Kenny Dalglish	1977-1990	27
4	Ronnie Whelan	1981-1994	14
5	Steve McMahon	1985-1991	13
6	Danny Murphy	1997-2004	11
7	David Fairclough	1975-1983	10
=	Steve McManaman	1990-1999	10
9	Michael Owen	1997-2004	9
=	David Johnson	1976-1982	9
=	Jan Molby	1984-1995	9
=	Graeme Souness	1978-1984	9
13	Steven Gerrard	1998-	7
=	Steve Heighway	1970-1981	7
=	Ian Callaghan	1960-1978	7
16	Kevin Keegan	1971-1977	6
=	Ray Kennedy	1974-1981	6

BIGGEST-EVER LEAGUE CUP VICTORIES

DATE	OPPONENTS	VENUE	OPPONENT DIVISION	SCORE
23rd Sept 1986	Fulham	Home	Three	10-0
29th Nov 2000	Stoke City	Away	Two	8-0
28th Oct 1981	Exeter City	Away	Three	6-0
23rd Sep 1980	Swindon Town	Home	Three	5-0
7th Oct 1981	Exeter City	Home	Three	5-0
5th Oct 1993	Fulham	Home	Two	5-0
24th Jan 2001	Crystal Palace	Home	One	5-0
19th Sept 1972	Carlisle United	Home	Two	5-1
25th Sept 1990	Crewe Alexandra	Home	Three	5-1
14th Sept 1999	Hull City	Away	Three	5-1

BIGGEST-EVER LEAGUE CUP DEFEATS

DATE	OPPONENTS	VENUE	OPPONENT DIVISION	SCORE
9th Jan 2007	Arsenal	Home	Prem	3-6
30th Nov 1988	West Ham United	Away	One	1-4
12th Nov 2008	Tottenham Hotspur	Away	Prem	2-4
6th Dec 1972	Tottenham Hotspur	Away	One	1-3
31st Oct 1990	Manchester United	Away	One	1-3
10th Nov 1998	Tottenham Hotspur	Home	Prem	1-3
6th Oct 1970	Swindon Town	Away	Two	0-2
18th Feb 1998	Middlesbrough	Away	One	0-2
19th Dec 2007	Chelsea	Away	Prem	0-2

Back in 2000 – Liverpool, 8-0 winners at Stoke City

FA CHARITY SHIELD/FA COMMUNITY SHIELD

Date	Round	Venue	Opponents	Opponent Division	Score	Scorers	Att
1922							
10th May		Old Trafford	Huddersfield Town	1	0-1		20,000
1964							
15th Aug		Anfield	West Ham United	1	2-2	Wallace, Byrne	38,858
1965							
14th Aug		Old Trafford	Manchester United	1	2-2	Stevenson, Yeats	48,502
1966							
13th Aug		Goodison Park	Everton	1	1-0	Hunt	63,329
1971							
7th Aug		Filbert Street	Leicester City	1	0-1		25,014
1974							
10th Aug		Wembley	Leeds United (Liverpool won 6-5 on penalties)	1	1-1	Boersma	67,000
1976							
14th Aug		Wembley	Southampton	2	1-0	Toshack	76,500
1977							
13th Aug		Wembley	Manchester United	1	0-0		82,000
1979							
11th Aug		Wembley	Arsenal	1	3-1	McDermott 2, Dalglish	92,000
1980							
9th Aug		Wembley	West Ham United	2	1-0	McDermott	90,000
1982							
21st Aug		Wembley	Tottenham Hotspur	1	1-0	Rush	82,500
1983							
20th Aug		Wembley	Manchester United	1	0-2		92,000
1984							
18th Aug		Wembley	Everton	1	0-1		100,000
1986							
16th Aug		Wembley	Everton	1	1-1	Rush	88,231
1988							
20th Aug		Wembley	Wimbledon	1	2-1	Aldridge 2	54,887
1989							
12th Aug		Wembley	Arsenal	1	1-0	Beardsley	63,149
1990							
18th Aug		Wembley	Manchester United	1	1-1	Barnes	66,558
1992							
8th Aug		Wembley	Leeds United	Prem	3-4	Rush, Saunders, Strachan o.g.	61,291
2001							
12th Aug		Cardiff	Manchester United	Prem	2-1	McAllister (pen), Owen	70,227
2002							
11th Aug		Cardiff	Arsenal	Prem	0-1		67,337
2006							
13th Aug		Cardiff	Chelsea	Prem	2-1	Riise, Crouch	56,275

SCREEN SPORT SUPER CUP

Created by the Football League as a replacement following the banning of English clubs from European club competition in 1985, the Screen Sport Super Cup lasted only one season. Every team invited to participate would have qualified for one of the three European competitions then still available to compete in in the 1985/86 season. The Reds came through a group phase and a two-legged semi-final. They would ease to the trophy courtesy of a 7-2 aggregate success over Everton, although the subsequent attendance of those two matches – and the fact that the games were played the following season – may give some indication as to why the tournament was shortlived. The Full Members Cup was similarly formed in 1985, to fill the financial and competitive void for clubs left by the absence of European competition, although Liverpool chose not to participate in the tournament, which lasted until 1992.

Date	Round	Venue	Opponents	Opponent Division	Score	Scorers	Att
1985/86							
			Group stage				
17th Sept	Group	(h)	Southampton	1	2-1	Molby, Dalglish	16,189
22nd Oct	Group	(a)	Southampton	1	1-1	Walsh	10,503
3rd Dec	Group	(h)	Tottenham Hotspur	1	2-0	MacDonald, Walsh	14,855
14th Jan	Group	(a)	Tottenham Hotspur	1	3-0	Rush 2, Lawrenson	10,078
5th Feb	SF Leg 1	(a)	Norwich City	1	1-1	Dalglish	15,330
6th May	SF Leg 2	(h)	Norwich City	1	3-1	MacDonald, Molby (pen), Johnston	26,696
1986/87							
16th Sept	F Leg 1	(h)	Everton	1	3-1	Rush 2, McMahon	20,660
30th Sept	F Leg 2	(a)	Everton	1	4-1	Rush 3, Nicol	26,068

MERCANTILE CREDIT CENTENARY TROPHY

As part of the Football League's centenary celebrations in 1988, Liverpool competed in two tournaments. A Football League Centenary Tournament in April 1988 saw 16 teams from the top four divisions compete in a straight knock-out format, with the games consisting of 40 minutes. The Reds would fall at the first hurdle, losing on penalties to Newcastle after a 0-0 draw.
In the 1988/89 season, the top eight teams from the First Division in the previous campaign were invited to compete in an early-season competition. Played on a straight knock-out basis, the Reds would win through to the last four before losing to eventual winners Arsenal, who beat Manchester United 2-1 at Villa Park. Incidentally, the attendance for the semi-final at Highbury was the highest for the tournament.

Date	Round	Venue	Opponents	Opponent Division	Score	Scorers	Att
1988/89							
29th Aug	QF	(h)	Nottingham Forest	1	4-1	Venison, Molby (pen), Houghton, Barnes	20,141
20th Sept	SF	(a)	Arsenal	1	1-2	Staunton	29,135

THE RECORDS

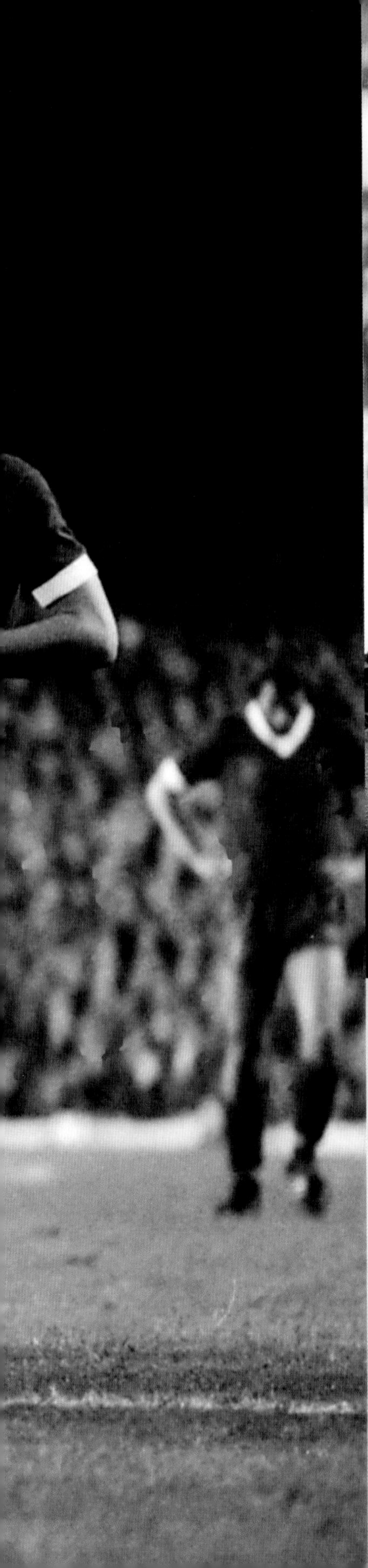

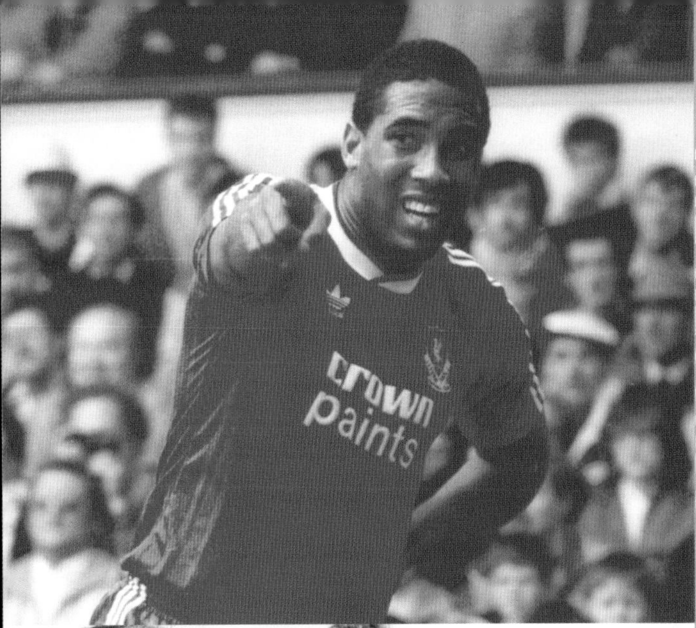

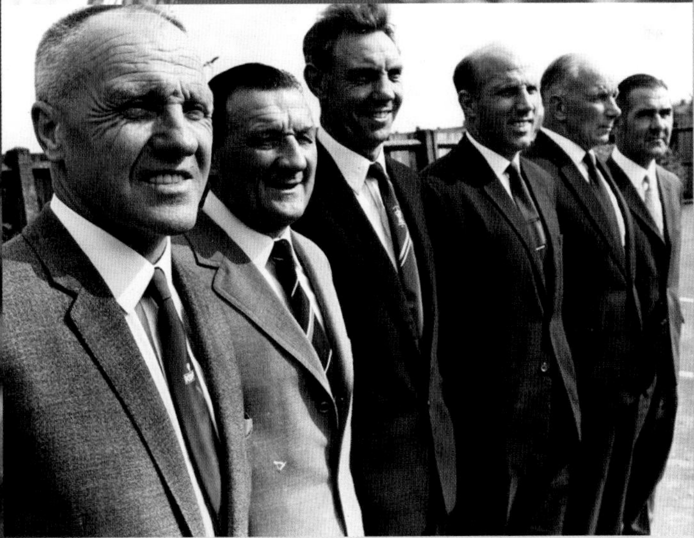

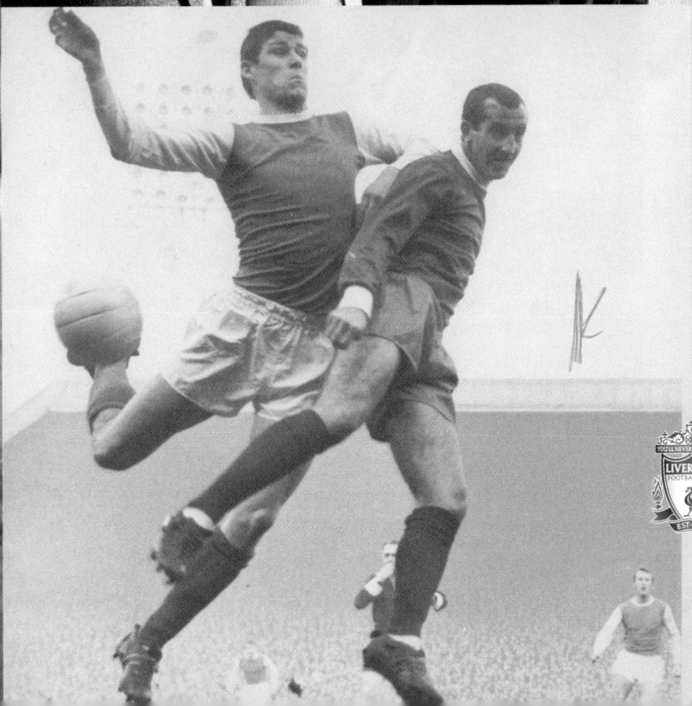

THE COMPLETE FIRST-TEAM RECORD

The following is a definitive statistical breakdown of every competitive first-team game the club have ever played. Amongst the landmarks reached during the 2008/09 season included 400 FA Cup matches, 200 League Cup games, 300 European Cup/Champions League goals, 300 fixtures in European competition and 2500 wins.

LIVERPOOL FOOTBALL CLUB 1892-2009

COMPETITION	PLAYED	WON	DRAWN	LOST	FOR	AGAINST
FA Premier League	658	331	168	159	1069	634
First Division	3096	1407	769	920	5094	3956
FA Premier League/First Division	**3754**	**1738**	**937**	**1079**	**6163**	**4590**
Second Division	428	243	82	103	977	571
All League Games	**4182**	**1981**	**1019**	**1182**	**7140**	**5161**
Test Matches	6	3	1	2	8	3
FA Cup	402	214	88	100	669	379
League Cup	202	120	42	40	411	193
European Cup/UEFA Champions League	169	99	36	34	312	137
European Cup Winners' Cup	29	16	5	8	57	29
Inter Cities Fairs Cup/UEFA Cup	95	52	23	20	162	70
European Super Cup/UEFA Super Cup	7	4	1	2	16	10
All European Competitions	**300**	**171**	**65**	**64**	**547**	**246**
World Club Championships	4	1	0	3	3	5
FA Charity/Community Shield	21	10	5	6	24	21
Screen Sport Super Cup	8	6	2	0	19	6
Football League Centenary Tournament	2	1	0	1	5	3
TOTAL	**5127**	**2507**	**1222**	**1398**	**8826**	**6017**

Peter Beardsley goes close during the successful 1987/88 campaign

CLUB BESTS

The 2008/09 campaign saw three impressive statistics added to the club roster – only two league defeats, a joint second best in the LFC annals; an unbeaten home campaign, the 10th in the club's history – and first for 21 season; and a joint-record number of away wins. The following tables show how those new marks compare to the existing records.

FEWEST LEAGUE DEFEATS IN A SEASON

SEASON	DEFEATS	GAMES	DIVISION	FINAL POSITION
1893/94	0	28	2	1st
1987/88	2	40	1	1st
2008/09	2	38	Prem	2nd
1904/05	3	34	2	1st
1978/79	4	42	1	1st
2007/08	4	38	Prem	4th
1975/76	5	42	1	1st
1989/90	5	38	1	1st

UNBEATEN HOME LEAGUE CAMPAIGNS

SEASON	GAMES	WINS	DRAWS
1893/94	14	14	0
1895/96	15	14	1
1904/05	17	14	3
1961/62	21	18	3
1970/71	21	11	10
1976/77	21	18	3
1978/79	21	19	2
1979/80	21	15	6
1987/88	20	15	5
2008/09	19	12	7

Kevin Keegan – Part of the 76/77 effort

MOST AWAY WINS IN A LEAGUE SEASON

SEASON	WINS	PLAYED	GOAL DIF.
1904/05	13	17	+20
2008/09	13	19	+22
2001/02	12	19	+18
1981/82	12	21	+23
1946/47	12	21	+14
1988/89	11	19	+15
1987/88	11	20	+23
1978/79	11	21	+22

John Aldridge – Prolific in 88/89

PLAYER RECORDS – APPEARANCES

Jamie Carragher could move into the top eight of the Liverpool all-time appearance holder table should be maintain the consistency which has been the hallmark of his career with the club. Steven Gerrard should make it lucky 13 – the number of players who will have played 500 games for the club – in the 2009/10 season.

TOTAL APPEARANCES - ALL COMPETITIONS

	PLAYER	FIRST-TEAM CAREER	GAMES
1	Ian Callaghan	1960-1978	857
2	Ray Clemence	1968-1981	665
=	Emlyn Hughes	1967-1979	665
4	Ian Rush	1980-1987 & 1988-1996	660
5	Phil Neal	1974-1985	650
6	Tommy Smith	1963-1978	638
7	Bruce Grobbelaar	1981-1994	628
8	Alan Hansen	1977-1990	620
9	Jamie Carragher	1997-	577
10	Chris Lawler	1963-1975	549
11	Billy Liddell	1946-1960	534
12	Kenny Dalglish	1977-1990	515
13	Ronnie Whelan	1981-1994	493
14	Roger Hunt	1959-1969	492
15	Steven Gerrard	1998-	483
16	Phil Thompson	1972-1983	477
17	Steve Heighway	1970-1981	475
18	Steve Nicol	1982-1994	468
=	Elisha Scott	1913-1934	468
20	Sami Hyypia	1999-2009	464
21	Ron Yeats	1961-1971	454
22	Donald MacKinlay	1910-1928	434
23	Ian St John	1961-1971	425
24	Peter Thompson	1963-1972	416
25	Arthur Goddard	1902-1914	414

PLAYER RECORDS – APPEARANCES

MOST CONSECUTIVE APPEARANCES - ALL COMPETITIONS

	PLAYER	TIME SPAN	GAMES
1	Phil Neal	Oct 1976-Sept 1983	417
2	Ray Clemence	Sept 1972-Mar 1978	336
3	Bruce Grobbelaar	Aug 1981-Aug 1986	317
4	Chris Lawler	Oct 1965-Apr 1971	316
5	David James	Feb 1994-Feb 1998	213
6	Alan Kennedy	Jan 1982-Mar 1985	205
7	Ian Callaghan	Aug 1971-Sept 1974	185
8	Kenny Dalglish	Aug 1977-Aug 1980	180
9	Emlyn Hughes	Oct 1972-Oct 1975	177
10	Peter Thompson	Sept 1965-Apr 1968	153

PLAYER RECORDS – GOALS

Nine more goals will see Steven Gerrard enter the hallowed top 10 Liverpool goalscorers of all time – and first predominantly midfield player to achieve this feat.

	PLAYER	FIRST-TEAM CAREER	GOALS
	TOTAL GOALS – ALL COMPETITIONS		
1	Ian Rush	1980-1987 & 1988-1996	346
2	Roger Hunt	1959-1969	286
3	Gordon Hodgson	1926-1935	241
4	Billy Liddell	1946-1960	228
5	Robbie Fowler	1993-2001 & 2006-2007	183
6	Kenny Dalglish	1977-1990	172
7	Michael Owen	1997-2004	158
8	Harry Chambers	1919-1928	151
9	Jack Parkinson	1903-1914	129
10	Sam Raybould	1900-1907	128
11	Dick Forshaw	1919-1927	124
12	Steven Gerrard	1998-	120
13	Ian St John	1961-1971	118
14	Jack Balmer	1935-1952	110
15	John Barnes	1987-1997	108
16	Kevin Keegan	1971-1977	100
17	John Toshack	1970-1977	96
18	Albert Stubbins	1946-1953	83
19	Terry McDermott	1974-1982	81
=	Jack Cox	1898-1909	81
21	Berry Nieuwenhuys	1933-1947	79
=	Jimmy Melia	1955-1964	79
23	David Johnson	1976-1982	78
24	Arthur Goddard	1902-1914	77
25	Steve Heighway	1970-1981	76

Roger Hunt (left) and Ian Rush – Top marksmen for the Reds

GOALSCORERS

MOST GOALS IN A SEASON – ALL COMPS

NAME	SEASON	GAMES	GOALS
Ian Rush	1983/84	65	47
Roger Hunt	1961/62	46	42
Ian Rush	1986/87	57	40
Roger Hunt	1964/65	58	37
Gordon Hodgson	1930/31	41	36
Robbie Fowler	1995/96	53	36
John Evans	1954/55	42	33
Billy Liddell	1955/56	44	33
Roger Hunt	1963/64	46	33
Roger Hunt	1965/66	46	33
Fernando Torres	2007/08	46	33
Ian Rush	1985/86	56	33
Sam Raybould	1902/03	34	32
Gordon Hodgson	1928/29	41	32
Billy Liddell	1954/55	44	31
Robbie Fowler	1996/97	44	31
John Aldridge	1988/89	47	31
Ian Rush	1982/83	51	31
Robbie Fowler	1994/95	57	31
Kenny Dalglish	1977/78	62	31
Jack Parkinson	1909/10	32	30
Ian Rush	1981/82	49	30
Roger Hunt	1967/68	57	30

MOST GOALS IN A LEAGUE SEASON

NAME	SEASON	DIV	GA	GLS
Roger Hunt	1961/62	2	41	41
Gordon Hodgson	1930/31	1	40	36
Ian Rush	1983/84	1	41	32
Sam Raybould	1902/03	1	33	31
Roger Hunt	1963/64	1	41	31
Jack Parkinson	1909/10	1	31	30
Gordon Hodgson	1928/29	1	38	30
Billy Liddell	1954/55	2	40	30
Ian Rush	1986/87	1	42	30
Roger Hunt	1965/66	1	37	29
John Evans	1954/55	2	38	29
Robbie Fowler	1995/96	Prem	38	28
Dick Forshaw	1925/26	1	32	27
Gordon Hodgson	1934/35	1	34	27
Billy Liddell	1955/56	2	39	27
John Aldridge	1987/88	1	36	26
Gordon Hodgson	1931/32	1	39	26
George Allan	1895/96	2	20	25
Roger Hunt	1964/65	1	40	25
Roger Hunt	1967/68	1	40	25
Robbie Fowler	1994/95	Prem	42	25

Kenny Dalglish (left) and Ian Rush – 30+ in a season

LIVERPOOL HAT-TRICK MEN

Steven Gerrard joined club legends in the form of Dalglish, Stubbins and team-mate Torres on three hat-tricks for the club following his treble against Aston Villa in March 2009. It was the 128th league hat-trick at Anfield scored by a Liverpool player, with the all-time list noted as follows:

FULL RECORD OF LIVERPOOL HAT-TRICKS

17	Gordon Hodgson
16	Ian Rush
12	Roger Hunt
10	Robbie Fowler, Michael Owen
8	Dick Forshaw, Jack Parkinson
6	Sam Raybould
5	Harry Chambers, Billy Liddell
4	George Allan, Joe Hewitt
3	John Aldridge, Jack Balmer, Kenny Dalglish, Steven Gerrard, Tony Hateley, Fred Howe, Albert Stubbins, Fernando Torres, John Toshack, John Wark
2	John Barnes, Harold Barton, Frank Becton, Yossi Benayoun, Jimmy Case, William Devlin, Cyril Done, John Evans, Dick Johnson, Terry McDermott, Steve McMahon, Malcolm McVean, Fred Pagnam, Henry Race, Robert Robinson, Jimmy Ross, Antonio Rowley, Ian St John, Dean Saunders, Graeme Souness, Paul Walsh
1	Alan Arnell, Alf Arrowsmith, Milan Baros, Peter Beardsley, Patrik Berger, Louis Bimpson, Phil Boersma, Ian Callaghan, Stan Collymore, Peter Crouch, Alun Evans, David Fairclough, Gary Gillespie, Bobby Graham, Jimmy Harrower, Emile Heskey, Dave Hickson, 'Sailor' Hunter, David Johnson, Kevin Keegan, Kevin Lewis, Andy McGuigan, William McPherson, Arthur Metcalfe, Jan Molby, Steve Nicol, Ronald Orr, Tom Reid, Michael Robinson, Ronny Rosenthal, Danny Shone, Jimmy Smith, Steve Staunton, James Stewart, James Stott, John Walker, Jimmy Walsh, Mark Walters, Johnny Wheeler, Ronnie Whelan, Jack Whitham, Dave Wright

85 players have scored a total of 219 hat-tricks

WHERE HAT-TRICKS HAVE BEEN SCORED

	AT ANFIELD	AWAY	TOTAL
League	128	43	171
FA Cup	12	5	17
League Cup	8	6	14
Europe	14	2	16
Other Games	0	1	1
TOTAL	**162**	**57**	**219**

50-UP

Fernando Torres impressive start to his Liverpool career sees him lying joint second in terms of the number of goals scored in his first 50 appearances, and the sixth quickest to reach 50 goals.

MOST GOALS SCORED IN FIRST 50 GAMES

PLAYER	GOALS	YEAR OF 50TH GAME
George Allan	41	1897
Antonio Rowley	34	1957
Fernando Torres	34	2008
John Evans	33	1955
Jack Parkinson	33	1906
Jim Smith	32	1930
Robert Robinson	32	1905
Albert Stubbins	32	1947
Robbie Fowler	32	1994
Dave Hickson	31	1960

OTHER RECENT COMPARISONS

PLAYER	GOALS	YEAR
John Aldridge	29	1988
Michael Owen	28	1998
Roger Hunt	28	1960
Ian Rush	27	1982
Kenny Dalglish	23	1978

Fernando Torres – Joint second

QUICKEST TO ACHIEVE 50 GOALS IN FEWEST GAMES FOR LIVERPOOL (ALL COMPETITIONS)

PLAYER	GAMES	PLAYER	GAMES
Albert Stubbins	77	Jack Balmer	144
Jack Parkinson	78	Peter Beardsley	144
Roger Hunt	79	Willie Fagan	156
George Allan	81	Berry Niewenhuys	164
Sam Raybould	81	Kevin Keegan	165
Fernando Torres	84	Alf Hanson	171
Ian Rush	87	Billy Liddell	174
John Evans	90	Emile Heskey	185
John Aldridge	92	Ronnie Whelan	212
Michael Owen	93	Jan Molby	219
Gordon Hodgson	94	Jack Cox	223
Robbie Fowler	94	Terry McDermott	235
Harry Chambers	96	Ray Kennedy	266
Kenny Dalglish	102	Steve McMahon	275
Joe Hewitt	111	Steve Heighway	279
Ian St John	111	Arthur Goddard	282
Robert Robinson	120	Steve McManaman	291
David Johnson	121	Alan A'Court	296
John Barnes	126	Steven Gerrard	297
Dick Forshaw	128	Graeme Souness	327
Harry Bradshaw	132	Peter Thompson	344
Tom Miller	132	Chris Lawler	430
Jimmy Melia	134	Ian Callaghan	442
David Fairclough	138	Phil Neal	493
John Toshack	143		

SUPER SUBS

LIVERPOOL'S MOST PROLIFIC GOALSCORING SUBSTITUTES						
	LEAGUE	FA CUP	LGE CUP	EUROPE	OTHERS	TOTAL
David Fairclough	7	2	7	2	0	18
Ryan Babel	4	0	0	5	0	9
Djibril Cisse	2	1	0	4	0	7
Michael Owen	4	0	1	1	0	6
Ian Rush	2	3	0	1	0	6
Vladimir Smicer	4	0	1	1	0	6
Robbie Fowler	3	1	0	1	0	5
Emile Heskey	2	3	0	0	0	5
David Johnson	3	0	1	1	0	5
Milan Baros	1	0	2	1	0	4
Phil Boersma	0	0	2	2	0	4
Jimmy Case	2	1	0	1	0	4
Peter Crouch	3	0	0	1	0	4
Luis Garcia	4	0	0	0	0	4
Craig Johnston	2	1	1	0	0	4
Jari Litmanen	3	0	0	1	0	4
Danny Murphy	4	0	0	0	0	4
Ronny Rosenthal	4	0	0	0	0	4
Florent Sinama-Pongolle	1	2	0	1	0	4
2008/09 squad members						
Xabi Alonso	3	0	0	0	0	3
Steven Gerrard	0	0	0	3	0	3
Fernando Torres	2	1	0	0	0	3
Yossi Benayoun	2	0	0	0	0	2
Andrea Dossena	1	0	0	1	0	2
Dirk Kuyt	2	0	0	0	0	2
Andriy Voronin	2	0	0	0	0	2
Lucas Leiva	1	0	0	0	0	1
David Ngog	1	0	0	0	0	1

LIVERPOOL SUBSTITUTES WHO HAVE SCORED IN THE SAME GAME			
PLAYERS	YEAR	OPPOSITION	COMPETITION	RESULT
---	---	---	---	---
Alun Evans & Roger Hunt	1969	Vitoria Setubal	Fairs Cup	3-2
Ian Rush & Mark Lawrenson	1981	Oulu Palloseura	European Cup	7-0
Michael Owen & Nick Barmby	2000	Fulham	League Cup	3-0
Nick Barmby & Emile Heskey	2001	Leeds United	FA Cup	2-0
Vladimir Smicer & Nicolas Anelka	2002	Ipswich Town	League	5-0
Danny Murphy & Florent S-Pongolle	2003	Leeds United	League	3-1
Xabi Alonso & Igor Biscan	2004	Fulham	League	4-2
Florent S-Pongolle & Neil Mellor	2004	Olympiakos	European Cup	3-1
Steven Gerrard & Djibril Cisse	2005	FBK Kaunas	European Cup	2-0
Luis Garcia & Djibril Cisse	2005	Birmingham City	League	2-2
Peter Crouch & Stephen Warnock	2006	Fulham	League	5-1
Fernando Morientes & Djibril Cisse	2006	Birmingham City	FA Cup	7-0
Peter Crouch & Djibril Cisse	2006	Portsmouth	League	3-1
Xabi Alonso & Harry Kewell	2007	Charlton Athletic	League	2-2
Dirk Kuyt & Fernando Torres	2009	Portsmouth	League	3-2

PENALTY KINGS

Steven Gerrard moved into sixth place courtesy of the successful conversation of seven spot-kicks during the 2008/09 season – still some way short of the club record, held by Jan Molby – still the only Liverpool player to score a hat-trick of penalties for the club.
Xabi Alonso also netted two penalties in 08/09 to take his Liverpool career tally to three.

COMPLETE RECORD – SCORERS IN SHOOT-OUTS NOT INCLUDED	
PLAYER	**PENALTIES**
Jan Molby	42
Phil Neal	38
Billy Liddell	34
Tommy Smith	22
Robbie Fowler	20
Steven Gerrard	18
John Aldridge	17
Terry McDermott	16
Gordon Hodgson	15
Michael Owen	13
Kevin Keegan	11
John Barnes	10
Willie Fagan	9
Alec Lindsay	8
Ronnie Moran	=
Danny Murphy	=
Sam Raybould	=
Willie Stevenson	=
Arthur Goddard	7
Jackie Sheldon	=
Robert Done	6
Jack Parkinson	=
Mark Walters	=
Gary McAllister	5
Jack Balmer	4
Peter Beardsley	=
Tom Chorlton	=
Donald MacKinlay	=
Alec Raisbeck	=
Alf West	=
Xabi Alonso	3
Frank Becton	=
Djibril Cisse	=
Dick Edmed	=
Kevin Lewis	=
Jari Litmanen	=
Tommy Lucas	=
Mike Marsh	=
Jamie Redknapp	=
Tommy Robertson	=
Ian Rush	=
Graeme Souness	=
John Wark	=
Milan Baros	2

Jan Molby – Prolific from 12 yards

PLAYER	PENALTIES
Patrik Berger	2
Harry Chambers	=
Julian Dicks	=
John Evans	=
Dick Forshaw	=
Alf Hanson	=
Dirk Kuyt	=
Ray Lambert	=
Andrew McCowie	=
Duncan McLean	=
Jimmy Melia	=
Jimmy Ross	=
George Allan	1
Lance Carr	=
Robert Crawford	=
El-Hadji Diouf	=
George Fleming	=
Gary Gillespie	=
Gordon Gunson	=
Brian Hall	=
Jimmy Harrower	=
Roger Hunt	=
Harry Kewell	=
Fred Morris	=
Ronald Orr	=
Robert Robinson	=
Florent Sinama-Pongolle	=
Vladimir Smicer	=
Geoff Strong	=
Albert Stubbins	=
Geoff Twentyman	=

OLDEST/YOUNGEST LIVERPOOL PLAYERS

One club record likely to exist for many years to come is that of Ted Doig's, the oldest player to represent the club in a first-team game. Kenny Dalglish's farewell appearance in a red shirt, when he was player/manager, remains the post-war oldest with the longest-serving current first-teamer, Jamie Carragher, needing to play for another eight years before beating that mark.

Carragher retains a presence as one of the youngest goalscorers ever for the club, although he is unlikely to be displaced from the top 10 in 2009/10.

OLDEST PLAYER

PLAYER	FINAL GAME	AGE
Ted Doig	11th April 1908	41 years & 165 days

OLDEST PLAYER (POST-WAR)

PLAYER	FINAL GAME	AGE
Kenny Dalglish	1st May 1990	39 years & 58 days
Billy Liddell	31st August 1960	38 years & 234 days
Gary McAllister	11th May 2002	37 years & 137 days
Paul Jones	17th January 2004	36 years & 274 days
Bruce Grobbelaar	19th February 1994	36 years & 136 days
Phil Taylor	25th December 1953	36 years & 98 days
Jack Balmer	16th February 1952	36 years & 10 days
Ian Callaghan	4th February 1978	35 years & 300 days
Sami Hyypia	24th May 2009	35 years & 229 days
Berry Nieuwenhuys	1st February 1947	35 years & 88 days
Bob Paisley	13th March 1954	35 years & 49 days

YOUNGEST PLAYER (POST-WAR)

PLAYER	DEBUT	AGE
Max Thompson	8th May 1974	17 years & 128 days
Michael Owen	6th May 1997	17 years & 144 days
Johnny Morrissey	23rd September 1957	17 years & 158 days
Reginald Blore	17th October 1959	17 years & 213 days
Phil Charnock	16th September 1992	17 years & 215 days

YOUNGEST-EVER GOALSCORERS FOR LIVERPOOL

PLAYER	DEBUT	AGE	OPPONENTS
Michael Owen	6th May 1997	17 years & 143 days	Wimbledon
Jimmy Melia	17th December 1955	18 years & 46 days	Nottingham Forest
Jamie Redknapp	7th December 1991	18 years & 165 days	Southampton
Alan A'Court	14th March 1953	18 years & 165 days	Sunderland
Robbie Fowler	22nd September 1993	18 years & 166 days	Fulham
John McLaughlin	22nd August 1970	18 years & 178 days	Huddersfield Town
Phil Taylor	28th March 1936	18 years & 192 days	Derby County
Brian Jackson	10th November 1951	18 years & 223 days	Bolton Wanderers
Gordon Wallace	8th May 1963	18 years & 329 days	Birmingham City
Jamie Carragher	18th January 1997	18 years & 356 days	Aston Villa

LONG-SERVING

Sami Hyypia and Steven Gerrard joined the 10-season club during 2008/09, marking the fact that they had both scored at least one goal in each of the last ten campaigns for the club. The Finn will remain on 10 seasons after ending his Anfield career during the summer of 2009, although Gerrard could go on to equal Ronnie Whelan's 14-season mark should he net in each of the next four seasons – the length of contract he signed in July 2009.

Elisha Scott's record as the club's longest-serving player should not be troubled anytime soon, the goalkeeper having made his first-team debut on New Year's Day 1913 (a career that would last until February 1934). Jamie Carragher is the current longest-server, having made his bow in January '97. In terms of most games played for the club without scoring, Ephraim Longworth remains way ahead, based on outfield players only. In in terms of the current squad at the start of the 2009/10 season, Martin Skrtel has made the most appearances for the Reds without scoring – 50 games.

PLAYERS TO SCORE FOR LIVERPOOL IN AT LEAST TEN SUCCESSIVE SEASONS

PLAYER	NO. OF SEASONS	SEASONS
Billy Liddell	15	1946-1960
Ronnie Whelan	14	1981-1994
Jack Cox	12	1898-1909
Arthur Goddard	12	1902-1913
Emlyn Hughes	12	1968-1979
Gordon Hodgson	11	1926-1936
Alan A'Court	11	1953-1963
Roger Hunt	11	1960-1970
Donald MacKinlay	11	1913-1927
Phil Neal	11	1976-1986
Jack Parkinson	11	1904-1914
Tommy Smith	11	1965-1975
Jack Balmer	10	1936-1951
John Barnes	10	1988-1997
Kenny Dalglish	10	1978-1987
Chris Lawler	10	1965-1974
Ian St John	10	1962-1971
Steven Gerrard	10	2000-2009
Sami Hyypia	10	2000-2009

Sami Hyypia – 10-season wonder

LONGEST-SERVING LIVERPOOL PLAYERS

PLAYER	LFC CAREER	TIME SPAN
Elisha Scott	1913-1934	21 yrs, 51 days
Donald MacKinlay	1910-1928	18 yrs, 134 days
Ian Callaghan	1960-1978	17 yrs, 347 days
Phil Taylor	1936-1954	17 yrs, 287 days
Ephraim Longworth	1910-1928	17 yrs, 215 days
Jack Balmer	1935-1952	16 yrs, 155 days
Tommy Smith	1963-1978	14 yrs, 352 days
Billy Liddell	1946-1960	14 yrs, 239 days
Ian Rush	1980-1987	14 yrs, 40 days
	1988-1996	
Billy Dunlop	1895-1909	14 yrs, 23 days

OUTFIELD PLAYERS WHO HAVE PLAYED MOST GAMES WITHOUT EVER SCORING

PLAYER	LFC CAREER	NUMBER OF GAMES
Ephraim Longworth	1910-1928	371
Rob Jones	1991-1998	243
Stephane Henchoz	1999-2004	205
Tom Cooper	1934-1939	160
Jim Harley	1935-1948	131
Willie Steel	1931-1934	128
Bob Pursell	1911-1919	112
Barry Wilkinson	1953-1959	79
Fred Rogers	1934-1939	75
Ernie Blenkinsop	1934-1937	71
Thomas Fairfoul	1913-1915	71

PLAYER HONOURS

The 2008/09 performances of Steven Gerrard saw the Liverpool captain become the 10th different Liverpool player to win the prestigious Football Writers' Football of the Year award. Having become the first Reds player to collect the honour for 19 years, unusually he is the only Liverpool winner to scoop the accolade in a season when the club have not collected any silverware.

FOOTBALL WRITERS' FOOTBALLER OF THE YEAR

YEAR	PLAYER	HONOURS WON (THAT SEASON)
1974	Ian Callaghan	FA Cup
1976	Kevin Keegan	First Division, UEFA Cup
1977	Emlyn Hughes	First Division, European Cup, FA Charity Shield
1979	Kenny Dalglish	First Division
1980	Terry McDermott	First Division, FA Charity Shield
1983	Kenny Dalglish	First Division, League Cup, FA Charity Shield
1984	Ian Rush	First Division, League Cup, European Cup
1988	John Barnes	First Division
1989	Steve Nicol	FA Cup, FA Charity Shield
1990	John Barnes	First Division, FA Charity Shield
2009	Steven Gerrard	-

PFA PLAYER OF THE YEAR

1980	Terry McDermott	First Division, FA Charity Shield
1983	Kenny Dalglish	First Division, League Cup, FA Charity Shield
1984	Ian Rush	First Division, League Cup, European Cup
1988	John Barnes	First Division
2006	Steven Gerrard	FA Cup, European Super Cup

PFA YOUNG PLAYER OF THE YEAR

1983	Ian Rush	First Division, League Cup, FA Charity Shield
1995	Robbie Fowler	League Cup
1996	Robbie Fowler	-
1998	Michael Owen	-
2001	Steven Gerrard	FA Cup, League Cup, UEFA Cup

EUROPEAN FOOTBALLER OF THE YEAR

2001	Michael Owen	FA Cup, League Cup, UEFA Cup

MANAGER OF THE YEAR

1973	Bill Shankly	First Division, UEFA Cup
1976	Bob Paisley	First Division, UEFA Cup
1977	Bob Paisley	First Division, European Cup, European Super Cup, FA Charity Shield
1979	Bob Paisley	First Division
1980	Bob Paisley	First Division, FA Charity Shield
1982	Bob Paisley	First Division, League Cup
1983	Bob Paisley	First Division, League Cup, FA Charity Shield
1984	Joe Fagan	First Division, League Cup, European Cup
1986	Kenny Dalglish	First Division, FA Cup
1988	Kenny Dalglish	First Division
1990	Kenny Dalglish	First Division, FA Charity Shield

CLEAN SHEETS – TEAM

Defensive solidity has proved the hallmark of Rafael Benitez's spell at the helm. Apart from his first season in charge, his teams from each subsequent season have found their way onto the following lists (minus 2007/08 in the % clean sheet table). Regardless, it could still be some years before the 1978/79 vintage is bettered.

MOST CLEAN SHEETS IN A SEASON (ALL COMPS)

SEASON	CLEAN SHEETS	GAMES PLAYED
1978/79	34	54
1970/71	34	62
1983/84	34	67
2005/06	33	62
1977/78	32	62
1981/82	31	62
1973/74	30	61
1975/76	29	59
1984/85	29	64
1971/72	28	53
2006/07	28	58
2001/02	28	59
2000/01	28	63
1987/88	27	50
1979/80	27	60
1982/83	27	60
1976/77	27	62
1995/96	26	53
2008/09	26	55
1972/73	26	66
1968/69	25	51
1994/95	25	57
2007/08	25	59
1974/75	24	53
1986/87	24	57
1980/81	24	63
1985/86	24	63

HIGHEST % OF CLEAN SHEETS IN SEASON (ALL COMPS)

SEASON	%	CLEAN SHEETS	GAMES PLAYED
1978/79	62.96	34	54
1970/71	54.84	34	62
1987/88	54.00	27	50
2005/06	53.23	33	62
1971/72	52.83	28	53
1977/78	51.61	32	62
1983/84	50.75	34	67
1893/94	50.00	16	32
1922/23	50.00	23	46
1981/82	50.00	31	62
1973/74	49.18	30	61
1975/76	49.15	29	59
1995/96	49.06	26	53
1968/69	49.02	25	51
2006/07	48.28	28	58
2001/02	47.46	28	59
2008/09	47.27	26	55
1984/85	45.31	29	64
1974/75	45.28	24	53
1898/99	45.00	18	40
1979/80	45.00	27	60
1982/83	45.00	27	60

MOST CLEAN SHEETS IN LEAGUE SEASON

SEASON	CLEAN SHEETS	GAMES
1978/79	28	42
1975/76	23	42
1977/78	23	42
1970/71	22	42
1971/72	22	42
2005/06	22	38
1922/23	21	42
1968/69	21	42
1987/88	21	40
1981/82	20	42
1983/84	20	42
2006/07	20	38
2008/09	20	38

Phil Neal – Defensive rock in 78/79

CLEAN SHEETS – GOALKEEPERS

Pepe Reina's impressive displays in the Liverpool goal compare impressively with previous incumbents in the keeper's jersey. The following tables highlight his prowess in terms of clean sheets for the club, having reached the 200-game landmark during 2008/09. He created a new landmark in terms of clean sheets achieved, while also conceding the least amount of goals during the same period.

His career statistics relate favourably with other Liverpool stoppers, and he has already kept more clean sheets than David James during his entire career with the club – having played nearly 70 games fewer. Ray Clemence retains the accolade of greatest goalkeeper statistically, although at the current shut-out rate, Reina would go close to Clem's mark of 323 clean sheets in 665 games. The Spanish goalkeeper does top the list of players who have not conceded in a game though, having taken the fewest games to reach 100 clean sheets. Reina overcame Clemence's previous best by three matches.

Please note that a goalkeeper has to play the full 90 minuts for the clean sheet to be awarded. However, if injured, substituted or sent off having conceded in that game, the appearance counts.

CLEAN SHEETS ACHIEVED BY LIVERPOOL GOALKEEPERS IN FIRST 200 FULL GAMES

PLAYER	CLEAN SHEETS	GOALS CONCEDED
Pepe Reina	102	138
Ray Clemence	100	145
Bruce Grobbelaar	95	158
David James	78	187
Elisha Scott	74	203
Tommy Lawrence	65	229
Sam Hardy	54	283
Arthur Riley	35	394

Tommy Lawrence – 65 shut-outs

LIVERPOOL CAREER STATISTICS – AT END OF 2008/09 SEASON

PLAYER	GAMES PLAYED	CLEAN SHEETS	GOALS CONCEDED
Ray Clemence	665	323	488
Bruce Grobbelaar	628	266	532
Elisha Scott	468	137	647
Tommy Lawrence	390	133	404
Arthur Riley	338	69	608
David James	275	102	273
Sam Hardy	239	63	340
Pepe Reina	207	105	150

QUICKEST TO 100 CLEAN SHEETS IN ALL COMPETITIONS

PLAYER	GAMES
Pepe Reina	197
Ray Clemence	200
Bruce Grobbelaar	209
David James	261
Elisha Scott	272
Tommy Lawrence	311

Ray Clemence – 200 games

MANAGER LANDMARKS

Rafael Benitez's statistics continue to remain amongst the moss impressive amongst the great Liverpool managers. The following tables reflect his overall record in charge, his record after 250 games in charge, his record compared to the other men who have resided over at least 250 fixtures in the Anfield hot seat, and his 100 win landmark.

RAFAEL BENITEZ'S OVERALL LIVERPOOL RECORD

COMPETITION	P	W	D	L	F	A	POINTS
Premier League	190	108	46	36	310	148	370
FA Cup	15	9	2	4	36	18	–
League Cup	15	10	0	5	29	25	–
FA Community Shield	1	1	0	0	2	1	–
Champions League	70	41	15	14	118	53	–
European Super Cup	1	1	0	0	3	1	–
Club World C'ship	2	1	0	1	3	1	–
TOTAL	**294**	**171**	**63**	**60**	**501**	**247**	**–**

RAFAEL BENITEZ'S RECORD AFTER 250 GAMES IN CHARGE OF LIVERPOOL

COMPETITION	P	W	D	L	F	A	% WINS
Premier League	158	87	37	34	240	123	55.1
FA Cup	12	8	1	3	33	17	66.7
League Cup	14	10	0	4	27	21	71.4
European Competition	63	38	12	13	105	44	60.3
FA Community Shield	1	1	0	0	2	1	100.0
World Club Championship	2	1	0	1	3	1	50.0
TOTAL	**250**	**145**	**50**	**55**	**410**	**207**	**58.0**

MOST SUCCESSFUL LIVERPOOL BOSS AFTER 250 GAMES IN CHARGE

MANAGER	SEASON OF 250 GAMES	P	W	D	L	F	A	% W
Kenny Dalglish	1989/90	250	152	61	37	493	204	60.8
Rafael Benitez	2008/09	250	145	50	55	410	207	58.0
Bob Paisley	1978/79	250	140	62	48	419	192	56.0
Gerard Houllier	2002/03	250	134	57	59	424	239	53.6
Bill Shankly	1964/65	250	133	54	63	502	307	53.2
Tom Watson	1902/03	250	110	55	85	391	314	44.0
George Kay	1948/49	250	100	63	87	400	376	40.0
George Patterson	1933/34	250	94	58	98	462	486	37.6

FASTEST TO 100 LEAGUE WINS AS BOSS

MANAGER	NUMBER OF GAMES TAKEN
Kenny Dalglish	167
Bob Paisley	179
Rafael Benitez	181
Bill Shankly	184
Gerard Houllier	197
Tom Watson	227
George Kay	262
George Patterson	271

Rafael Benitez – Third fastest

NATIONALITIES

The 2009/10 season should see the club's first Greek first-team player in the form of defender Sotirios Kyrgiakos, while Italian new-boy Alberto Aquilani and Spanish prospect Daniel Ayala were others set to be added to the list of 93 overseas players who have represented the club in competitive first-team games.

OVERSEAS LIVERPOOL FIRST-TEAM PLAYERS

COUNTRY	NO. OF PLAYERS	PLAYERS
France	13	Jean-Michel Ferri, Pegguy Arphexad, Bernard Diomede, Gregory Vignal, Nicolas Anelka, Bruno Cheyrou, Patrice Luzi, Anthony Le Tallec, Florent Sinama-Pongolle, Djibril Cisse, Charles Itandje, Damien Plessis, David Ngog
Spain	11	Josemi, Luis Garcia, Xabi Alonso, Antonio Nunez, Fernando Morientes, Pepe Reina, Antonio Barragan, Miki Roque, Alvaro Arbeloa, Fernando Torres, Albert Riera
South Africa	10	Lance Carr, Hugh Gerhadi, Gordon Hodgson, Dirk Kemp, Berry Nieuwenhuys, Robert Priday, Arthur Riley, Doug Rudham, Charlie Thompson, Harman Van Den Berg
Holland	6	Erik Meijer, Sander Westerveld, Bolo Zenden, Jan Kromkamp, Dirk Kuyt, Ryan Babel
Norway	=	Stig Inge Bjornebye, Oyvind Leonhardsen, Bjorn Tore Kvarme, Vegard Heggem, Frode Kippe, John Arne Riise
Argentina	5	Mauricio Pellegrino, Gabriel Paletta, Javier Mascherano, Emiliano Insua, Sebastian Leto
Germany	=	Karlheinz Riedle, Dietmar Hamann, Markus Babbel, Christian Ziege, Sean Dundee
Brazil	3	Fabio Aurelio, Lucas Leiva, Diego Cavalieri
Denmark	=	Jan Molby, Torben Piechnik, Daniel Agger
Czech Republic	=	Patrik Berger, Vladimir Smicer, Milan Baros
Israel	=	Avi Cohen, Ronny Rosenthal, Yossi Benayoun
Finland	2	Sami Hyypia, Jari Litmanen
Italy	=	Daniele Padelli, Andrea Dossena
Mali	=	Djimi Traore, Mohamed Sissoko
Senegal	=	El-Hadji Diouf, Salif Diao
Switzerland	=	Stephane Henchoz, Philipp Degen
USA	=	Brad Friedel, Zak Whitbread
Australia	1	Harry Kewell
Cameroon	=	Rigobert Song
Chile	=	Mark Gonzalez
Croatia	=	Igor Biscan
Guinea	=	Titi Camara
Hungary	=	Istvan Kozma
Morocco	=	Nabil El Zhar
Poland	=	Jerzy Dudek
Portugal	=	Abel Xavier
Slovakia	=	Martin Skrtel
Sweden	=	Glenn Hysen
Ukraine	=	Andriy Voronin
Zimbabwe	=	Bruce Grobbelaar

INTERNATIONAL CAPS

LFC PLAYERS CAPPED FOR THEIR COUNTRIES - HOME NATIONS (END OF 2008/09 SEASON)

PLAYER	COUNTRY	CAPS	PLAYER	COUNTRY	CAPS
Steven Gerrard	England	74	George Lathom	Wales	=
Ian Rush	Wales	67	Alex Raisbeck	Scotland	=
Michael Owen	England	60	Dean Saunders	Wales	=
Emlyn Hughes	England	59	Cyril Sidlow	Wales	7
Ray Clemence	England	56	Alan A'Court	England	5
Kenny Dalglish	Scotland	55	Tom Bromilow	England	=
Ronnie Whelan	Republic of Ireland	51	David Johnson	England	=
Phil Neal	England	50	Ray Lambert	Wales	=
John Barnes	England	48	Ephraim Longworth	England	=
Phil Thompson	England	42	Richard Morris	Wales	=
Steve Staunton	Republic of Ireland	38	Edward Parry	Wales	=
Graeme Souness	Scotland	37	Michael Robinson	Republic of Ireland	=
Emile Heskey	England	35	Mark Wright	England	=
Peter Beardsley	England	34	Ian Callaghan	England	4
Jamie Carragher	England	=	Robbie Keane	Republic of Ireland	=
Ray Houghton	Republic of Ireland	=	Chris Lawler	England	=
Roger Hunt	England	=	Alec Lindsay	England	=
Steve Heighway	Republic of Ireland	33	Ken Campbell	Scotland	3
Steve Finnan	Republic of Ireland	28	Jack Cox	England	=
Kevin Keegan	England	=	Gordon Hodgson	England	=
Billy Liddell	Scotland	=	John Hughes	Wales	=
Peter Crouch	England	27	Laurie Hughes	England	=
Steve Nicol	Scotland	=	Tommy Lawrence	Scotland	=
Elisha Scott	Northern Ireland	=	Larry Lloyd	England	=
Alan Hansen	Scotland	26	Tommy Lucas	England	=
John Toshack	Wales	=	David McMullan	Northern Ireland	=
Phil Babb	Republic of Ireland	25	John Scales	England	=
Terry McDermott	England	=	Phil Taylor	England	=
Mark Lawrenson	Republic of Ireland	24	John Wark	Scotland	=
Steve McManaman	England	=	Gerry Byrne	England	2
Robbie Fowler	England	22	Scott Carson	England	=
John Aldridge	Republic of Ireland	19	Bill Jones	England	=
Joey Jones	Wales	18	Alan Kennedy	England	=
Mark Kennedy	Republic of Ireland	17	Donald MacKinlay	Scotland	=
Ray Kennedy	England	=	Jimmy McDougall	Scotland	=
Steve McMahon	England	=	Frank McGarvey	Scotland	=
Jamie Redknapp	England	=	Jimmy Melia	England	=
Maurice Parry	Wales	16	Jack Parkinson	England	=
Peter Thompson	England	=	Ron Yeats	Scotland	=
Yommy Younger	Scotland	=	George Allan	Scotland	1
Jim Beglin	Republic of Ireland	15	John Bamber	England	=
Sam Hardy	England	14	Frank Becton	England	=
Sammy Lee	England	=	Thomas Bradshaw	England	=
Jason McAteer	Republic of Ireland	=	Ken De Mange	Republic of Ireland	=
Gordon Milne	England	=	Billy Dunlop	Scotland	=
Ian St John	Scotland	=	Raby Howell	England	=
Gary Gillespie	Scotland	13	David James	England	=
Paul Ince	England	12	Lee Jones	Wales	=
Billy Lacey	Northern Ireland	=	Chris Kirkland	England	=
Craig Bellamy	Wales	11	Robert Matthews	Wales	=
Ernest Peake	Wales	10	Jock McNab	Scotland	=
Danny Murphy	England	9	Tom Miller	Scotland	=
Nick Barmby	England	8	Hugh Morgan	Scotland	=
Harry Chambers	England	=	Neil Ruddock	England	=
Rob Jones	England	=	Tommy Smith	England	=

INTERNATIONAL GOALS

LFC PLAYERS WHO HAVE SCORED FOR THEIR COUNTRIES – HOME NATIONS (END OF 2008/09)

PLAYER	COUNTRY	GOALS	PLAYER	COUNTRY	GOALS
Michael Owen	England	26	Terry McDermott	England	=
Ian Rush	Wales	=	Ronnie Whelan	Republic of Ireland	=
Roger Hunt	England	18	Frank Becton	England	2
Peter Crouch	England	14	Robbie Keane	Republic of Ireland	=
Steven Gerrard	England	=	Billy Lacey	Northern Ireland	=
Kenny Dalglish	Scotland	13	Sammy Lee	England	=
John Barnes	England	8	Tom Miller	Scotland	=
Ian St John	Scotland	=	Dean Saunders	Wales	=
John Toshack	Wales	=	Steve Staunton	Republic of Ireland	=
Kevin Keegan	England	7	Alan A'Court	England	1
Peter Beardsley	England	6	John Aldridge	Republic of Ireland	=
Billy Liddell	Scotland	=	Nick Barmby	England	=
Harry Chambers	England	5	Steve Finnan	Republic of Ireland	=
Robbie Fowler	England	=	Gordon Hodgson	England	=
Emile Heskey	England	=	Emlyn Hughes	England	=
Phil Neal	England	=	Chris Lawler	England	=
Craig Bellamy	Wales	4	Jason McAteer	Republic of Ireland	=
Graeme Souness	Scotland	=	Jimmy Melia	England	=
Ray Houghton	Republic of Ireland	3	Danny Murphy	England	=
David Johnson	England	=	Ernest Peake	Wales	=
Ray Kennedy	England	=	Jamie Redknapp	England	=
Mark Lawrenson	Republic of Ireland	=	Phil Thompson	England	=

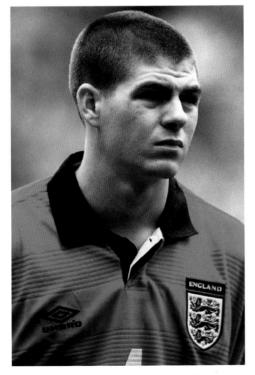

Steven Gerrard (left) and Robbie Fowler – England goalscorers

4-4 DRAWS – A HISTORY

The unusual spectacle of two eight-goal thrillers in the space of seven days in April 2009 brought to light an interesting variable in Liverpool's history. The 4-4 draws against Chelsea and Arsenal respectively saw the club's grand total of games which have seen that very scoreline into double figures – 10 – out of a grand total of 5,127 first-team fixtures. Each Liverpool XI is noted, with only one man being involved in three Liverpool 4-4 games – Billy Liddell – while Pepe Reina is the only goalkeeper to have played in more than one 4-4 fixture.

Date	Comp.	H/A	Liverpool team	Liverpool scorers
1898/99 v SHEFFIELD UNITED				
23rd Mar	FAC 3 Rep, aet	(a)	Storer, A. Goldie, Dunlop, Howell, Raisbeck, W. Goldie, Cox, Walker, Allan, Morgan, Robertson	Walker (20), Allan (50), Boyle (70, o.g.), Cox (72)
1927/28 v ARSENAL				
27th Oct	League	(a)	Scott, Jackson, Done, Morrison, Davidson, McBain, Edmed, Hodgson, Salisbury, McDougall, Clark	Edmed (1), Hodgson (31, 32, 44)
1938/39 v PORTSMOUTH				
11th Mar	League	(h)	Riley, Cooper, Harley, Busby, Rogers, Bush, Nieuwenhuys, Taylor, Fagan, Balmer, Kinghorn	Fagan (16), Taylor (27, 51), Nieuwenhuys (62)
1953/54 v MANCHESTER UNITED				
22nd Aug	League	(h)	Ashcroft, Lambert, Spicer, Taylor, Hughes, Paisley, Payne, Baron, Bimpson, W. Jones, Liddell	Liddell (20), W. Jones (44), Bimpson (54, 58)
1954/55 v LUTON TOWN				
2nd Apr	League	(h)	Rudham, Lambert, Moran, Saunders, Saunders, South, Twentyman, Payne, Anderson, Liddell, Evans, A'Court	Evans (3, 22), Anderson (14), South (85)
1959/60 v ASTON VILLA				
30th Mar	League	(a)	Slater, Molyneux, Moran, Wheeler, White, Leishman, Liddell, Hunt, Hickson, Harrower, A'Court	Hunt (19), Hickson (24, 60), Molyneux (44)
1990/91 v EVERTON				
20th Feb	FAC 5 Rep. aet	(a)	Grobbelaar, Hysen, Burrows, Nicol, Molby, Ablett, Beardsley, Staunton, Rush, Barnes, Venison. Unusued subs: Speedie, Houghton	Beardsley (37, 71), Rush (77), Barnes (103)

4-4 DRAWS – A HISTORY

Date	Comp.	H/A	Liverpool team	Liverpool scorers
1992/93 v CHESTERFIELD				
22nd Sept	LC 2, L.1	(h)	James, Marsh, Burrows, Tanner, Redknapp, Wright, Rosenthal, Charnock (Kozma), Hutchison, Molby, Walters. Unused sub: Harkness	Rosenthal (51), Hutchison (57), Walters (72), Wright (85)
2008/09 v CHELSEA				
14th Apr	CL QF, L. 2	(a)	Reina, Arbeloa (Babel), Skrtel, Carragher, Aurelio, Alonso, Mascherano (Riera), Kuyt, Lucas, Benayoun, Torres (Ngog). Unused subs: Cavalieri, Dossena, Hyypia, Agger	Aurelio (19), Alonso (28, pen), Lucas (81), Kuyt (83)
2008/09 v ARSENAL				
21st Apr	League	(h)	Reina, Arbeloa, Carragher, Agger, Aurelio, Benayoun, Alonso, Mascherano, Riera (Babel), Torres, Kuyt (El Zhar). Unused subs: Cavalieri, Dossena, Lucas, Ngog, Skrtel	Torres (49, 72), Benayoun (55, 90)

Fernando Torres, on target during the 4-4 draw against Arsenal in April 2009

ARSENAL

2008/09 OVERVIEW

Final position: 4th, Premier League
Best cup runs: SF, Champions Lge, FA Cup
Player of season: Robin van Persie
Top scorer (all): 20, Robin van Persie

ALL-TIME RECORD

(League matches only)

	PL	W	D	L
Home:	85	48	16	21
Away:	85	20	28	37
Overall:	170	68	44	58

LAST 2 MEETINGS (LEAGUE)

21/04/2009

Liverpool	4-4	Arsenal
Torres 48, 72		Arshavin 36, 67, 70, 90
Benayoun 55, 90		

21/12/2008

Arsenal	1-1	Liverpool
Van Persie 24		Keane 42

CLUB DETAILS

Nickname: The Gunners
Ground: Emirates Stadium, capacity 60,432 (08/09 away alloc. 2,956)
Manager: Arsene Wenger (app. 01/10/96)
Major signing: Thomas Vermaelen
Year formed: 1886

USEFUL INFORMATION

Website: www.arsenal.com
Address: Emirates Stadium, Highbury House, 75 Drayton Park N5 1BU
Switchboard: 0207 704 4000

TRAVEL INFORMATION

By Car (from Anfield): 209 miles/3 hours 45 mins.
By Tube: Arsenal (Piccadilly Line) is a three-minute walk. Finsbury Park and Highbury & Islington are also within 10 minutes of the stadium.
By Bus: Main bus stops are located on Holloway Road, Nag's Head, Seven Sisters Road, Blackstock Road and Highbury Corner. Regular services will take you to within 10 minutes walk of the ground.

ASTON VILLA

2008/09 OVERVIEW

Final position: 6th, Premier League
Best cup runs: R5, FA Cup, L32, UEFA Cup
Player of season: Ashley Young
Top scorer (all): 15, John Carew

ALL-TIME RECORD

(League matches only)

	PL	W	D	L
Home:	84	53	17	14
Away:	84	26	21	37
Overall:	168	79	38	51

LAST 2 MEETINGS

22/03/2009

Liverpool	5-0	Aston Villa
Kuyt 8, Riera 33,		
Gerrard 39 (p), 50, 65 (p)		

31/08/2008

Aston Villa	0-0	Liverpool

CLUB DETAILS

Nickname: The Villans
Ground: Villa Park, capacity 42,573 (08/09 away allocation 2,771)
Manager: Martin O'Neill (app. 04/08/06)
Major signing: Stewart Downing
Year formed: 1874

USEFUL INFORMATION

Website: www.avfc.co.uk
Address: Villa Park, Trinity Road, Birmingham B6 6HE
Switchboard: 0871 423 8100

TRAVEL INFORMATION

By Car (from Anfield): 96 miles/1 hour 50 mins.
By Train: Witton station is a five-minute walk, while Aston is 15 minutes away. From New Street Station, a taxi should take 15 minutes.
By Bus: The number 7 West Midlands Travel Bus runs from Birmingham City Centre to the stadium (Witton). For services check www.travelwm.co.uk

BIRMINGHAM CITY

2008/09 OVERVIEW

Final position: 2nd, Championship
Best cup runs: R3, FA Cup, R2, League Cup
Player of season: Frank Queudrue
Top scorer (all): 14, Kevin Phillips

ALL-TIME RECORD

(League matches only)

	PL	W	D	L
Home:	48	31	10	7
Away:	48	15	12	21
Overall:	96	46	22	28

LAST 2 MEETINGS

26/04/2008
Birmingham City   2-2   Liverpool
Forssell 34,   Crouch 63,
Larsson 55   Benayoun 76

22/09/2007
Liverpool   0-0   Birmingham City

CLUB DETAILS

Nickname: Blues
Ground: St Andrew's, capacity 30,009
(07/08 away allocation 2,665)
Manager: Alex McLeish (app. 28/11/07)
Major signing: Christian Benitez
Year formed: 1875

USEFUL INFORMATION

Website: www.bcfc.com
Address: St Andrew's Stadium,
Birmingham, West Midlands
B9 4RL
Switchboard: 0844 557 1875

TRAVEL INFORMATION

By Car (from Anfield): 99 miles/1 hour 55 mins.
By Train: From Birmingham New Street, you can take a five-minute walk to Moor Street station. Take a train to Bordesley, which is 10 minutes from the stadium.
By Bus: The following services serve the stadium from Birmingham city centre – near Moor Street station on Queensway: 57A, 58, 60. Look for bus stop MF.

BLACKBURN ROVERS

2008/09 OVERVIEW

Final position: 15th, Premier League
Best cup runs: R5, League Cup, R5, FA Cup
Player of season: Stephen Warnock
Top scorer (all): 13, Benni McCarthy

ALL-TIME RECORD

(League matches only)

	PL	W	D	L
Home:	61	36	16	9
Away:	61	15	21	25
Overall:	122	51	37	34

LAST 2 MEETINGS

11/04/2009
Liverpool   4-0   Blackburn Rovers
Torres 5, 33,
Agger 83, Ngog 90

06/12/2008
Blackburn Rovers 1-3   Liverpool
Santa Cruz 86   Alonso 69,
Benayoun 79,
Gerrard 90

CLUB DETAILS

Nickname: Rovers
Ground: Ewood Park, capacity 31,367
(08/09 away allocation 7,035)
Manager: Sam Alladyce (app. 17/12/08)
Major signing: Nicola Kalinic
Year formed: 1875

USEFUL INFORMATION

Website: www.rovers.co.uk
Address: Ewood Park, Bolton Road,
Blackburn, Lancashire BB2 4JF
Switchboard: 08701 113232

TRAVEL INFORMATION

By Car (from Anfield): 40 miles/45 minutes.
By Train: Blackburn station is a mile and a half away, Mill Hill is one mile. Direct trains run from Manchester Victoria, Salford Crescent and Preston.
By Bus: The central bus station is next to the railway station. Services 3, 3A, 3B, 46, and 346 all go from Blackburn to Darwen. Ewood Park is a mile and a half along the journey.

BOLTON WANDERERS

2008/09 OVERVIEW

Final position: 13th, Premier League
Best cup runs: R3, FA Cup, R2, League Cup
Player of season: Kevin Davies
Top scorer (all): 12, Kevin Davies

ALL-TIME RECORD

(League matches only)

	PL	W	D	L
Home:	56	30	16	10
Away:	56	18	13	25
Overall:	112	48	29	35

LAST 2 MEETINGS

26/12/2008
Liverpool   3-0   Bolton Wanderers
Riera 26,
Keane 53, 58

15/11/2008
Bolton Wanderers 0-2   Liverpool
                        Kuyt 28, Gerrard 73

CLUB DETAILS

Nickname: The Trotters
Ground: Reebok Stadium, capacity 28,000 (08/09 away alloc. 4,425)
Manager: Gary Megson (app. 26/10/07)
Major signing: Sean Davis
Year formed: 1874

USEFUL INFORMATION

Website: www.bwfc.co.uk
Address: Reebok Stadium, Burnden Way, Lostock, Bolton BL6 6JW
Switchboard: 01204 673673

TRAVEL INFORMATION

By Car (from Anfield): 27 miles/40 minutes.
By Train: Horwich Parkway station is a few minutes walk from the stadium. Regular trains run from Bolton, while from Liverpool you can change at Manchester Oxford Road.
By Bus: The club operate regular buses to and from Bolton town centre.

BURNLEY

2008/09 OVERVIEW

Final position: 5th, Championship
Best cup runs: SF, League Cup, R5, FA Cup
Player of season: Robbie Blake
Top scorer (all): 19, Martin Paterson

ALL-TIME RECORD

(League matches only)

	PL	W	D	L
Home:	37	19	10	8
Away:	37	10	9	18
Overall:	74	29	19	26

LAST 2 MEETINGS (LEAGUE)

27/03/1976
Liverpool   2-0   Burnley
Fairclough 39, 61

06/12/1975
Burnley   0-0   Liverpool

CLUB DETAILS

Nickname: The Clarets
Ground: Turf Moor, capacity 22,547 (away allocation 2,000-2,500)
Manager: Owen Coyle (app. 22/11/07)
Major signing: Steven Fletcher
Year formed: 1882

USEFUL INFORMATION

Website: www.burnleyfootballclub.com
Address: Turf Moor, Harry Potts Way, Burnley, Lancashire BB10 4BX
Switchboard: 0871 221 1882

TRAVEL INFORMATION

By Car (from Anfield): 54 miles/1 hour.
By Train: Burnley Central and Burnley Manchester Road stations are within 20 minutes' walk. The latter is served by a faster express service, with the ground visible when you leave the station.
By Bus: The main bus station is less than one mile from the stadium, just off Centenary Way.

CHELSEA

2008/09 OVERVIEW

Final position: 3rd, Premier League
Best cup runs: W, FA Cup, SF, Ch. League,
Player of season: Frank Lampard
Top scorer (all): 25, Nicolas Anelka

ALL-TIME RECORD

(League matches only)

	PL	W	D	L
Home:	66	44	14	8
Away:	66	16	14	36
Overall:	132	60	28	44

LAST 2 MEETINGS (LEAGUE)

01/02/2009

Liverpool	2-0	Chelsea
Torres 89, 90		

26/10/2008

Chelsea	0-1	Liverpool
		Alonso 10

CLUB DETAILS

Nickname: The Blues
Ground: Stamford Bridge, capacity 41,841 (08/09 away alloc. 3,107)
Manager: Carlo Ancelotti (app. 01/06/09)
Major signing: Yuri Zhirkov
Year formed: 1905

USEFUL INFORMATION

Website: www.chelseafc.com
Address: Stamford Bridge, Fulham Road, London SW6 1HS
Switchboard: 0870 300 2322

TRAVEL INFORMATION

By Car (from Anfield): 216 miles/4 hours.
By Tube: Fulham Broadway (District Line) is five minutes' walk away. Take a tube to Earls Court and change for Wimbledon-bound tubes. West Brompton overground station is 15 minutes away.
By Bus: Numbers 14, 211 and 414 go along Fulham Road from central London via West Brompton station.

EVERTON

2008/09 OVERVIEW

Final position: 5th, Premier League
Best cup runs: F, FA Cup, R3, League Cup
Player of season: Phil Jagielka
Top scorer (all): 9, Tim Cahill, Marouane Fellaini

ALL-TIME RECORD

(League matches only)

	PL	W	D	L
Home:	90	38	29	23
Away:	90	30	27	33
Overall:	180	68	56	56

LAST 2 MEETINGS (LEAGUE)

19/01/2009

Liverpool	1-1	Everton
Gerrard 68		Cahill 87

27/09/2008

Everton	0-2	Liverpool
		Torres 59, 62

CLUB DETAILS

Nickname: The Toffees
Ground: Goodison Park, capacity 40,260 (08/09 away allocation 2,881)
Manager: David Moyes (app. 14/03/02)
Major signing: Diniyar Bilyaletdinov
Year formed: 1878

USEFUL INFORMATION

Website: www.evertonfc.com
Address: Goodison Park, Goodison Road, Liverpool L4 4EL
Switchboard: 0151 330 2200

TRAVEL INFORMATION

By Car (from Anfield): 0.8 miles/3 minutes.
By Train: From Liverpool Central, take any train heading for Ormskirk or Kirkby and get off at Kirkdale - from there it is a 10-minute walk.
By Bus: From Queen's Square Bus Station in Liverpool city centre, numbers 1, 2, 19, 20, 21, 311, 345 and 350 go past or near the stadium.

FULHAM

2008/09 OVERVIEW

Final position: 7th, Premier League
Best cup runs: R6, FA Cup, R3, League Cup
Player of season: Mark Schwarzer
Top scorers (all): 10, Andrew Johnson

ALL-TIME RECORD

(League matches only)

	PL	W	D	L
Home:	22	16	6	0
Away:	22	9	6	7
Overall:	44	25	12	7

LAST 2 MEETINGS

04/04/2009

Fulham	0-1	Liverpool
		Benayoun 90

22/11/2008

Liverpool	0-0	Fulham

CLUB DETAILS

Nickname: Cottagers
Ground: Craven Cottage, capacity 25,678 (08/09 away allocation 2,835)
Manager: Roy Hodgson (app. 30/12/07)
Major signing: Damien Duff
Year formed: 1879

USEFUL INFORMATION

Website: www.fulhamfc.com
Address: Craven Cottage, Stevenage Road, Fulham, London SW6 6HH
Switchboard: 0870 442 1222

TRAVEL INFORMATION

By Car (from Anfield): 216 miles/4 hours.
By Tube: Alight at Putney Bridge (District Line), from central London. The stadium is a 10-minute walk. Bishop's Park, along the Thames is the quickest route – note it's closed after night games.
By Bus: The following run down nearby Fulham Palace Road: 74, 190, 211, 220, 295. London Transport's website is www.tfl.gov.uk

HULL CITY

2008/09 OVERVIEW

Final position: 17th, Premier League
Best cup runs: R6, FA Cup, R2, League Cup
Player of season: Michael Turner
Top scorers (all): 8, Geovanni

ALL-TIME RECORD

(League matches only)

	PL	W	D	L
Home:	4	3	1	0
Away:	4	3	1	0
Overall:	8	6	2	0

LAST 2 MEETINGS

25/04/2009

Hull City	1-3	Liverpool
Geovanni 72		Alonso 45, Kuyt 63, 89

13/12/2008

Liverpool	2-2	Hull City
Gerrard 24, 32		McShane 12, Carragher 22 (o.g.)

CLUB DETAILS

Nickname: The Tigers
Ground: The KC Stadium, capacity 25,404 (08/09 away allocation 2,475)
Manager: Phil Brown (app. 04/12/06)
Major signing: Stephen Hunt
Year formed: 1904

USEFUL INFORMATION

Website: www.hullcityafc.premiumtv.co.uk
Address: The Circle, Walton Street, Hull HU3 6HU
Switchboard: 08708 370 003

TRAVEL INFORMATION

By Car (from Anfield): 123 miles/2 hours 10 mins.
By Train: Hull Paragon is 15 minutes away. Leave on the south side, turn right and follow Anlaby Road.
By Road: Leave M62 (J38) and join the A63, towards Hull. Stay on A63 and KC Stadium is signposted. One mile from Hull leave A63 (signposted Hull Royal Infirmary) and take the 2nd exit at the roundabout. Turn left at the lights and then over the flyover, right at the next lights and the stadium is on the right.

MANCHESTER CITY

2008/09 OVERVIEW

Final position: 10th, Premier League
Best cup runs: QF, UEFA Cup, R3 FA Cup
Player of season: Stephen Ireland
Top scorer (all): 15, Robinho

ALL-TIME RECORD

(League matches only)

	PL	W	D	L
Home:	73	45	15	13
Away:	73	29	20	24
Overall:	146	74	35	37

LAST 2 MEETINGS

22/02/2009

Liverpool	1-1	Manchester City
Kuyt 78		Bellamy 51

05/10/2008

Manchester City	2-3	Liverpool
Ireland 18,		Torres 55, 73
Garrido 42		Kuyt 90

CLUB DETAILS

Nickname: Blues/The Citizens
Ground: City of Manchester Stadium, capacity 48,000 (08/09 away allocation 2,786)
Manager: Mark Hughes (app. 05/06/08)
Major signing: Carlos Tevez
Year formed: 1887

USEFUL INFORMATION

Website: www.mcfc.co.uk
Address: City of Manchester Stadium, SportCity, Rowsley Street, Manchester M11 3FF
Switchboard: 0870 062 1894

TRAVEL INFORMATION

By Car (from Anfield): 36 miles/50 minutes.
By Train: Ashburys station is a 15-minute walk, a five-minute train journey from Manchester Piccadilly (20-25 minutes on foot).
By Bus: The following services run direct from Piccadilly Gardens: 216, 217, 218, 231, 236 and 237. See www.gmpte.com for more information.

MANCHESTER UNITED

2008/09 OVERVIEW

Final position: 1st, Premier League
Best cup runs: W, League Cup, W, Club World
Player of season: Nemanja Vidic
Top scorer (all): 26, Cristiano Ronaldo

ALL-TIME RECORD

(League matches only)

	PL	W	D	L
Home:	76	36	18	22
Away:	76	15	25	36
Overall:	152	51	43	58

LAST 2 MEETINGS

14/03/2009

Manchester Utd	1-4	Liverpool
Ronaldo 23 (p)		Torres 28, Gerrard 44 (p),
		Aurelio 77, Dossena 90

13/09/2008

Liverpool	2-1	Manchester Utd
Brown 26 (o.g.),		Tevez 3
Babel 77		

CLUB DETAILS

Nickname: Red Devils
Ground: Old Trafford, capacity 76,312 (08/09 away allocation 3,026)
Manager: Sir Alex Ferguson (app. 06/11/86)
Major signing: Antonio Valencia
Year formed: 1878

USEFUL INFORMATION

Website: www.manutd.com
Address: Old Trafford, Manchester M16 0RA
Switchboard: 0870 442 1994

TRAVEL INFORMATION

By Car (from Anfield): 33 miles/45 minutes.
By Train: Services run from Piccadilly to the club's railway station. There is also a Metrolink service, with the station located next to Lancashire CCC on Warwick Road, which leads to Sir Matt Busby Way.
By Bus: The 250, 255, 256, 263, 290 and 291 run from Piccadilly Gardens in the city centre.

PORTSMOUTH

2008/09 OVERVIEW

Final position: 14th, Premier League
Best cup runs: R4, FA Cup, Gr. Stage, UEFA Cup
Player of season: Glen Johnson
Top scorer (all): 15, Peter Crouch

ALL-TIME RECORD

(League matches only)

	PL	W	D	L
Home:	29	15	10	4
Away:	29	9	5	15
Overall:	58	24	15	19

LAST 2 MEETINGS

07/02/2009

Portsmouth	2-3	Liverpool
Nugent 62,		Aurelio 69, Kuyt 85,
Hreidarsson 78		Torres 90

29/10/2008

Liverpool	1-0	Portsmouth
Gerrard 76 (p)		

CLUB DETAILS

Nickname: Pompey
Ground: Fratton Park, capacity 20,700
(08/09 away allocation 2,381)
Manager: Paul Hart (app. 21/07/09)
Major signing: Aruna Dindane
Year formed: 1898

USEFUL INFORMATION

Website: www.pompeyfc.co.uk
Address: Fratton Park,
Frogmore Road,
Portsmouth,
Hants PO4 8RA
Switchboard: 0239 273 1204

TRAVEL INFORMATION

By Car (from Anfield): 255 miles/4 hours 30 mins.
By Train: Fratton Bridge is a 10-minute walk from the stadium – on arrival by train you pass the ground on your left. Portsmouth station is a 30-minute walk.
By Bus: 13, 17 and 18 all run to the stadium from Portsmouth city centre.

STOKE CITY

2008/09 OVERVIEW

Final position: 12th, Premier League
Best cup runs: R5, League Cup, R3, FA Cup
Player of season: Abdoulaye Faye
Top scorers (all): 11, Ricardo Fuller

ALL-TIME RECORD

(League matches only)

	PL	W	D	L
Home:	54	41	10	3
Away:	54	12	19	23
Overall:	108	53	29	26

LAST 2 MEETINGS

10/01/2009

Stoke City	0-0	Liverpool

20/09/2008

Liverpool	0-0	Stoke City

CLUB DETAILS

Nickname: The Potters
Ground: Britannia Stadium, capacity
27,500 (away allocation 2,800)
Manager: Tony Pulis (app. 13/06/06)
Major signing: Tuncay
Year formed: 1863

USEFUL INFORMATION

Website: www.stokecityfc.premiumtv.co.uk
Address: Stanley Matthews Way,
Stoke-on-Trent
ST4 4EG
Switchboard: 01782 592 222

TRAVEL INFORMATION

By Car (from Anfield): 60 miles/1 hour 10 minutes.
By Train: Stoke-on-Trent is two minutes from Glebe Street, where buses to the stadium run. Turn right out of the station and then next right. Follow the road to the end then turn left, down a bank into Glebe Street.
By Bus: From Hanley Bus Station take the 23 to Glebe Street where shuttle bus services to the stadium depart. Service is at 15-minute intervals.

SUNDERLAND

2008/09 OVERVIEW

Final position: 16th, Premier League
Best cup runs: R4, FA Cup, R4, League Cup
Player of season: Danny Collins
Top scorer (all): 12, Kenwyne Jones

ALL-TIME RECORD

(League matches only)

	PL	W	D	L
Home:	72	36	18	18
Away:	72	28	13	31
Overall:	144	64	31	49

LAST 2 MEETINGS

03/03/2009

Liverpool	2-0	Sunderland
Ngog 52,		
Benayoun 65		

16/08/2008

Sunderland	0-1	Liverpool
		Torres 83

CLUB DETAILS

Nickname: The Black Cats
Ground: Stadium of Light, capacity 49,000 (08/09 away alloc. 2,361)
Manager: Steve Bruce (app. 03/06/09)
Major signing: Darren Bent
Year formed: 1879

USEFUL INFORMATION

Website: www.safc.com
Address: The Sunderland Stadium of Light, Sunderland SR5 1SU
Switchboard: 0191 551 5000

TRAVEL INFORMATION

By Car (from Anfield): 169 miles/3 hours.
By Train: Sunderland mainline station is a 10-15 minute walk. The Metro service also runs from here, with St Peter's or the Stadium of Light stations nearest the stadium.
By Bus: Numbers 2, 3, 4, 12, 13, 15 and 16 all stop within a few minutes walk of the ground. All routes connect to the central bus station, Park Lane Interchange.

TOTTENHAM HOTSPUR

2008/09 OVERVIEW

Final position: 8th, Premier League
Best cup runs: RU, League Cup, L32, UEFA Cup
Player of season: Aaron Lennon
Top scorers (all): 17, Darren Bent

ALL-TIME RECORD

(League matches only)

	PL	W	D	L
Home:	66	42	19	5
Away:	66	20	15	31
Overall:	132	62	34	36

LAST 2 MEETINGS (LEAGUE)

24/05/2009

Liverpool	3-1	Tottenham H.
Torres 31, Hutton 64 (o.g.),		Keane 77
Benayoun 81		

01/11/2008

Tottenham H.	2-1	Liverpool
Carragher 70 (o.g.),		Kuyt 3
Pavlyuchenko 90		

CLUB DETAILS

Nickname: Spurs
Ground: White Hart Lane, capacity 36,240 (08/09 away alloc. 2,929)
Manager: Harry Redknapp (app. 26/10/08)
Major signing: Peter Crouch
Year formed: 1882

USEFUL INFORMATION

Website: www.spurs.co.uk
Address: 748 High Road, Tottenham, London N17 0AP
Switchboard: 0208 365 5000

TRAVEL INFORMATION

By Car (from Anfield): 214 miles/3 hours 45 mins.
By Tube: The nearest tube station is Seven Sisters (Victoria - a 25-minute walk), with trains running to Liverpool Street. The nearest mainline station is White Hart Lane, approx 5 minutes walk.
By Bus: A regular service runs from Seven Sisters past the stadium entrance (numbers 149, 259, 279).

WEST HAM UNITED

2008/09 OVERVIEW

Final position: 9th, Premier League
Best cup runs: R5, FA Cup, R3, League Cup
Player of season: Scott Parker
Top scorer (all): 12, Carlton Cole

ALL-TIME RECORD

(League matches only)

	PL	W	D	L
Home:	52	35	14	3
Away:	52	19	15	18
Overall:	104	54	29	21

LAST 2 MEETINGS

09/05/2009

West Ham	0-3	Liverpool
		Gerrard 2, 38,
		Babel 84

01/12/2008

Liverpool	0-0	West Ham

CLUB DETAILS

Nickname: The Hammers
Ground: Upton Park, capacity 35,647
(08/09 away allocation 2,938)
Manager: Gianfranco Zola (app. 09/09/08)
Major signing: Luis Jimenez
Year formed: 1895

USEFUL INFORMATION

Website: www.whufc.com
Address: Boleyn Ground, Green Street, Upton Park, London E13 9AZ
Switchboard: 0208 548 2748

TRAVEL INFORMATION

By Car (from Anfield): 224 miles/4 hours 5 mins.
By Tube: Upton Park is the closest tube station, around 45 minutes from Central London (District Line). When you exit the station turn right, the stadium is then a two-minute walk. East Ham and Plaistow Stations, which are further away, may also be worth using to avoid match congestion.
By Bus: Routes 5, 15, 15A, 58, 58A, 104, 147 and 238 all serve Upton Park.

WIGAN ATHLETIC

2008/09 OVERVIEW

Final position: 11th, Premier League
Best cup runs: R4, League Cup, R3, FA Cup
Player of season: Titus Bramble
Top scorer (all): 11, Amr Zaki

ALL-TIME RECORD

(League matches only)

	PL	W	D	L
Home:	4	3	1	0
Away:	4	3	1	0
Overall:	8	6	2	0

LAST 2 MEETINGS

28/01/2009

Wigan Athletic	1-1	Liverpool
Mido 83 (p)		Benayoun 41

18/10/2008

Liverpool	3-2	Wigan Athletic
Kuyt 37, 85,		Zaki 29, 45
Riera 80		

CLUB DETAILS

Nickname: The Latics
Ground: DW Stadium, capacity 25,023
(08/09 away allocation 4,520)
Manager: Roberto Martinez (app. 15/06/09)
Major signing: Jason Scotland
Year formed: 1932

USEFUL INFORMATION

Website: www.wiganlatics.co.uk
Address: DW Stadium, Robin Park, Newtown, Wigan WN5 0UZ
Switchboard: 01942 774000

TRAVEL INFORMATION

By Car (from Anfield): 21 miles/30 minutes.
By Train: Wigan Wallgate and Wigan North Western are a 15-minute walk. From either station head under the railway bridge and keep to the right – following the road (A49) for 10 minutes.
By Bus: No particular route, as the venue is within easy distance of the station.

WOLVERHAMPTON WANDERERS

2008/09 OVERVIEW

Final position: 1st, Championship
Best cup runs: R4, FA Cup, R2, League Cup
Player of season: Kevin Foley
Top scorer (all): 25, Sylvan Ebanks-Blake

ALL-TIME RECORD

(League matches only)

	PL	W	D	L
Home:	44	29	7	8
Away:	44	14	9	21
Overall:	88	43	16	29

LAST 2 MEETINGS

20/03/2004

Liverpool	1-0	Wolves
Hyypia 90		

21/01/2004

Wolves	1-1	Liverpool
Miller 90		Cheyrou 42

CLUB DETAILS

Nickname: Wolves
Ground: Molineux, capacity 29,400
(03/04 away allocation 3,028)
Manager: Mick McCarthy (app. 21/07/06)
Major signing: Kevin Doyle
Year formed: 1877

USEFUL INFORMATION

Website: www.wolves.co.uk
Address: Waterloo Road, Wolverhampton,
West Midlands WV1 4QR
Switchboard: 0871 222 2220

TRAVEL INFORMATION

By Car (from Anfield): 88 miles/1 hour 35 minutes.
By Train: The stadium is a 15-minute walk from Wolverhampton station. Follow the Ring Road, walking down the side of the Chubb buildings. At the crossroads you will see the stadium on your left.
By Bus: The 503 and 504 from stand R in the city centre bus station stop at the stadium – this is opposite the railway station, in easy walking distance.

Liverpool at Fulham – October 31

TICKETS

ADDRESS

Ticket Office,
PO Box 204,
Liverpool
L69 4PQ

TELEPHONE NUMBER

0844 844 0844 (24-Hour Ticket Information Line)
0844 844 2005 (Customer Services)
++44 870 2202151

TICKET OFFICE HOURS

Monday-Friday 8.15am-5.30pm
Matchdays 9.15am to kick-off, then 15 minutes after end of game
Non Match Saturdays 9.15am-1.00pm

PRICES

	Category A	Category B
Kop		
Adult	£36	£34
Over 65	£27	£25.50
Disabled and Visually Impaired	£27	£25.50
Main Stand		
Adult	£38	£36
Over 65	£28.50	£27
Centenary		
Adult	£38	£36
Over 65	£28.50	£27
Paddock		
Adult	£38	£36
Over 65	£28.50	£27
Disabled and Visually Impaired	£28.50	£27
Anfield Road		
Adult	£38	£36
Over 65	£28.50	£27
Combined 1 Adult/1 Child (16 or under)	£57	£54
Disabled and Visually Impaired	£28.50	£27

CATEGORY A MATCHES

Arsenal, Aston Villa, Blackburn Rovers, Chelsea, Everton, Manchester City, Manchester United, Tottenham Hotspur, West Ham United.

FAMILY TICKETS

For adult/child combined tickets a ratio of two adults to one child, or two children to one adult is allowed. In the event that the number of children exceeds the ratio of 2:1 the additional tickets will be charged at the adult rate.

BUYING TICKETS

General sales begin 18 days before a home fixture and are available through the credit card hotline (Monday-Friday 8.30am-5.30pm - a maximum of four tickets, minimum booking fee of 50p per ticket applies), postal application and for Fan Card holders, online (subject to a booking fee of £2.50 per ticket).

TICKETS

BY POST

State the match and number of tickets you require, with the correct remittance and a stamped addressed envelope, to LFC Ticket Office, PO Box 204, Liverpool L69 4PQ. You can pay by cheque, postal order, credit or debit card. Cheques must be made payable to Liverpool FC. If you want to pay by credit or debit card, include card number and expiry date, plus debit card issue number where applicable. If applications exceed the number of tickets, they will be allocated through a ballot.

BY PHONE

You can apply for a maximum of four tickets, by calling the credit card hotline, quoting your credit or debit card number and expiry date. A minimum booking fee of 50p per ticket will be charged. Tickets booked more than three days before the match will be sent out by post, those booked after this must be collected from the credit card collections window at the ticket office, and you must produce the card used to book the tickets.

IN PERSON

Any remaining tickets will go on sale at the ticket office 11 days in advance. A maximum of four tickets may be purcased in one transaction (subject to change). However, tickets usually sell out through phone and postal bookings.

AWAY MATCHES (BARCLAYS PREMIER LEAGUE)

Tickets go on sale first based on a priority system (i.e. to supporters who have attended the most away fixtures in the Premiership during season 2007/08 - and subsequently 2008/09). The number of matches attended will be determined from the information held on the ticket office database.

CUP MATCHES

Ticket information concerning European and domestic Cup match allocations are made as soon as possible after each draw has taken place. Supporters are advised that they should quote their Fan Card number for all ticket purcahses, and to retain their ticket stubs for potential use for any additional fixtures allocated on a voucher system or in the ven of a home match being abandoned.

ABOUT ANFIELD

ADDRESS

Liverpool Football Club
Anfield Road
Liverpool
L4 0TH

ABOUT

First used in 1884 to house Everton FC, the Reds have called Anfield their home since 1892. Originally owned by John Orrell, fellow brewer and friend John Houlding bought the ground in 1891, soon after Everton won the league title. His proposed increase in rent to Everton – some records state a four-fold increase on their original agreement with Orrell – saw the club leave. With an empty ground and no team, Houlding formed his own club – and so Liverpool FC were born. Their first match at Anfield saw a 7-0 victory over Rotherham Town on September 1 1892, with the first Football League match played a year later, the Reds seeing off Lincoln City 4-0 on September 8, 1893 in front of an estimated 5,000 spectators.

On its original inauguration in 1884 Anfield housed 20,000. Extensive redevelopment, has seen Anfield hold upwards of 60,000, the stadium's record attendance of 61,905 coming against Wolves on February 2, 1952.

The ground, which hosted European Championship games in 1996 and is rated a 4-star stadium by UEFA, holds 45,522 – with this figure taking into account the Press and disabled areas and all seating, some of which is not used due to segregation. Anfield, or a new stadium, is also due to host games during the 2015 rugby union World Cup, while Liverpool has been pencilled in as a host for games should England win the right to stage the 2018 or 2022 World Cup.

THE KOP GRANDSTAND

Built in 1906, after the Reds won the league championship for a second time. It was named 'The Spion Kop' after a South African hill in Natal which was the scene of a bloody Boer War battle. In 1928 it was rebuilt and a roof was added with the capacity reaching close to 30,000 – the largest covered terrace in the Football League at that time. It was rebuilt in summer 1994 to its current splendour after an emotional send-off against Norwich City at the end of the 1993/94 campaign.

CENTENARY STAND

The original Kemlyn Road Stand incorporated a barrel roof and was fronted by an uncovered paddock. It was demolished in 1963 to make way for a new cantilever stand. In 1992 a second tier was added, and the stand was renamed to mark the club's 100th anniversary.

MAIN STAND/PADDOCK

The original structure was erected in the late 19th century, a 3,000-capacity stand with a distinctive red and white tudor style with the club's name in the centre. In 1973 it was redeveloped with a new roof and officially opened by HRH the Duke of Kent. Seats were added to the Paddock in 1980.

ANFIELD ROAD STAND

In 1903 the first Anfield Road stand was built. Once a simple one-tier stand which contained a covered standing enclosure (the roof was first added in 1965), it was demolished to make way for a two-tier development in 1998 – the stand having been originally altered to accomodate multi-coloured seating in the early 1980s.

GETTING TO ANFIELD

HOW TO GET THERE - BY CAR

Follow the M62 until you reach the end of the motorway. Then follow the A5058 towards Liverpool for 3 miles, then turn left at the traffic lights into Utting Avenue (there is a McDonald's on the corner of this junction). Proceed for one mile and then turn right at The Arkles pub for the ground. It is recommended that you arrive at least two hours before kick-off in order to secure your parking space. Otherwise, you can park in the streets around Goodison Park and walk across Stanley Park to Anfield, or you can park in a secure parking area at Goodison.

HOW TO GET THERE - BY TRAIN

Kirkdale Station is the closest to Anfield (about a mile away), although Sandhills Station the stop before has the benefit of a bus service to the ground (Soccerbus). Both stations can be reached by first getting a train from Liverpool Lime Street (which is over 3 miles from the ground) to Liverpool Central (Merseyrail Northern Line), and then changing there for trains to Sandhills (2 stops away) or Kirkdale (3 stops). Note: only trains to Ormskirk or Kirkby go to Kirkdale station. A taxi from Liverpool Lime Street should cost between £5 and £7.

HOW TO GET THERE - SOCCERBUS

There are frequent shuttle buses from Sandhills Station, to Anfield for all Liverpool home Premiership and Cup matches. Soccerbus will run for two hours before each match (last bus from Sandhills Station is approximately 15 minutes before kick-off) and for 50 minutes after the final whistle (subject to availability). You can pay as you board the bus. Soccerbus is FREE for those who hold a valid TRIO, SOLO or SAVEAWAY ticket or Merseytravel Free Travel Pass.

HOW TO GET THERE - BY BUS

Take a 26 (or 27) from Paradise Street Bus Station or a 17B, 17C, 17D, or 217 from Queen Square bus station directly to the ground. The 68 and 168 which operate between Bootle and Aigburth and the 14 (from Queen Square) and 19 stop a short walk away.

HOW TO GET THERE - BY AIR

Liverpool John Lennon Airport is around 10 miles from the ground, and taxis should be easily obtainable. Alternatively, you can catch the 80A bus to Garston Station and change at Sandhills for the Soccerbus service.

HOW TO GET THERE - ON FOOT

From Kirkdale Station, turn right and then cross the railway bridge, where you will see the Melrose Abbey pub. Walk past up Westminster Road for around 1/3 of a mile before you arrive at the Elm Tree pub. Follow the road around the right-hand bend and then turn left into Bradwell Street. At the end of the road you will come to County Road (A59). Cross over at the traffic lights and then go down the road to the left of the Aldi superstore. At the end of this road you will reach Walton Lane (A580). You should be able to see Goodison Park on your left and Stanley Park in front of you. Cross Walton Lane and either enter Stanley Park, following the footpath through the park (keeping to the right) which will exit into Anfield Road. As an alternative to going through Stanley Park, bear right down Walton Lane and then turn left down the road at the end of Stanley Park to the ground.

TO CHECK BUS AND TRAIN TIMES (8AM-8PM, 7 DAYS A WEEK):

Traveline Merseyside   0871 200 22 33
Soccerbus   0151 330 1066

MUSEUM & STADIUM TOUR

"The very word Anfield means more to me than I can describe."
Bill Shankly

Anfield - the name alone conjures up a million memories; many associated with success.
It is one of the oldest and most famous football grounds in the world. Originally the home of Everton Football Club between 1884 and 1892, Anfield has long since become synonymous with Liverpool Football Club and the amazing success achieved by the Reds.
Over the years some of football's greatest names have graced the hallowed turf and contributed to some of the most memorable matches ever played.

STADIUM TOUR

Join many thousands of visitors every year on the Liverpool FC Stadium Tour. It's a 'must-see' experience for any visitor to the region:

- Follow the journey taken by the home and away players at every game, taking you behind the scenes at Anfield.
- Walk in through the players' entrance, imagining the excitement and atmosphere which reaches fever pitch on match day.
- Visit the home team changing room – stopping for pictures next to your favourite player's shirt.
- Get wrapped up in the pre-match rituals as described by your entertaining tour guides.
- It's your big chance to shine next as you take in the interview areas, used after every game by the world's media to capture those post-match headlines...
- You have another perfect photo opportunity touching the famous "This Is Anfield" sign before you make your way down the player's tunnel to the sounds of the legendary Anfield crowd.
- Once you enter the stadium you take your seat in the team dug out, maybe even the managers seat!
- Your tour of Anfield finishes in the Kop End, one of the iconic structures in world football. Steeped in history and success, this has been witness to many famous and legendary matches. In crucial games the Kop has been known as the 12th man with legend suggesting on occasion they have helped the ball over the line, such is the power of the Kopites roar!

BETTER AVAILABILITY ON STADIUM TOUR – INTRODUCING THE FREE FLOW TOUR...

During our peak times we will be launching a free flow element to the tour with lots of fun and activity happening at every turn. Many people have been disappointed that they have not been able to book onto the tour in its current format, especially at weekends and school holidays.

We're opening a few new, never seen before areas giving you to peace of mind that you'll never be disappointed again by not getting in to see this iconic stadium. Launch date is Tuesday 27th October – see **www.liverpoolfc.tv/tours** for details.

LEGENDS TOUR

To make the visit to Anfield unforgettable, join one of our fantastic Legends Tours. You will be shown around Anfield with a hero from our past who will guide you through our historic stadium and reminisce on his time playing for Liverpool giving you his superstitions, funny stories and lots more. The Tour will finish off with am entertaining question and answer session from the inner sanctum of Liverpool Football Club where our photographer will take a photograph of you and the Liverpool Legend before you leave with a limited edition Legends Tour gift.

This is available as the perfect gift purchase

STADIUM TOUR & MUSEUM

LIVERPOOL FC MUSEUM

The Liverpool FC Museum captures the glory & catalogues the success of Britain's most successful football club. Amongst many other notable collections it is home to 5 European Cups, including the original trophy won for the 5th time against AC Milan in 2005.

You can soak up the memories of the many legends to have worn the famous red strip, relive many of our famous triumphs & get lost in the nostalgia.

If you've visited the museum before you'll find plenty of reasons to come back with enhancements to the museum and a changeable exhibition area, giving you a perfect reason to come back.

Museum opening times:	9am–5pm (last admission 4.30pm) Match days (last admission in museum is one hour before kick-off).
Stadium opening times:	9.30am–3.30pm There are seasonal variances with tours running later in summer months, see **www.liverpoolfc.tv/tours** for more information
Mini stadium tours:	Before some home games when we are preparing the stadium, there are restrictions with some of the areas we can visit. These tours will still give you limited access to the stadium & the LFC Museum (at a reduced cost).
Booking information:	**www.liverpoolfc.tv/tours** 0151 260 6677 Check online for promotions and other important information about bookings.

THE ANFIELD EXPERIENCE

Liverpool Football Club offers you the perfect opportunity to treat yourself or anybody else to a choice of two exclusive VIP days. These can be purchased either as an open voucher giving you the flexibility to redeem the day over the next nine months (subject to availability) or on a specific date. As they come in a stylish presentation pack which can be personalised for the lucky recipient, they make the perfect gift for any Liverpool fan.

The stadium tour takes you behind the scenes at Anfield, visiting the dressing rooms, down the tunnel to the sound of the crowd, a chance to touch the famous "This Is Anfield" sign and sit in the team dug-out. Informative tour guides will tell you about the historic Anfield Stadium and escort you on to The Kop - the most famous terrace in world football. Bring your cameras and hand-held video recorders to take those precious pictures of the stadium and museum.

You'll enjoy a luxurious "Heathcotes at Anfield" three-course lunch in one of our executive boxes overlooking the pitch - expect one of our Legends to drop in and make a special personal appearance. Before you leave with your limited edition gift, join the rest of the guests for a fun question and answer session with your Liverpool Legend. A great day out for all Liverpool fans!

THE ULTIMATE ANFIELD EXPERIENCE

What if you could live a life in the day of a Liverpool Legend? Take a nostalgic tour around Anfield Stadium and Museum, and revel in the club's great history. Then play with Reds' Legends at the Liverpool Academy in a unique training session before dining with them in one of our luxury suites. The Ultimate Anfield Experience is truly unique.

You'll be spending a day at the club you love...meeting past greats, collecting autographs and accessing areas of Liverpool FC that few fans are privileged to see. It's a real once-in-a-lifetime VIP experience.

For more information please call **0151 263 7744** or visit **www.theanfieldexperience.com**

CLUB STORES

Selling everything from the new replica kits to the latest toys and games, the club stores provide Reds fans with a wealth of souvenirs. With the new adidas range having been unveiled, there remains a wealth of choice for the new season.
Addresses and contact details are as follows:

WILLIAMSON SQUARE OFFICIAL CLUB STORE

11 Williamson Square, Liverpool, L1 1EQ
United Kingdom
Tel +44 (0)151 330 3077
Opening times: Mon-Wed 9.00am - 5.30pm
Thursday 9.00am - 8.00pm
Fri-Sat 9.00am - 5.30pm
Sundays 10.00am - 4.00pm

LIVERPOOL ONE SUPERSTORE

7 South John Street, Liverpool, L1 8BU
United Kingdom
Tel +44 (0)151 709 4345
Opening times: Mon-Fri 9.30am - 8.00pm
Saturdays 9.00am - 7.00pm
Sundays 11.00am - 5.00pm

ANFIELD OFFICIAL CLUB STORE

Telephone +44 (0)151 263 1760
Fax +44 (0)151 264 9088
Opening times Mon-Sat 9.00am - 5.00pm
Sundays 10.00am - 4.00pm
The store will have varying opening hours on match days, depending on kick-off times.
Please call for details.

CHESTER OFFICIAL CLUB STORE

48 Eastgate Street, Chester, CH1 1LE
United Kingdom
Tel +44 (0)1244 344 608
Opening times: Mon-Sat 9.00am - 5.30pm
Sundays 10.00am - 4.00pm

ONLINE STORE

www.liverpoolfc.tv/store

ORDERING BY PHONE

0844 800 4239
(International calls) 00 44 138 684 8247
Lines open: Mon-Fri 8.00am - 9.00pm
Saturday 8.00am - 7.00pm
Sunday 9.00am - 6.00pm

Liverpool One official club superstore

OFFICIAL WEBSITE

WWW.LIVERPOOLFC.TV

ABOUT

Despite being the last Premier League club to launch an official website in 1999, Liverpool FC can now boast one of the most popular sports sites anywhere in the world.

Liverpoolfc.tv was officially launched in 2001 and within a year it was recognised as the most visited football club website in the world – with fans from 139 countries viewing 13.3 million pages a month.

In May 2005, Liverpoolfc.tv set a new record as 2.8 million fans viewed 48 million pages in a single month as Reds fans all over the world logged on to bask in the glory of that remarkable comeback in Istanbul.

In July 2007, the month Fernando Torres swapped Madrid for Merseyside, 2.9 million supporters from 238 different countries visited the site to read all about the Spaniard's move to Anfield with an incredible 65 million pages viewed within 31 days.

Two years on and Liverpoolfc.tv has been relaunched to ensure the website stays ahead of the chasing pack in delivering the best possible online service to fans desperate to interact with the football club they love. Whether it's reading the latest official news as it breaks, watching goals, highlights and interviews, buying the new kit from the online store, checking out the stats and pictures from the last game or sharing your opinions on the ever-vibrant discussion forums, Liverpoolfc.tv offers something for every supporter. Make sure it's the first place you visit when you hit the web.

www.liverpoolfc.tv homepage, August 2009

OFFICIAL CLUB TV CHANNEL

ABOUT

The only place on TV to savour every minute of every Barclays Premier League and UEFA Champions League game Liverpool play, LFC TV is a must watch for supporters in the UK. Bringing you unrivalled access to Liverpool FC on and off the pitch, past and present, LFC TV allows you to follow the team like never before from the comfort of your own home.

'LFC Now' is our daily news show, 'The Match' features every kick of every game while 'A Closer Look' sees LFC TV's resident expert Gary Gillespie analyse every game we play in detail.

'This is Anfield' is your chance to have your say on the issues that matter, 'The Academy' follows the progress of the kids just starting out while 'Cup Kings' allows fans everywhere to wallow in the glory of the moments that made this football club what it is today. Whatever your age, you'll always find something worth watching on LFC TV.

LFC TV can be viewed online with an e-Season Ticket (**www.liverpoolfc.tv/eseason**), Sky Channel 434 or Virgin Media Channel 544.

Visit **www.liverpoolfc.tv/tv**

e-SEASON TICKET

ABOUT

NOW TAKE YOUR SEAT!

The Liverpool FC e-Season Ticket takes you to the heart of the club you love:

- Watch LFC TV, the club's TV channel LIVE or catch up with the best bits, at your leisure
- Watch selected pre-season matches LIVE
- LIVE match commentary & picture slideshow of every LFC game
- Goal clips & video highlights of all our Premier League and Champions League matches
- Live and exclusive coverage of every Reserve match Liverpool FC play
- Exclusive video interviews with players, managers and legends
- The only place to watch every Reds' press conference - IN FULL
- Relive KOP classics – live and breathe Liverpool's history
- Enter our exclusive match ticket ballot

... all from your computer and all from as little as 13 pence per day!

e-Season Ticket is available to fans the world over.

For a FREE PREVIEW, visit **www.liverpoolfc.tv/preview**

ALL RED – THE NEW OFFICIAL MEMBERSHIP SCHEME

ABOUT

Become a member of ALL RED, the new LFC Official Membership Scheme.

With a whole host of new benefits including access to priority tickets, an exclusive 'Real Rafa Benitez' DVD and 10% off retail purchases – and much more. Make sure you don't miss out!

ADULT MEMBERSHIP BENEFITS

- Access to 5,000 priority tickets for all Barclays Premier League home games.
- 10% retail discount.
- Exclusive 'Real Rafa Benitez' DVD.
- Exclusive ALL RED merchandise including beanie hat, scarf, mouse mat and limited edition Shankly print.
- LFC members card.
- Exclusive access to the ticket exchange.
- Exclusive club competitions and prize draws, plus discounts for LFC reserve games, entry into the LFC museum and tour, e-Season Ticket discount and LFC Magazine subscription.
- Exclusive offers from LFC Partners.

JUNIOR MEMBERSHIP BENEFITS

- Access to 5,000 priority tickets for all Barclays Premier League home games.
- 10% retail discount.
- Exclusive 'Real Rafa Benitez ' DVD.
- Exclusive merchandise including boot bag, mini cones, training bib, training cards and wall chart.
- LFC members card.
- Personalised certificate.
- Chance to be a mascot.
- Opportunity to attend LFC soccer school.
- Exclusive club competitions and prize draws plus discounts for LFC reserve games, entry into the LFC museum and tour, e-Season Ticket discount and LFC Magazine subscription.

TODDLER MEMBERSHIP BENEFITS

- Bag.
- LFC dinner set.
- Liver toy.
- Blanket.
- LFC members card.
- Personalised certificate.
- Exclusive club competitions and prize draws.

PRICES

Adult Members: £29 (Inc P&P)
Junior Members: £20 (Inc P&P)

HOW TO JOIN

Visit **www.liverpoolfc.tv/ALLRED** or telephone **0844 499 3000**.
International calls **+44 151 261 1444**.

OFFICIAL PUBLICATIONS

Official Matchday Programme

Redesigned for the 2009/10 season, the award-winning 84-page souvenir matchday publication offers even more value for money for supporters. Including exclusive interviews with players and management, facts, statistics, quizzes, match action, club news and a host of regular features for Liverpudlians. Regulars like Kop 'n' Goal Years, Files of Anfield Road and LFC Uncut have been joined by World Service and The Shankly Seasons in 09/10.

How to subscribe

Phone: 0845 143 0001 (Monday-Friday 9am-5pm)
Website: www.liverpoolfc.tv/match/magazine
(Also available in braille and other formats - contact community department on 0151 264 2316 for details)

LFC Weekly

Established as the only weekly publication produced by a Barclays Premier League club in 2002, the new-look club magazine continues to inform and entertain fans of all ages. Packed with more fresh content and analysis, the magazine offers greater interaction with fans and liverpoolfc.tv. The very best match previews, reports, on-field action, interviews and statistics are guaranteed, while columnists Kenny Dalglish and Alan Hansen offer their expert opinion.

How to subscribe

Phone: 0845 143 0001 (Monday-Friday 9am-5pm)
Website: www.liverpoolfc.tv/match/magazine

Play Like Liverpool FC

Imagine sitting in the dressing room before a match or having a kick-about in the park with your mates when, suddenly, Steven Gerrard, Fernando Torres, Jamie Carragher and Rafa Benitez turn up to give you advice on how to play. This exciting official book does exactly that. Perfect for helping young footballers improve their game and even giving tips on how to eat, sleep and think like a Liverpool player, it is also a revealing behind-the-scenes insight for fans of all ages who want to know more about the secrets of success that make the club so special.

How to order

Phone: 0845 143 0001 (Monday-Friday 9am-5pm)
Website: www.merseyshop.com

LFC IN THE COMMUNITY

ABOUT

The tremendous work undertaken by Liverpool Football Club's community department has been recognised through its achievement of the **CommunityMark** from Business in the Community. It is one of only 28 companies nationally to be recognised by this independently-assessed standard. LFC delivers these programmes directly and in partnership with others.

LFC's programmes in schools such as **Truth 4 Youth** assemblies deliver hard-hitting messages such as: *Give Bullying the Boot*, *Kick Drugs into Touch*, *Show Racism the Red Card*, *Shoot Goals not Guns*.

LFC utilises sports coaching in its **Coaching 4 All** programme, which provides free football coaching to schools, after-school and holiday programmes. **Football 4 All** unites young people from different ethnic groups. **PL 4 Sport** involves young people in multi-sports activities, including table tennis, badminton, volleyball and judo. **Kickz** engages 12 to 18-year-olds and has reduced anti-social behaviour by promoting good citizenship.

The **Respect 4 All** disability centre accommodates children and adults with the most severe disabilities. Football coaching takes place in Liverpool's special schools each week, and there is a full complement of teams in the **Ability Counts** league.

Through the **Tactics 4 Families** project, LFC supports whole families, helping community organisations to run family fun days, parenting support groups and parent/child activity sessions. The schools programme – through which LFC works with year 5 and 6 pupils to deliver specially designed lessons covering the Tactics 4 Families key messages – is particularly well regarded in Merseyside primary schools.

In its seventh year, the **Sweeper Zone** project has 15 groups of young people who collect litter on match days and get to attend the game. In 2008 LFC gave 750 tickets to these youngsters, who are nominated by their schools or community groups. LFC also supports the Sweeper Zone cleansing vehicle in partnership with Liverpool City Council.

Young people who have displayed courage, bravery, caring and commitment to others are rewarded at the **Young Persons of the Year Award** event – a prestigious evening attended by a first-team player.

Health 4 All covers a wide-range of programmes that deliver health and fitness sessions to young people and courses, information and health checks to adults. Healthy stadia promotes the health of visitors, fans, players, employees and the surrounding community. Action 4 Health encourages life-style changes leading to measurably better health and longer lives.

Charity 4 All involves sending old and unused kit to poor communities in third world countries. The Community Department also carries out coaching in these areas in conjunction with other charities.

LFC IN ANFIELD

LFC has worked with Liverpool City Council and local community on the delivery of significant improvements to the local area including the restoration of Stanley Park and the Isla Gladstone Conservatory, improved highways/pedestrian access, and the renovation of four community centres in North Liverpool as part of a wider regeneration programme for new schools, new and restored housing and new health centre.

LFC IN THE COMMUNITY

LFC'S WIDER COMMUNITY

LFC also communicates with its huge national and international fan base through the **PR Section of the Community Department**. Thousands of letters are received and answered each year with requests concerning just about every aspect of life at LFC.

Because of the high demand for signed items, the club prioritises requests from special needs and terminally ill youngsters/adults. Similarly, visits to Melwood are prioritised for these individuals. Charities can also request items to be used for fundraising purposes and decisions will be made in accordance with club criteria.

The sheer volume of mail, especially with requests for players' autographs, requires us to answer most letters in a standard format with pre-printed signed photos of the team and individual players.

**Please note: The PR Section of the Community Department
do not deal with requests for matchday tickets.**

OTHER PR INITIATIVES

"**Football Aid**" is a charity supported by LFC for many years. In 2008, £61,000 was raised, the largest amount by any one club. If you have ever dreamed of playing at Anfield, visit their website:
www.footballaid.com

Alder Hey Children's Hospital is another major charity partner. The annual visit by the first-team squad each Christmas is a highlight of the year when each child receives a present from the club.

LFC takes an active part in the national anti-racism campaign, "**Kick it Out**." In 2008, LFC made a film, "*From Gayle to Babel*" released during Black History Month. The club is working with the Anthony Walker Foundation and Merseyside Police on future projects addressing critical social issues.

Jamie Carragher with local pupils in Reducate

REDUC@TE

ABOUT

Reduc@te is preparing to celebrate a decade of delivering innovative educational activities to school children in Liverpool from across the key stages. Over 35,000 pupils have now benefited from the varied educational opportunities available. Reduc@te continues to inspire and motivate children with a wide range of specially made curriculum materials created and delivered by an exceptionally dedicated team of 'Study Supporters'. All materials are available on the Reduc@te website for young people to access anywhere in the world.

Liverpool players have continued to support Reduc@te this year with visits. Most recently Jamie Carragher spent two hours in Reduc@te helping Liverpool school children improve their reading skills.

Visits to the centre for schools can be arranged by contacting the centre manager, Keith White:

Phone: **0151 263 1313**
Email: **krwhite.lfc.study@talk21.com** or **keith.white@liverpoolfc.tv**

LFC is committed to being a good neighbour and responsible world citizen whilst being responsive to its global fan base. For more details please visit:

www.liverpoolfc.tv/community

ASSOCIATION OF INTERNATIONAL BRANCHES

ABOUT

There are currently over 200 official branches registered to Liverpool Football Club and these are located both in the UK and internationally. It is an opportunity for fellow Reds to meet on a local level to show their loyalty and dedication to LFC.
All registered branches are listed at **www.liverpoolfc.tv/club/aib**

LIVERPOOL DISABLED SUPPORTERS' ASSOCIATION

AIMS AND OBJECTIVES

To act in partnership with Liverpool Football Club to promote inclusiveness for the disabled fans of the club, the disabled fans of visiting clubs as well as those individuals who support disabled people and those with impairments.
This association recognises that all fans should have an equal opportunity to participate in an enjoyable matchday experience and that people with disabilities and/or impairments must have their interests recognised and promoted by LFC with equal status to that of all other Liverpool fans.

CONTACT DETAILS

Disability liaison officer Colin McCall continues to develop the LDSA, acting as a link between the club and its supporters. The LDSA committee is made up of 10 members who are all Liverpool supporters and they meet once a month with the liaison officer to discuss disability issues at LFC.

If you would like any more information about the LDSA then please email **LDSA@liverpoolfc.tv** or write to **LDSA, Liverpool Football Club, Anfield Road, Liverpool, L4 0TH**.

OFFICIAL CLUB PARTNERS

Carlsberg
www.partofthegame.tv

adidas
www.adidas.com/liverpoolfc

Bank of America
www.liverpoolfc.tv/creditcard

Britannia
www.britannia.co.uk/home/lfc

Courts
Malaysia: www.courts.com.my
Singapore: www.courts.com.sp

Konami
www.pesunites.com

Lucozade Sport
www.lucozade.com/sport/football

Maxxis
www.maxxis.co.uk

Thomas Cook
www.thomascooksport.com/liverpoolfc

2010	Jan	Feb	March	April	May	June
Monday		1	1			
Tuesday		2	2			1
Wednesday		3	3			2
Thursday		4	4	1		3
Friday	1	5	5	2		4
Saturday	2	6	6	3	1	5
Sunday	3	7	7	4	2	6
Monday	4	8	8	5	3	7
Tuesday	5	9	9	6	4	8
Wednesday	6	10	10	7	5	9
Thursday	7	11	11	8	6	10
Friday	8	12	12	9	7	11
Saturday	9	13	13	10	8	12
Sunday	10	14	14	11	9	13
Monday	11	15	15	12	10	14
Tuesday	12	16	16	13	11	15
Wednesday	13	17	17	14	12	16
Thursday	14	18	18	15	13	17
Friday	15	18	18	16	14	18
Saturday	16	20	20	17	15	18
Sunday	17	21	21	18	16	20
Monday	18	22	22	18	17	21
Tuesday	18	23	23	20	18	22
Wednesday	20	24	24	21	18	23
Thursday	21	25	25	22	20	24
Friday	22	26	26	23	21	25
Saturday	23	27	27	24	22	26
Sunday	24	28	28	25	23	27
Monday	25		29	26	24	28
Tuesday	26		30	27	25	29
Wednesday	27		31	28	26	30
Thursday	28			29	27	
Friday	29			30	28	
Saturday	30				29	
Sunday	31				30	
Monday					31	
Tuesday						

July	Aug	Sept	Oct	Nov	Dec	
				1		Monday
				2		Tuesday
		1		3	1	Wednesday
		2		4	2	Thursday
		3	1	5	3	Friday
		4	2	6	4	Saturday
	1	5	3	7	5	Sunday
	2	6	4	8	6	Monday
	3	7	5	9	7	Tuesday
	4	8	6	10	8	Wednesday
	5	9	7	11	9	Thursday
	6	10	8	12	10	Friday
10	7	11	9	13	11	Saturday
11	8	12	10	14	12	Sunday
12	9	13	11	15	13	Monday
13	10	14	12	16	14	Tuesday
14	11	15	13	17	15	Wednesday
15	12	16	14	18	16	Thursday
16	13	17	15	18	17	Friday
17	14	18	16	20	18	Saturday
18	15	18	17	21	18	Sunday
19	16	20	18	22	20	Monday
20	17	21	18	23	21	Tuesday
21	18	22	20	24	22	Wednesday
22	18	23	21	25	23	Thursday
23	20	24	22	26	24	Friday
24	21	25	23	27	25	Saturday
25	22	26	24	28	26	Sunday
26	23	27	25	29	27	Monday
27	24	28	26	30	28	Tuesday
28	25	29	27		29	Wednesday
29	26	30	28		30	Thursday
30	27		29		31	Friday
31	28		30			Saturday
	29		31			Sunday
	30					Monday
	31					Tuesday

OTHER USEFUL CONTACTS

The Premier League
30 Gloucester Place,
London W1U 8PL
Phone: 0207 864 9000
Email: **info@premierleague.com**

The Football Association
Wembley Stadium,
PO Box 1966,
London SW1P 9EQ
Phone: 0844 980 8200

The Football League
Edward VII Quay, Navigation Way,
Preston PR2 2YF
Email: **fl@football-league.co.uk**

Professional Footballers' Association
2 Oxford Court,
Bishopsgate,
Off Lower Mosley Street,
Manchester M2 3WQ
Phone: 0161 236 0575
Email: **info@thepfa.co.uk**

Hillsborough Family
Support Group
c/o Liverpool FC,
Anfield Road,
Liverpool L4 0TH
Email: **hfsg@worthside.co.uk**

Liverpool FC logo and name are registered trademarks of
The Liverpool Football Club and Athletics Grounds Ltd and are reproduced under license.
Published in Great Britain in 2009 by: Trinity Mirror Sport Media, PO Box 48, Old Hall Street, Liverpool, L69 3EB

All Rights Reserved. No part of this publication may be reproduced, stored in a retrieval system, or transmitted in any form, or by
any means, electronic, mechanical, photocopying, recording or otherwise without the prior permission in writing of the copyright
holders, nor be otherwise circulated in any form of binding or cover other than in which it is published and without a similar
condition being imposed on the subsequent publisher.

ISBN: 1 9068 0222 6
978 1 9068 0222 6

Photographs: PA Photos, Trinity Mirror, John Cocks, John Powell
Printed and finished by Korotan